Study Guide
for use with

ACCOUNTING
THE BASIS FOR BUSINESS DECISIONS
SIXTH EDITION

Walter B. Meigs
University of Southern California

Robert F. Meigs
San Diego State University

McGraw-Hill Book Company

New York   St. Louis   San Francisco   Auckland   Bogotá   Hamburg   Johannesburg
London   Madrid   Mexico   Montreal   New Delhi   Panama   Paris   São Paulo
Singapore   Sydney   Tokyo   Toronto

Study Guide for use with
ACCOUNTING: THE BASIS FOR BUSINESS DECISIONS

4 5 6 7 8 9 0   WEBWEB   8 9 8 7 6

ISBN 0-07-041588-9

This book was set in Century Schoolbook by Intergraphic Technology, Inc.
The editors were Jim DeVoe, Elisa Adams, and Edwin Hanson;
the production supervisor was Phil Galea.
The cover was designed by Charles A. Carson;
the cover photograph was taken by Fern Logan.
Webcrafters, Inc., was printer and binder.

CONTENTS

TO THE STUDENT

This self-study guide is designed for your use as a student taking your first course in accounting at either the undergraduate or the graduate level. It is prepared to accompany *Accounting: The Basis for Business Decisions*, sixth edition, by Meigs and Meigs. However, it can be used effectively with other introductory accounting texts. The key purposes of this study guide are:

1 To help you in *mastering the material* as you initially study each chapter.

2 To *summarize the essential points* in each chapter and to *test your knowledge* with a series of objective questions and exercises, thus making it possible for you to *review the material quickly* from time to time, particularly before examinations.

3 To make the study of accounting *more enjoyable and less tedious* for you. This is accomplished by presenting an informal and concise summary of each chapter, followed by three groups of objective questions and some short exercises. The answers to these questions and exercises are provided at the back of the study guide *in order to give you immediate feedback and point out areas that need additional attention.*

The manner in which each student uses this study guide may differ. However, we recommend the following approach:

1 Study the chapter in your textbook.

2 Read the *Highlights of the Chapter* section of the study guide. If you encounter any statements that you do not understand, refer to the textbook for a more detailed discussion of the topic.

3 Work the questions and exercises in the *Test Yourself* section of the study guide, and compare your answers and solutions with those provided in the back of the guide. This will show you how well you really understand the material contained in the related chapter of your textbook. Again, if you find something you do not understand, refer to your text for a thorough discussion of the subject.

4 Work the problems assigned as homework in your text.

Once you have mastered the material in this manner, rereading the *Highlights of the Chapter* section of the study guide will assist you in quickly reviewing the material before examinations.

Walter B. Meigs
Robert F. Meigs

1

ACCOUNTING: THE LANGUAGE OF BUSINESS

HIGHLIGHTS OF THE CHAPTER

1 The basic purpose of accounting is to provide financial information about a business enterprise or any other economic entity. This information is needed internally by managers and also by outsiders such as bankers, other creditors, investors, and certain government agencies. In short, anyone who must make *decisions* regarding a business enterprise has need of *accounting information*.

2 Most businesses enter into so many different transactions every year that a complete list of these transactions would be too long to be useful to decision makers. An accounting system creates *useful* information by (a) *recording* business events as they occur, (b) *classifying* these events into related groups, and (c) *summarizing* this information into accounting reports designed to meet the information needs of decision makers.

3 The major types of accounting reports include (a) financial statements, (b) tax returns, (c) specialized reports to management, and (d) reports to governmental regulatory agencies. In this accounting course, we shall emphasize the information contained in financial statements.

4 Financial statements are useful to management and also are the primary source of accounting information to persons outside the business enterprise. These statements show the financial position of the business at a given date and also the operating results which caused it to arrive at this position.

5 The accounting concepts, measurement techniques, and standards of presentation used in the preparation of financial statements are called *generally accepted accounting principles*. Developing accounting information in conformity with generally accepted accounting principles is often termed *financial accounting*. Developing accounting information to fill the specialized needs of management, on the other hand, is called *managerial accounting*.

6 *Bookkeeping* refers to the mechanical aspects of recording and classifying transactions, and is but a small part of the field of accounting. *Accounting* includes the design of the financial information system, preparation of financial statements, development of forecasts, cost studies, tax consulting, and the *analysis* and *interpretation* of accounting information to assist decision makers in making *informed* decisions.

7 Careers in accounting may be divided into three broad areas: (a) the public accounting profession, (b) private accounting, and (c) governmental accounting.

8 Public accounting is practiced by *certified public accountants*, called CPAs. CPAs are granted a license to practice by the state, and perform professional accounting services for clients for a fee. These services include:

a *Auditing* An audit is an investigation of a company's accounting system to determine that the financial statements *present fairly* its financial positions and operating results. All large corporations and many small companies are audited annually by a CPA firm.

b *Tax services*   Taxes often play an important role in financial decisions. CPA firms offer "tax planning" services to minimize the impact of taxes on their clients, and also assist in the preparation of their clients' income tax returns.

c *Management advisory services*   CPA firms may become familiar with their clients' problems and be able to recommend corrective action. This service is actually *management consulting.*

9 *Private accounting* refers to the work of accountants employed directly by private industry. The functions of accountants in private industry include:

a *Design of accounting systems*   Although most business concerns follow the same basic accounting principles, each firm will require its own individually tailored accounting system.

b *Cost accounting*   This is the specialized field of determining the cost of manufacturing a product or performing a specific process.

c *Financial forecasting*   A financial *forecast (budget) is a plan* of financial operations for the future. The forecast helps management to set goals, and then to measure actual performance relative to these goals.

d *Tax accounting*   Tax specialists play as important a role in private accounting as they do in public accounting.

e *Internal auditing*   Internal auditors are responsible for seeing that the objectives of a company are being carried out efficiently in all departments. Unlike CPAs, internal auditors are *not* responsible for determining the fairness of annual financial statements.

10 *Governmental accounting* includes many specialized areas such as monitoring regulated industries, auditing tax returns, and preparing budgets for governmental agencies. Two important governmental agencies using accounting information are:

a *Internal Revenue Service*   The IRS processes the federal income tax returns filed by individuals and corporations.

b *Securities and Exchange Commission*   The SEC reviews and approves the financial disclosure by corporations which offer their securities for sale to the public.

11 In the United States, four groups which have been influential in improving accounting principles and practices are the *American Institute of Certified Public Accountants* (AICPA), the *Securities and Exchange Commission* (SEC), the *American Accounting Association* (AAA), and the *Financial Accounting Standards Board* (FASB). The FASB conducts research and issues Statements of Financial Accounting Standards which represent authoritative expressions of generally accepted accounting principles.

12 Two primary objectives of most business concerns are to make a profit and remain solvent. Being *solvent* means having the cash to pay debts on time. The accounting system is the means by which profitability and solvency are measured.

13 Steps taken to ensure the reliability of accounting information and to safeguard the resources of a business against waste, fraud, or inefficient use are called the system of *internal control.*

14 Accounting information is gathered for specific business entities. A business *entity* is any economic unit which enters into business transactions. The business entity is regarded as separate from its owners; the entity owns its own property and has its own debts.

15 The three most common forms of business entities are single proprietorships, partnerships, and corporations. Accounting principles and concepts apply to all three forms of organization.

a A single proprietorship is a business owned by one individual.

b A partnership is a business owned by two or more people who have agreed to act as partners.

c A corporation is a business granted a charter by the state and owned by *stockholders.* Ownership is evidenced by shares of capital stock which may be sold by one investor to another.

16 The two most widely used financial statements are the *balance sheet* and the *income statement.* A balance sheet shows the financial position of a business at a particular date. It consists of a list of the company's assets, liabilities, and owner's equity. (The income statement will be discussed in Chapter 3.)

17 Assets are economic resources owned by a business, such as land, buildings, and cash. Assets are valued on a balance sheet at their *cost,* rather than at current market prices,

because cost is more factual and can be more *objectively determined* than current market value. Another reason for valuing assets at cost is that a business is assumed to be a *going concern* that will keep and use such assets as land and buildings rather than sell them.

18 The validity of the *cost principle* is weakened by inflation. Inflation has caused many accountants to recommend valuing assets at appraised value or replacement cost rather than at original (historical) cost. In Great Britain, for example, current values are used in accounting for assets. The problem of asset valuation is complex and will be given much attention in later chapters.

19 Liabilities are debts. Either borrowing money or buying on credit will create a liability. Liabilities represent the claims of *creditors* to the resources of the business. Examples of liabilities are accounts payable and notes payable.

20 Owner's equity represents the owner's investment in the business; it is equal to total assets minus liabilities. The equity of the owner is a *residual* amount. It is the claim to all resources (assets) of the business *after* the claims of the creditors have been satisfied. If a loss occurs, it is the owner's equity rather than the creditors' claims which must absorb the loss. Thus, creditors view the owner's equity as a "buffer" which protects the safety of their claims to the resources of the business.

21 Increases in owner's equity results from (a) investment of cash or other assets by the owner or (b) earnings from profitable operation of the business. Decreases in owner's equity result from (a) withdrawal of cash or other assets by the owner or (b) losses from unprofitable operation of the business. Earnings and losses will be discussed in Chapter 3.

22 The "accounting equation" is *Assets = Liabilities + Owner's Equity*. The listing of assets shows us what things the business owns; the listing of liabilities and owner's equity tells us who supplied these resources to the business and how much each group supplied.

23 You should become familiar with the effects of various transactions upon a balance sheet.

a Purchasing an asset for cash is merely trading one kind of asset for another. Total assets will not change.

b Purchasing an asset on credit will cause total assets to increase because additional resources are being acquired and none are being given up. However, total liabilities will increase by the same amount.

c Paying a liability with cash will cause both total assets and total liabilities to decrease.

TEST YOURSELF ON THIS INTRODUCTORY CHAPTER

True or False

For each of the following statements, circle the T or the F to indicate whether the statement is true or false.

T F 1 The basic purpose of accounting is to provide financial information to economic decision makers.

T F 2 Bookkeeping is only a small part of the field of accounting and probably the simplest part.

T F 3 The most useful financial statement would be a detailed list of every business transaction in which the business enterprise has been involved.

T F 4 Financial statements are confidential documents made available only to the top management of a business enterprise.

T F 5 The chief accounting officer of a corporation is usually called the *controller.*

T F 6 A forecast for a business enterprise is always prepared by the CPA firm conducting the annual audit.

T F 7 The Financial Accounting Standards Board is an authoritative source of generally accepted accounting principles in the United States.

T F 8 A business may be profitable, but not solvent.

T F 9 A business may be solvent, but not profitable.

T F 10 One characteristic of corporations is that ownership cannot be transferred easily from one person to another.

T F 11 Assets are valued on the balance sheet at current liquidation values to show how much cash would be realized if the business went broke.

T F 12 The cost principle is especially valid during periods of severe inflation.

T F 13 Losses from unprofitable operations cause the owner's equity in a business enterprise to decrease.

T _F_ **14** The purchase of a building for cash will cause total assets to increase.

T (F) **15** The payment of a liability will not affect total assets, but will cause total liabilities to decrease.

Completion Statements

Fill in the necessary words or amount to complete the following statements:

1 Two major financial statements are the ___balance___ ___sheet___ and the ___income___ ___statement___.

2 The three basic steps in the accounting process are (a) ___record___ transactions, (b) ___classify___ these events into groups, and (c) ___summarize___ the information in accounting reports.

3 The accounting concepts, measurement techniques, and standards of presentation used in the preparation of financial statements are called ___generally___ ___accepted___ ___accounting___ ___principles___.

4 An investigation of the accounting system of a business to determine the fairness of the firm's financial statements is called an ___audit___.

5 The governmental agency which reviews and approves the financial disclosure by companies which offer their securities to the public is the ___Securities___ ___exchange___ ___commission___.

6 *Statements of Financial Accounting Standards* are authoritative expressions of generally accepted accounting principles issued by the ___Financial___ ___accounting___ ___Standards___ ___board___.

7 Two primary objectives of most business concerns are (a) making a ___profit___ and (b) remaining ___solvent___.

8 The steps taken to ensure the reliability of the accounting information and to safeguard the assets of the firm against waste, fraud, or inefficient use make up the system of ___internal___ ___control___.

9 The three common forms of business organizations are ___single___ ___proprietorship___, ___partnership___, and ___corporations___.

10 The heading of a balance sheet should include ___company name___, ___name of finance sheet___, and ___date___.

11 Two reasons supporting the cost principle of asset valuation are the "___going concern___" assumption and the ___objectivity___ principle. Some accountants, however, suggest that assets should be valued at appraisal value or ___replacement___ cost rather than at ___historical___ cost.

12 Since the claims of ___creditors___ have priority over those of the ___owners___ of a business, the owner's equity is called a ___residual___ claim.

13 The accounting equation states that ___Assets___ = ___liabilities___ + ___owners equity___.

14 Land advertised for sale at $90,000 was purchased for $80,000 cash by a development company. For property tax purposes, the property was assessed by the county at $65,000. The development firm intended to sell the property in parcels for a total of $150,000. The land would appear on the balance sheet of the development company among the ___assets___ at a value of $ ___80,000___.

15 On December 15, Shadow Mountain Golf Course had a contractor install a $90,000 sprinkler system. Since no payment to the contractor was required until the following month, the transaction was not recorded in December and was not reflected in any way in the December 31 balance sheet. Indicate for each of the following elements of the balance sheet whether the amounts were overstated, understated, or correct. Total assets ___understated___, total liabilities ___understated___, owner's equity ___o.k.___.

16 The owner's equity in a business comes from two sources: ___investments___ and ___profit___.

17 A transaction which causes total liabilities to increase but which has no effect on owner's equity must cause total assets to ___increase___.

Multiple Choice

Choose the best answer for each of the following questions and enter the identifying letter in the space provided.

_____ **1** Which of the following best describes the nature of an asset?

a Something with a ready market value.

b An economic resource, which will provide some future benefits, owned by a business.

c Tangible property (something with physical form) owned by a business.

d The amount of the owner's investment in a business.

_____ **2** The principal reason for an annual audit of a business corporation by a firm of certified public accountants (CPAs) is:

a To obtain an independent expert opinion on the fairness and dependability of the financial statements prepared by the company and distributed to stockholders, bankers, and other outsiders.

b To detect fraud on the part of company personnel.

c To assist the accounting department of the company in handling the heavy year-end work of preparing financial statements.

d To relieve management of the responsibility for financial reporting to creditors and other outsiders.

_____ **3** The primary objective of the internal auditor is to:

a Conduct an annual audit of a company's accounting system to determine that the financial statements present fairly its financial position and operating results.

b Observe the business transactions of the firm to be sure the annual tax returns are accurately prepared.

c Aid management by investigating and reporting on accounting, financial, and other operations of the company.

d Render a professional opinion as to the fairness and accuracy of the budget.

_____ **4** Which of the following equations *cannot* be derived from the basic accounting equation (Assets = liabilities + owner's equity)?

a Assets — liabilities = owner's equity.

b Liabilities = assets — owner's equity.

c Owner's equity = liabilities — assets.

d Assets — owner's equity = liabilities.

_____ **5** Magic Forest Land Development Company sold a parcel of land at a profit. This will cause:

a A decrease in assets and liabilities.

b An increase in assets and liabilities.

c An increase in assets and owner's equity.

d A decrease in liabilities and owner's equity.

_____ **6** Lake Arrowhead Boat Shop bought a $700 electric hoist to lift engines out of boats. The boat shop paid $200 in cash for the hoist and signed a note to pay the balance in 60 days. This transaction will cause:

a The boat shop's assets to increase by $700 and liabilities to increase by $500.

b Assets to increase by $500 and owner's equity to decrease.

c No change in total assets, but a $500 increase in liabilities and a similar decrease in owner's equity.

d No change in owner's equity, but a $500 increase in both assets and liabilities.

Exercises

1 In the space on page 6, indicate the effect of each of the following transactions on various balance sheet items of the Billiard Den. Indicate the new account balances after the transaction of July 3 and each subsequent transaction. (The effects of the July 1 transaction are already filled in to provide you with an example.)

July **1** Robert Neal began the business by depositing $20,000 cash in a bank account in the name of the business.

3 Purchased an existing pool hall at a price of $21,000 for the land and $30,000 for the building. Neal paid the former owner $10,000 in cash and issued a short-term note payable for the balance of the purchase price.

10 Purchase 10 pool tables for $1,000 each, paying $6,000 cash and agreeing to pay the balance due in 30 days.

14 Sold one pool table to a friend for $1,000. The friend paid $500 cash to the Billiard Den and promised to pay the balance within 30 days.

20 Paid $2,000 of the amount owed on the pool tables.

24 Collected $200 from the friend who had bought the pool table.

30 Purchased one used pool table from another pool hall, paying $600 cash.

	Assets					=	Liabilities		+	Owner's Equity
	Cash	Accounts Receivable	Land	Building	Pool Tables		Notes Payable	Accounts Payable		Capital Stock
July 1	+$20,000									+$20,000
3	−10,000		+21000	+30000			+41000			
Balances	+10,000		+21000	+30000			+41000			+20000
10	−6000				+10,000			+4000		
Balances	+4000		+21000	+30000	+10000		+41000			+20000
14	+800	+800			−1600					
Balances	+4800	+800	+21000	+30000	+9000		+41000			+20000
20	−2000							−2000		
Balances	+2800	+800	+21000	+30000	+9000		+41000			+20000
24	+200	−200								
Balances	+2700	+300	+21000	+30000	+9000		+41000			+20000
30	−600				+600					
Balances	+2100	+300	+21000	+30000	+9600		+41000	2000		+20000

2 In the space provided below, prepare a balance sheet for the McCall Company at December 31, 19___, from the following alphabetical list of accounts.

Accounts payable	$21,000
Accounts receivable	24,000
Building	45,000
Cash	7,000
Delivery equipment	12,000
Land	29,000
Notes payable	53,000
Office equipment	6,000
Daniel McCall, capital	49,000

McCALL COMPANY
Balance Sheet
December 31, 19___

Assets		Liabilities & Owner's Equity	
Cash	$ 7000	A/P	$ 21000
A/R	24000	N/P	53000
Building	45000	Dan McCall, capital	49000
Delivery Equip	12000		
Land	29000		123,000
Office Equip	6000		
	123,000		

2

RECORDING CHANGES IN FINANCIAL POSITION

HIGHLIGHTS OF THE CHAPTER

1 Many businesses engage in hundreds or even thousands of business transactions every day. Obviously, it would be too costly and time-consuming to prepare a new balance sheet after each transaction. Instead, the effects of these transactions are stored in the *ledger* until the end of a month or year, when new financial statements are prepared.

2 A *ledger account* is maintained for every item on the balance sheet. Thus, we have a ledger account for each type of asset (such as Cash), for each type of liability (such as Accounts Payable), and for each element of owner's equity (such as John Scott, Capital).

3 Each ledger account occupies a separate page in a loose-leaf book called a *ledger*. The ledger is a permanent, important, and basic accounting record. For example, the first page in a ledger might be the ledger account entitled *Cash*. It would show increases and decreases in cash, resulting from the many transactions in which cash is received or paid.

4 A balance sheet is usually prepared at the end of each month by listing the cumulative balances of accounts contained in the ledger.

5 In its simplest form, a ledger page is divided into two sections by a vertical line drawn down the center of the page. The left half of the page is called the *debit* side; the right half of the page is the *credit* side.

6 An amount recorded on the left side of a ledger page is called a *debit entry*; an amount recorded on the right side is called a *credit entry*.

7 Asset accounts normally have debit balances; that is, the sum of the amounts entered on the debit (or left) side is larger than the sum of the amounts entered on the credit (or right) side. For example, Cash is an asset account and has a debit balance.

8 Liability accounts and owner's equity accounts normally have credit balances because the sum of the amounts entered on the credit (right-hand) side of such accounts is greater than the sum of the amounts entered on the debit (left-hand) side.

9 For all *asset* accounts, increases are recorded by debits, and decreases are recorded by credits.

10 For all *liability* accounts and *owner's equity* accounts, increases are recorded by credits, and decreases are recorded by debits.

11 The double-entry system of accounting (which is almost universally used) requires that *equal debits and credits* be recorded for *every* transaction.

12 Most ledger accounts are actually designed in a *running balance* form. This means there is a third column, on the extreme right side of the account, which shows the *balance* (the amount by which the debits exceed the credits, or vice versa) of the account.

13 Since every transaction results in recording equal dollar amounts of debits and credits (double entry), it follows that the total of the debit entries in the ledger must equal the total of the credit entries. It also follows that the total of the debit balance accounts must equal the total of the credit balance accounts. When this equality of debits and credits exists, we say the ledger is *in balance*.

Otherwise, one or more errors must have been made in recording transactions.

14 Accounts are arranged in the ledger in the same sequence as they appear on the balance sheet: asset accounts first, then liabilities, and finally owner's equity. Each account has a number, but many numbers are skipped, so that later a new account may be inserted in the ledger if the business acquires a new type of asset, liability, or owner's equity.

15 A very small business could record transactions directly in the ledger as they occurred. However, this procedure would be inefficient and it would be difficult to locate errors because you could not locate all the parts of one transaction. Therefore, virtually every business also maintains a *journal*, or *book of original entry*. A journal is a chronological record listing the transactions in the order they occur.

16 The journal shows all information about one transaction in one place. It shows (a) the date of the transaction, (b) the account(s) debited, (c) the account(s) credited, and (d) a written explanation of the transaction.

17 After a transaction has first been recorded in the journal, each debit and credit is later transferred to the proper ledger accounts. This transfer is called *posting*.

18 At month-end, when all entries in the journal have been posted to the ledger, the debit or credit balance of each account is computed (unless running balance form ledger accounts are maintained). These balances are listed in a *trial balance*. The trial balance is a two-column schedule listing the names and balances of all accounts in the order they appear in the ledger. Debit balances are listed in the left-hand column of the trial balance, and credit balances are listed in the right-hand column. Since the total of the debit balances should equal the total of the credit balances, the totals of the two columns of the trial balance *should be equal*, if the ledger is in balance.

19 The trial balance proves that equal dollar amounts of debits and credits were posted to the ledger and also that the arithmetic of determining the account balances was correct. However, it does not prove that all transactions were correctly recorded in the journal. For example, the trial balance would not disclose the omission of an entire transaction (both the debit and credit parts) from the journal. Also if the *right amount*

of debits or credits was entered in the ledger but the entry was made to the *wrong account*, the trial balance would not reveal the error.

20 The trial balance is not a formal financial statement, but merely a preliminary step to preparing financial statements.

21 The balance sheet is prepared from the trial balance.

22 Businesses using computers maintain accounting records on magnetic disks instead of loose-leaf notebooks (ledgers), but the accounting principles of analyzing and recording transactions and preparing financial statements *are the same* as for a manual system. An understanding of accounting concepts is more easily acquired by studying a manual system.

TEST YOURSELF ON RECORDING CHANGES IN FINANCIAL POSITION

True or False

For each of the following statements, circle the T or the F to indicate whether the statement is true or false.

T F 1 In a prosperous and solvent business the accounts with credit balances will normally exceed in total dollar amount the accounts with debit balances.

T F 2 The term *debit* may signify either an increase or a decrease; the same is true of the term *credit*.

T F 3 All transactions are recorded in the ledger accounts by equal dollar amounts of debits and credits.

T F 4 A business transaction is always recorded in the ledger by entries to two or more different ledger accounts.

T F 5 An entry on the left side of a ledger account is called a debit entry and an entry on the right side is called a credit entry, regardless of whether the account represents an asset, a liability, or owner's equity.

T F 6 Accounts representing items which appear on the left-hand side of the balance sheet usually have credit balances.

T F 7 Decreases in a ledger account are recorded by debits and increases are recorded by credits, regardless of whether the account represents an asset, a liability, or owner's equity.

T F 8 The balance of a T account is entered in small pencil figures opposite the last entry on the side having the larger column total.

T F 9 A trial balance with equal debit and credit totals proves that all transactions have been correctly journalized and posted to the proper ledger accounts.

T F 10 The sequence of the account titles in a trial balance depends upon the size of the account balances.

T F 11 A journal entry may include debits to more than one account and credits to more than one account, but the total of the debits must always equal the total of the credits.

T F 12 One advantage of using a journal and a ledger rather than recording transactions directly in the ledger accounts is that the journal provides all information about a particular transaction in one place.

T F 13 The purchase of a typewriter on account would be recorded as a debit to Accounts Payable and a credit to Office Equipment.

T F 14 Of the following 10 accounts, 6 normally have debit balances and 4 have credit balances: Accounts Receivable; Accounts Payable, Buildings; C. Barr, Capital; Cash; Land; Machinery; Mortgage Payable; Notes Payable; Notes Receivable.

T F 15 A transposition error means a posting of a journal entry to the wrong ledger account.

T F 16 The footings, or memoranda totals of the entries in a ledger account, do not relate to a specific transaction, but are merely a step in determining the balance of the account.

T F 17 If a business transaction is recorded correctly, it cannot possibly upset the equality of debits and credits in the ledger.

T F 18 More knowledge of accounting is required to post amounts from the journal to the ledger than is required to record transactions in journal entry form.

T F 19 In a journal entry recording the purchase of a desk for $275.80, both the debit and credit were recorded

and posted as $257.80. This *transposition error* would *not* be disclosed by the preparation of a trial balance.

T F 20 The double-entry accounting system means that transactions are recorded both in the journal and in the ledger.

Completion Statements

Fill in the necessary words to complete the following statements:

1 A T account is a simplified model of a formal ledger account and consists of only three elements: an account *name*, a *debit* _____, and a *credit side*.

2 Increases in assets are recorded by *debits*, and decreases in assets are recorded by credits; increases in accounts appearing on the right side of a balance sheet are recorded by *credits*, while decreases in those accounts are recorded by *debits*.

3 In accounting, the term *debit* refers to the *right* side of a *T account*, while the term *credit* refers to the *left* side.

4 Asset accounts appear on the *left* side of the balance sheet and normally have *debit* balances. Liability and owner's equity accounts appear on the *right* side of the balance sheet and normally have *credit* balances.

5 When a company borrows from a bank, two accounts immediately affected are *cash* and *note payable*. The journal entry to record the transaction requires a *dr* to the first account and a *Cr* to the second one.

6 If you charge a sweater at a clothing store where you have an account, the store will *debit* your account for the amount of your purchase.

7 The journal may also be called the *book of original entry*.

8 A journal entry shows (a) the *date* of the transaction, (b) the *account* to be *debited*, (c) the *account* to be *credited*; and also (d) an *explanation* of the transaction.

9 A _trial balance_ is prepared from the ledger accounts at the end of the month (or other accounting period) in order to prove that the total of accounts with _debit balances_ is equal to the total of accounts with _credit balances_.

10 When a journal entry is made, the _ledger page_ column just to the left of the debit column is left blank. When the debits and credits are later _posted_ to the ledger, the _numbers_ of the ledger accounts are listed in this column to provide a convenient _cross reference_ with the ledger.

11 With respect to (a) posting, (b) journalizing, (c) preparation of a balance sheet, (d) preparation of a trial balance, and (e) occurrence of a business transaction, the normal sequence of these events is denoted by the following order of letters: _e, b, a, d, c_ .

Multiple Choice

Choose the best answer for each of the following questions and enter the identifying letter in the space provided.

___a___ 1 Mohawk Company completed a transaction which caused both its total assets and its total liabilities to increase by $6,000. The transaction could have been:
a Purchase of a fork lift by paying $14,000 cash and issuance of a note payable for $6,000.
b Purchase of a drill press by a payment of $2,000 in cash and issuance of a $4,000 note payable.
c Sale of land costing $24,000 for $30,000 in cash.
d None of the above.

___c___ 2 Red Hill Vineyards completes a transaction which causes an asset account to decrease. Which of the following related effects may also occur?
a An increase of an equal amount in a liability account.
b An increase of an equal amount in owner's equity.
c An increase of an equal amount in another asset account.
d None of the above.

___b___ 3 The term _posting_ means:
a Entering transactions in a book of original entry.

b Transferring debit and credit amounts from the journal to the ledger.
c Proving the equality of debits and credits in the ledger.
d Determining the balances of individual ledger accounts.

___d___ 4 If a computer is acquired by paying $10,000 in cash and signing a note payable for $40,000:
a Total assets are increased and total owner's equity is increased.
b Total liabilities are increased and total owner's equity is decreased.
c Total assets are decreased and total liabilities are increased.
d Total assets are increased and total liabilities are increased.

___c___ 5 Which of the following errors would _not_ be disclosed by the trial balance?
a The collection of a $520 account receivable was journalized as a $520 debit to Cash and a $5,202 credit to Accounts Receivable.
b The collection of a $200 account receivable was journalized as a $200 debit to Cash and a $200 debit to Accounts Receivable.
c The collection of a $1,000 account receivable was journalized correctly, but the debit was posted to the Land account instead of to Cash.
d None of the above.

___d___ 6 The accountant of the Midas Company made an error in posting from the journal to the ledger accounts. A debit to Office Equipment was posted as a debit to Accounts Receivable. The procedure which is most likely to disclose this error is:
a Refooting all the accounts in the ledger.
b Sending month-end bills to all customers.
c Taking a trial balance.
d Comparing the written explanation of the journal entry with the accounts mentioned in the journal.

___c___ 7 If a trial balance is out of balance, a possible cause is:
a A transaction calling for a debit to an asset account and a credit to a liability account was entered in the journal as a debit to a liability account and a credit to an asset account.
b A transaction was entirely omitted from the records.
c An error was made in determining the balance of the Cash account.
d The balance of the Cash account and the Accounts Receivable account were switched in the preparation of the trial balance.

8 Peckham Investment Company entered into a transaction which did not change total assets, total liabilities, or total owner's equity. The transaction could have been:

a The sale of land for cash at a price equal to the cost of the land.

b An investment of cash in the business by the owner.

c The settlement of a liability by paying the creditor some asset other than cash.

d None of the above.

Exercises

1 Show the change in total assets, total liabilities, and total owner's equity that will be caused by posting each amount in the following journal entries. In the *effect of transaction* row, show the total change in assets, liabilities, and owner's equity that has occurred after all parts of the transaction have been posted. *Hint:* The effect of each transaction should be that the total change on the left side of the balance sheet (change in assets) should equal the change on the right side (change in liabilities + change in owner's equity). Explanations have been omitted from journal entries to conserve space.

Journal Entry	Dr	Cr	Assets	=	Lia-bilities	+	Owner's Equity
Example:							
Office Equipment.	600		+ 600				
Cash		150	− 150				
Accounts Payable.		450			+ 450		
Effect of Transaction			+ 450	=	+ 450	+	
a Cash	1,230		+1230				
Accounts Receivable		1,230	−1230				
Effect of transaction				=		+	
b Cash	5,000		+5000				
Ray Scott, Capital		5,000					+5000
Effect of transaction			+5000	=		+	+5000
c Cash	3,800		+3800				
Notes Payable.		3,800					
Effect of transaction			+3800	=	+3800	+	
d Accounts Payable.	350		−350				
Cash		350	−350				
Effect of transaction			−350	=	−350	+	
e Land	9,000		+9000				
Cash		1,000	−1000				
Notes Payable.		8,000					
Effect of transaction			+8000	=	+8000	+	

2 Enter the following transactions of Riviera Company in the T accounts provided, and then prepare a trial balance at September 30, 19___:

a The owner, Vivian DuPar, invested $70,000 in the business.

b Borrowed $12,000 cash from a bank and signed a note payable for that amount.

c Purchased land and building for $90,000, paying $40,000 in cash and issuing a $50,000 note payable. The land was estimated to represent one-third of the total purchase price.

d Purchased office equipment on credit at a cost of $6,000.

e Added a balcony to the building at a cost of $5,000; agreed to pay contractor in full in 30 days.

f Returned part of the office equipment to the supplier and received full credit of $600.

g Made a partial payment of $3,000 on the amount owed for office equipment.

Cash		Notes Payable	
70000	40000		12000
12000	3000		50000
39000			62000

Land		Accounts Payable	
30000		600	6000
30,000		3000	5000
			7400

Building		Vivian DuPar, Capital	
60000			70,000
5000			
65000			70,000

Office Equipment	
6000	6000
5400	

RIVIERA COMPANY
Trial Balance
September 30, 19___

	Debit	Credit
Cash .... $	39000	
Land	30,000	
Building	65000	
Office equipment	5400	62000
Notes payable		7400
Accounts payable		70000
Vivian DuPar, capital		
	$ 139,400	$ 139,400

3

MEASURING BUSINESS INCOME

HIGHLIGHTS OF THE CHAPTER

1 Two things can cause a change in the owner's equity in a business concern: (a) a change in the owner's investment (owner putting assets in or taking assets out of the business) and (b) profits or losses resulting from operation of the business.

2 The change in owner's equity resulting from profits or losses is very important to most business concerns. Profits increase owner's equity. These profits may be either withdrawn by the owner or retained in the business to help finance expansion and growth. Losses, however, reduce the owner's equity and make the owner economically worse off.

3 *Net income* is the term accountants use for the increase in owner's equity resulting from profitable operation of the business; *net loss* means a decrease in owner's equity resulting from unprofitable operations.

4 Net income (or loss) is measured by deducting the *expenses* of a given period from the *revenue* earned in that period. Thus, *revenue minus expenses equals net income.*

5 *Revenue is the price of goods sold and services rendered to customers.* Revenue comes into existence when the goods are sold or the service is rendered, even though cash is not collected until some later date. If a customer buys our product on credit in July and pays us in August, we should recognize the revenue from the sale in July. In August we are merely converting one asset (an account receivable) into another asset (cash).

6 Revenue causes both assets (accounts receivable or cash) and owner's equity to in-

crease. Sometimes revenue is defined as the inflow of cash and receivables from sales of goods and services during a period.

7 *Expenses are the cost of goods and services used up in the process of obtaining revenue.* Expenses are recorded when the goods or services are used up, even though cash payment is not made until later. If we use electricity in January but do not pay the electric company until February, we should recognize the expense from using the service (electricity) in January. In February, we are merely paying a liability owed to the electric company.

8 To measure net income, we first show all revenue earned during the period and then deduct all expenses incurred in producing that revenue. This policy of offsetting revenue with the related expenses is called the *matching principle.*

9 Not all cash payments are expenses; for instance, cash used to buy a building is a trade of assets, not an expense. *Expenses cause owner's equity to decrease.*

10 Withdrawals by the owner mean that the owner takes assets out of the business. This causes owner's equity to change but has nothing to do with net income. This kind of change in equity is a *change in the owner's investment* in the business. Withdrawals are disinvestments; they are *not expenses* of the business.

11 To be meaningful, net income must be measured *for some time period* (such as a month or year). To determine the net income of a time period, we must first measure the revenue and expenses of *that*

same time period. The span of time for which net income is determined is called the *accounting period*.

12 Many transactions affect two or more accounting periods. A building, for instance, is an asset which is used up over 20 or 30 years. The cost of the building should be recognized as expense as it is used up, but that period of time is not precisely determinable in advance.

13 The rules of debit and credit for revenue and expenses are based on the changes caused in owner's equity. Revenue increases owner's equity; therefore revenue is recorded by credits. Expenses decrease owner's equity; therefore expenses are recorded by debits.

14 Every transaction which affects a revenue or an expense account also affects a balance sheet account. For example, credits to revenue are usually offset by debits to asset accounts; debits to expense are offset by credits to asset or liability accounts.

15 A separate ledger account is maintained for each major category of revenue and expense. Revenue accounts have credit balances; examples are Fees Earned, Commissions Earned, and Interest Revenue. Expense accounts have debit balances; examples are Telephone Expense, Office Salaries, and Insurance Expense.

16 The sequence of accounts in the ledger is as follows: (a) assets, (b) liabilities, (c) owner's equity, (d) revenue, and (e) expenses. This sequence is called *financial statement order*, because the three groups of balance sheet accounts (assets, liabilities, owner's equity) come before the income statement accounts (revenue and expenses).

17 Buildings, office equipment, and other *plant assets* have limited useful lives over which the asset is used up. A portion of the cost of the asset becomes expense (price of goods used up) during each year of its use. This process of allocating the cost of a plant asset over its useful life is called *depreciation*. For example, if we acquire a $100,000 building with an estimated life of 25 years and no salvage value, the depreciation expense each year will be $\frac{1}{25}$ of $100,000, or $4,000. To ignore depreciation would cause expenses to be understated and therefore net income to be overstated.

18 Depreciation differs from most expenses in that no immediate or near-term cash outlay is required. The cash outlay was made *in advance* when the plant asset was acquired.

19 The journal entry to record depreciation is made at the end of the period by a debit to *Depreciation Expense* and a credit to *Accumulated Depreciation*. The Accumulated Depreciation account has a credit balance, and appears on the balance sheet as a deduction from the related asset account. The net amount (asset cost minus accumulated depreciation) represents the undepreciated cost (benefits remaining) of the asset. Undepreciated cost is also called *book value* or *carrying value*.

20 No one sends us a bill to show us how much of our building was "used up" in a specific accounting period. The entry to record depreciation expense is based on our understanding of what constitutes "expenses." Entries to record expenses and revenue that are not evidenced by transactions in the current period are called *adjusting entries*.

21 After the adjusting entries, such as recognizing depreciation expense, are made, an *adjusted trial balance* is prepared to prove that the ledger is still in balance.

22 The *income statement* is a formal financial statement which lists the revenue, deducts the expenses, and shows the net income of a business concern for a specified period of time (the accounting period).

23 The income statement is of great interest to managers, investors, and other groups, but it has certain limitations. It is not entirely accurate, because many transactions overlap accounting periods and their effect on any one period is merely an estimate. Also, the economic significance of some events (such as the discovery of an oil well) cannot be objectively measured and reflected in the income statement.

24 The *report form* of balance sheet contains the same information as the *account form* previously illustrated. However, in the report form the assets are listed and totaled in the upper half of the page. The liabilities and owner's equity constitute a separate section in the lower half of the page.

25 The income statement relates to the balance sheet because the net income figure is one of the causes of change in owner's equity.

26 *Closing the accounts* means transferring the balances of the revenue and expense accounts at the end of each accounting period into an account used to measure net income, called

the *Income Summary* account. If revenue (credit balances) exceeds expenses (debit balances), the Income Summary account will have a credit balance representing the net income for the period. If the expenses exceed the revenue, the Income Summary account will have a debit balance, representing a net loss. In either case, the Income Summary account is then closed by transferring its balance to the owner's capital account. Transferring a credit balance from the Income Summary (representing net income) causes the owner's capital account to increase; transferring a debit balance (net loss) into the capital account causes that account to decrease.

27 The *drawing* account, used to record the owner's withdrawals of assets from the business, is closed by transferring its debit balance into the owner's capital account. Drawings by the owner do not go through the Income Summary account because withdrawals are not an expense.

28 The principal purpose of closing the revenue and expense accounts is to reduce their balances to zero at the end of the period so that they are ready to measure the revenue and expenses of the next period.

29 Four journal entries are generally used to close the accounts: (a) close revenue accounts into Income Summary, (b) close expense accounts into Income Summary, (c) close the Income Summary into the owner's capital account, and (d) close the owner's drawing account into his or her capital account. These journal entries are called *closing entries.*

30 After the accounts are closed, an *after-closing trial balance* is prepared to prove that the ledger is still in balance. The after-closing trial balance will contain only balance sheet accounts since all others will have zero balances.

31 The accounting procedures covered thus far may be summarized in eight steps: (a) journalize transaction, (b) post amounts to ledger, (c) prepare a trial balance, (d) make end-of-period adjustments, (e) prepare an adjusted trial balance, (f) prepare financial statements, (g) journalize and post closing entries, and (h) prepare an after-closing trial balance.

32 We have defined revenue as the price of goods sold and services rendered and expenses as the price of goods and services used during the period. These definitions of revenue and expenses are called *accrual basis* accounting. An alternative to accrual basis accounting is *cash basis* accounting. Under cash basis accounting, revenue is not recorded until received in cash; expenses are recognized in the period in which cash payment is made. The cash basis does not give a fair measure of profitability. For instance, the cash basis ignores revenue earned but not yet received and expenses incurred but not yet paid. We shall therefore use only the *accrual basis* to determine net income.

TEST YOURSELF ON MEASURING BUSINESS INCOME

True or False

For each of the following statements, circle the T or the F to indicate whether the statement is true or false.

T F 1 If a real estate firm using the accrual basis of accounting sells a client's building in May but the commission is not collected until July, the revenue is earned in May and should be included in the May income statement.

T F 2 Expenses cause a decrease in owner's equity and are recorded by debits.

T (F) 3 If cash receipts are $10,000 greater than total expenses for a given period, the business will earn a net income of $10,000 or more.

T F 4 The journal entry to recognize a revenue or an expense must always affect an asset or liability account as well.

T F 5 Under accrual basis accounting, revenue is recognized when cash is received, and expenses are recognized when cash is paid.

T F 6 An expense may be recognized and recorded even though no cash outlay has been made.

T F 7 Buying a building for cash is just exchanging one asset for another and will not result in an expense even in future periods.

T F 8 Revenue increases owner's equity and is recorded by a credit.

T F 9 Revenue accounts are closed at the end of the period by debiting the revenue accounts and transferring their balances by crediting the Income Summary account.

T F   10 If a business is operating profitably, the entry to close the Income Summary account will consist of a debit to Income Summary and a credit to the owner's capital account.

T F   11 If expenses are larger than revenue, the Income Summary account will have a debit balance.

T F   12 The owner's drawing account is closed at the end of the period by transferring its balance to the Income Summary account.

T F   13 The entry to recognize depreciation is an example of an adjusting entry.

T F   14 An increase in an expense account is the equivalent of a decrease in owner's equity.

T F   15 An adjusted trial balance contains only balance sheet accounts.

T F   (16) In a well-established business which had been audited annually by a CPA, it would be reasonable to expect the Depreciation Expense account and the Accumulated Depreciation account to have equal balances.

Completion Statements

Fill in the necessary words or amounts to complete the following statements:

1 Owner's equity may be changed by either _____ and _____ or a change in the owner's _____ .

2 The Income Summary account is used to bring together the balances of the _____ _____ and _____ accounts.

3 The process of allocating the _____ of a plant asset to expense as that asset is used up is called _____ .

4 Performance Products Company began business on July 7. The company made the following total cash sales: July, $18,000; August, $26,000. Sales on 30-day credit were July, $31,000; August, $42,000. All the July credit sales were collected in August, and all accounts receivable originating in August were collected in September. The total revenue for July was $ _____ , and total revenue for August was $ _____ . Total cash receipts in August were $ _____ .

5 The principal distinction between expenses and withdrawals by the owner is that expenses are incurred for the purpose of _____ _____ . A similarity between the two is that both expenses and withdrawals cause a _____ in _____ _____ .

6 A credit balance in the Income Summary account indicates a _____ _____ for the period. This will cause owner's equity to _____ .

7 If expenses exceed revenue, the Income Summary account will be closed into the _____ _____ account by an entry which _____ the Income Summary account.

8 Assets, liabilities, and owner's equity are the only accounts that will have balances after the _____ _____ have all been posted.

9 An owner's withdrawing assets from a business will cause owner's equity to _____ . Such an event will be recorded by a debit to the owner's _____ account and a credit to the related asset accounts. The owner's investing assets in the business will cause owner's equity to _____ and will be recorded as a debit to the asset accounts and a credit to the owner's _____ account.

Multiple Choice

Choose the best answer for each of the following questions and enter the identifying letter in the space provided.

_____ 1 During March, the Campus Bike Shop had revenue of $3,000 and expenses of $1,800. The owner also withdrew $600 cash from the business. If owner's equity on March 1 was $8,600, owner's equity on March 31 must have been:
a $10,400
b $ 9,800
c $ 9,200
d $ 8,000

_____ 2 If a journal entry recognizes revenue, the other part of the entry might:
a Decrease an asset account.
b Increase the owner's capital account.
c Increase an asset account.
d Increase a liability account.

_____ 3 If a journal entry recognizes an expense, the other part of the entry might:
a Increase an asset account.

b Decrease the owner's equity account.
c Decrease a liability account.
d Increase a liability account.

_____ 4 The Dillingham Company had a net income in October of $6,040. During the month, the owner withdrew $2,160 cash from the business. The Income Summary account was closed at the end of October by:
a Debiting the account $6,040.
b Crediting the account $6,040.
c Debiting the account $3,880.
d Crediting the account $2,160.

_____ 5 On April 1, Hudson Company received and paid a $700 bill for advertising done in March. In addition to this bill, the company paid $6,100 during April for expenses incurred in that month. On May 2, Hudson Company paid a $4,600 payroll to employees for work done in April. Based on these facts, total expenses for the month of April were:
a $6,100
b $6,800
c $10,700
d $11,400

_____ 6 The principal difference between depreciation and most types of expense is that depreciation:
a Is deductible only in years in which a profit is earned.
b Does not require an immediate or near-term cash outlay.
c Can be avoided if management creates a cash fund for use in replacing worn-out assets.
d Is subject to more precise measurement.

Exercises

1 Using the adjusted trial balance to the right, prepare (a) an income statement and (b) a balance sheet in *report form* for Speedline Autor Repair.

a
SPEEDLINE AUTO REPAIR
Income Statement
For the Month Ended May 31, 19___

SPEEDLINE AUTO REPAIR
Adjusted Trial Balance
May 31, 19___

	Debit	Credit
Cash	$ 2,900	
Accounts receivable	12,400	
Garage equipment	24,000	
Accumulated depreciation: garage equipment		$ 7,600
Accounts payable		9,100
Wages payable		800
Robert Leo, capital, Apr. 30, 19___		19,200
Robert Leo, drawings	1,200	
Repair revenue		21,000
Rent expense	900	
Wages expense	14,000	
Supplies expense	2,000	
Utilities expense	100	
Depreciation expense: garage equipment	200	
	$57,700	$57,700

b
SPEEDLINE AUTO REPAIR
Balance Sheet
May 31, 19___

Assets		
Liabilities & Owner's Equity		

2 Indicate the effect of the following errors on each of the accounting elements described in the column headings below. Use the following symbols:

O = overstated, *U* = understated, *NE* = no effect

Error	Total Revenue	Total Expenses	Net Income	Total Assets	Total Liabilities	Total Owner's Equity
Example: Rendered services to a customer and received immediate payment in cash but made no record of the transaction.	*U*	*NE*	*U*	*U*	*NE*	*U*
1 Payment for repairs erroneously debited to Building account.						
2 Recorded collection of an account receivable by debiting cash and crediting a revenue account.						
3 Failed to record depreciation for the current period.						
4 Recorded twice a purchase of office equipment on credit.						
5 Recorded the purchase of office equipment for cash as a debit to Office Equipment and a credit to Depreciation Expense.						
6 Recorded cash payment for advertising by debiting Repairs Expense and crediting Cash.						

4
COMPLETION OF THE ACCOUNTING CYCLE

HIGHLIGHTS OF THE CHAPTER

1 For the purpose of measuring income, the life of a business is divided into accounting periods of *equal length*. This helps us to compare revenue and expenses of the current period with those of prior periods and determine whether operating results are improving or declining.

2 Many business transactions are begun in one accounting period and completed in a later period. A precise cutoff of transactions at the end of each accounting period is essential to the preparation of accurate financial statements.

3 *Adjusting entries* are made at the end of the accounting period to apportion transactions between periods. We want to be sure that the income statement contains all revenue earned and all expenses incurred in the period covered but does not contain any revenue or expense applicable to the following period. Similarly, the balance sheet must contain all the assets owned and all liabilities owed on the last day of the period.

4 Every adjusting entry affects both a balance sheet account and an income statement account. Two purposes are accomplished by adjusting entries: (a) the proper amount of revenue and expense is apportioned to the current accounting period, and (b) the proper amount of related asset or liability is established for the balance sheet.

5 Four types of transactions requiring adjusting entries are recorded costs, recorded revenue, unrecorded expenses, and unrecorded revenue. *Recorded costs* consist of costs which have been recorded in one period but will benefit more than one accounting period. A fire insurance policy, for example, may cost $3,600 and run for three years. In this case, $\frac{1}{36}$ of the policy is used up in each month and should be recognized as an expense of that month. A recorded-cost adjusting entry at the end of each month would transfer to expense the portion of the total cost that had been used up in the period. In journal entry form, we would debit Insurance Expense $100 and credit Unexpired Insurance $100. Depreciation is another recorded-cost adjusting entry.

6 *Recorded revenue* results when revenue has been received (and therefore recorded) before it has been earned. An example is a fee received in advance for services we are to render in the future. When we are paid in advance, a liability exists either to render the service or to refund the customer's money. As we render the service (or deliver the goods), we are earning the revenue and reducing our liability. At the end of the period, an adjusting entry would be made debiting (reducing) the liability and crediting a revenue account for the portion of the advance payments we have earned during the period.

7 *Unrecorded expenses* adjusting entries are necessary when an expense has been incurred, but payment will not have to be made until a future period. For example, if employees will not be paid until February 2 for work they did in January, the cost of this work should be recognized as expense

in January. Also, at the end of January, a liability exists to pay the employees. The unrecorded expense adjusting entry at the end of January would debit Wages Expense (to recognize the expense in January) and credit Wages Payable (to record the liability to make a future payment).

8 Revenue which has been earned but not yet recorded must be brought on the books by an *unrecorded revenue* adjusting entry. For example, at the end of a period, services may have been rendered but no accounting entry made and no bill sent to the customer. The necessary adjusting entry would debit an account receivable and credit a revenue account.

9 Because so much detailed work is necessary at the end of the period in adjusting and closing the books and preparing financial statements, it is easy to make errors. One way to simplify this work and avoid errors in the permanent accounting records is to use a *work sheet*.

10 A work sheet is a large columnar sheet of paper, prepared in pencil, organizing all accounting data required at the end of the period. An error made on the work sheet is easily corrected; furthermore, a work sheet is self-balancing so that many types of errors are automatically brought to light. The work sheet is a working tool of the accountant which is helpful in preparing accurate financial statements at the end of the period. It also serves as a guide to making the necessary adjusting and closing entries in the accounting records. The work sheet, as the name suggests, is not a financial statement nor part of the permanent accounting records. It is the source from which financial statements are prepared and from which adjusting and closing entries are made in the journal.

11 To prepare a work sheet, carry out the following steps:
 a Enter ledger account balances in the Trial Balance columns.
 b Enter all necessary adjusting entries in columns 3 and 4, the Adjustments columns.
 c Combine the trial balance amounts with the related adjustments and enter the adjusted balances in the Adjusted Trial Balance columns.
 d Extend the amounts in the Adjusted Trial Balance columns horizontally across the work sheet into one of the four remaining

columns. Revenue and expense accounts go to the Income Statement columns. Asset, liability, and owner's equity accounts go to the Balance Sheet columns.
 e Total the Income Statement columns and enter the net income or loss as the balancing figure. This net income or loss is also entered in the Balance Sheet columns, since net income or loss becomes a part of owner's equity. Total both pairs of columns.

12 Financial statements are easily prepared from the work sheet as the data needed are already classified in the last four columns.

13 Adjusting entries are entered in the journal by taking data directly from the Adjustments columns of the work sheet. Preparation of closing entries from the work sheet may be summarized as follows:
 a Close the revenue accounts by debiting each account listed in the credit column of the Income Statement columns, and credit Income Summary.
 b Close the expense accounts by crediting each account in the debit column of the Income Statement columns, and debit Income Summary.
 c To close the Income Summary account, transfer the balancing figure of the Income Statement columns of the work sheet (also the balance of the Income Summary account) to the owner's capital account.
 d Close the drawing account by debiting the owner's capital account and crediting the drawing account.

14 When a work sheet is used, the sequence of procedures making up the accounting cycle may be summarized in six steps:
 a Record all transactions daily in the journal.
 b Post journal entries to ledger accounts.
 c Prepare the work sheet.
 d Prepare financial statements from the work sheet.
 e Enter adjusting and closing entries in the journal using the work sheet as a source. Post these entries to ledger accounts.
 f Prepare an after-closing trial balance.

15 Most companies prepare *monthly* financial statements from work sheets, but close the books only once a year. Monthly and quarterly financial statements are called *interim statements*.

16 *Reversing entries* are an optional bookkeeping procedure in which certain year-end adjusting entries are reversed on the first day

of the next accounting period. The reversing entry is exactly the opposite of the related adjusting entry: it contains the same account titles and the same dollar amounts as the adjusting entry, but the debits and credits are the reverse of those in the adjusting entry. The purpose of reversing entries is to permit accounting personnel to record routine transactions in a standard manner, without referring to the amounts of revenue or expense accrued at year-end.

17 Reversing entries may be used for those adjusting entries which (a) accrue a liability for an expense or (b) accrue a receivable for revenue. Adjusting entries that apportion a recorded cost between accounting periods (such as the adjusting entry to record depreciation) are not reversed.

TEST YOURSELF ON COMPLETION OF THE ACCOUNTING CYCLE

True or False

For each of the following statements, circle the T or the F to indicate whether the statement is true or false.

T F   1 If all transactions were originally recorded in conformity with generally accepted accounting principles, there would be no need for adjusting entries at the end of the period.

T F   2 Adjusting entries contribute to accurate financial reporting by allocating revenues to the period in which they were earned and expenses to the period in which they were incurred.

T F   3 Every adjusting entry must change both an income statement account and a balance sheet account.

T F   4 An account called Unearned Commissions Revenue is a revenue account.

T F   5 The adjusting entry to allocate the cost of a three-year fire insurance policy to expense will cause total assets to increase.

T F   6 The adjusting entry to recognize that commission revenue not previously recorded (or billed to a customer) has now been earned will cause total assets to increase.

T F   7 The adjusting entry to recognize an expense which has not yet been recorded and will not be paid until some future period will cause total assets to decrease.

T F   8 The adjusting entry to recognize that a fee received in advance from a customer has now been earned will cause total liabilities to increase.

T F   9 If employees have worked eight days in a period for which they will not be paid until the first payday next period and if no adjusting entry is made at the end of this period, total liabilities will be understated and both net income and owner's equity will be overstated.

T F 10 The original cost of a building minus the accumulated depreciation is called the *book value*, or *carrying value*.

T F 11 The balance of the Accumulated Depreciation account will appear in the Balance Sheet credit column of a work sheet.

T F 12 The balances of any unearned revenue accounts will appear in the Income Statement credit column of the work sheet.

T F 13 The Balance Sheet credit column of the work sheet usually contains only liability accounts and owner's equity accounts.

T F 14 Net income will appear on the work sheet as a balancing figure in the Income Statement debit column and the Balance Sheet credit column.

T F 15 Sullivan's Car Wash borrowed $10,000 from its bank on June 1, signing a six-month 9% interest-bearing note for that amount. The proper adjusting entry at June 30 will be a $75 debit to an expense account and a $75 credit to a liability account.

T F 16 A separate trial balance is unnecessary when a work sheet is used.

T F 17 The total of the Balance Sheet columns of the work sheet will usually be the same as the totals appearing on a formal balance sheet.

T F 18 The Adjustments columns of the work sheet for Martin's Cabinet Shop contained only two adjustments: one to allocate a portion of the three-year fire insurance policy to expense, and the other to record the earnings of a revenue which had been received in advance. The totals of the Adjusted

Trial Balance columns would be larger than the totals of the Trial Balance columns.

T F 19 The adjusting entries to accrue fees earned and salaries expense through year-end may both be reversed on the first day of the next accounting period.

Completion Statements

Fill in the necessary words or amounts to complete the following statements:

1 The four types of transactions requiring adjusting entries are _____ _____, _____ _____, _____, _____, and _____ _____ transactions.

2 An adjusting entry at November 30 concerning the cost of an insurance policy serves two purposes: (a) it _____ the proper amount of _____ to November operations, and (b) it reduces the _____ account entitled _____ _____ _____ so that the correct amount will appear on the November 30 balance sheet.

3 Adjusting entries always recognize either a _____ or an _____ .

4 The adjusting entry to record receiving some of the benefits in the current period from an expenditure made in an earlier period consists of a _____ to an _____ account and a _____ to an _____ account.

5 If a customer pays in advance for services to be rendered, the entry to record the receipt of the payment consists of a _____ to an _____ account and a _____ to a _____ account.

6 If an expense has been accumulating from day to day (such as wages) without being recorded, the proper adjusting entry would _____ an _____

_____ account and _____ a _____ account.

7 If an expenditure will yield benefits to a business only during the period in which it is made, the entry for the expenditure consists of a _____ to an _____ _____ account and a _____ _____ to an _____ account and/or a _____ account.

8 If an expenditure will yield benefits to the business over several periods, the entry for the expenditure consists of a _____ to an _____ account and a credit to an _____ account and/or a _____ _____ account.

9 In the work sheet prepared by a business operating at a loss, the Income Statement _____ column will exceed the _____ column and the excess of the _____ over the _____ will be entered in the _____ column in order to bring the two Income Statement columns into balance.

10 The South Bay Management Company agreed to manage an apartment building beginning May 15, 19___, for 1 year at a management fee of $400 per month. The first $400 payment is received June 15, 19___. The adjusting entry at May 31, 19_ should consist of a debit to _____ _____ _____ and a credit to _____ _____ _____ _____ .When the first payment is received on June 15, the collection should be recorded by an entry debiting _____ for $400, and crediting _____ _____ _____ _____ for $_____ and _____ _____ _____ for $_____ .

11 On December 31, Year 4, the accountant of Morrow Company made an adjusting entry to accrue salaries expense through year-end. The appropriate reversing entry should consist of a debit to _____ _____ and a credit to _____ _____ and should be dated _____ , _____ .

Multiple Choice

Choose the best answer for each of the following questions and enter the identifying letter in the space provided.

_____ **1** An adjusting entry should never consist of:
a A debit to an asset and a credit to revenue.
b A debit to an asset and a credit to a liability.
c A debit to expense and a credit to a liability.
d A debit to a liability and a credit to revenue.

_____ **2** Assets would be overstated if a necessary adjusting entry were omitted for:
a Expired insurance.
b Accrued salaries.
c Accrued interest earned.
d Revenue collected in advance during the period.

_____ **3** The preparation of a work sheet:
a Constitutes creation of a formal financial statement.
b Eliminates the need for entering adjusting entries in the journal.
c Provides the information needed for adjusting and closing entries.
d Serves no purposes unless the books are to be closed.

_____ **4** The entry recording the liability to employees for work done during the period for which they have not yet been paid is an example of which type of adjusting entry?
a Recorded costs.
b Recorded revenue.
c Unrecorded expenses.
d Unrecorded revenue.

_____ **5** Both the accounts for Depreciation Expense and Accumulated Depreciation:
a Are closed at the end of the period.
b Appear in the Trial Balance columns of the work sheet.
c Appear in the Adjusted Trial Balance columns of the work sheet.
d Appear in the after-closing trial balance.

_____ **6** Failure to make an adjusting entry to recognize accrued interest receivable would cause:
a An understatement of assets, net income, and owner's equity.
·b An understatement of liabilities and an overstatement of net income and owner's equity.
c An overstatement of assets, net income, and owner's equity.
d No effect on assets, liabilities, net income, and owner's equity.

_____ **7** Which of the following adjusting entries will result in a decrease in assets and owner's equity?
a The entry to record the earned portion of rent received in advance.
b The entry to record accrued wages payable.
c The entry to record a revenue earned but not yet received.
d None of the above.

_____ **8** A balance sheet account was debited in the amount of $1,240 for office supplies purchased during the first year of operations. At year-end, the office supplies on hand were counted and determined to represent a cost of $360. The appropriate adjusting entry would:
a Have no effect on net income.
b Consist of a debit to expense of $360 and a credit to the balance sheet account.
c Decrease assets of $1,240.
d Increase expenses $880.

_____ **9** Which of the following amounts appears in both the Income Statement credit column and the Balance Sheet debit column of a work sheet?
a Net income.
b Net loss.
c Accumulated depreciation.
d Drawings.

_____ **10** When a work sheet is used, the normal sequence of accounting procedures would call for:
a Journalizing the adjusting entries before preparing the work sheet.
b Posting adjusting entries to the ledger after preparing an after-closing trial balance.
c Preparing a work sheet before journalizing adjusting and closing entries.
d Journalizing closing entries before preparing an adjusted trial balance.

Exercises

1 Use the adjustments below to complete the work sheet on page 24 for the month ended June 30, 19__.

a Unexpired insurance at June 30 amounted to $300.

b Office supplies on hand were determined by count to amount to $250.

c The office equipment is being depreciated on the basis of a 10-year life with no salvage value. Record one month's depreciation.

d Accrued interest on notes payable at June 30 amounted to $50.

e Commissions still unearned at June 30 amounted to $700.

f Accrued salaries payable at June 30 were $200.

	Trial Balance		Adjustments		Adjusted Trial Balance		Income Statement		Balance Sheet	
	Debit	Credit	Debit	Credit	Debit	Credit	Debit	Credit	Debit	Credit
Cash	5,100									
Accounts receivable	17,300									
Unexpired insurance	360									
Office supplies	900									
Office equipment	4,800									
Accumulated depreciation: office equipment		560								
Notes payable		8,000								
Accounts payable		1,800								
Unearned commissions		1,500								
Steven Nuccio, capital, May 31, 19__		16,000								
Steven Nuccio, drawing	1,000									
Commissions earned		15,000								
Rent expense	2,400									
Salaries expense	11,000									
	42,860	42,860								
Insurance expense										
Office supplies expense										
Depreciation expense: office equipment										
Interest expense										
Interest payable										
Salaries payable										
Net income										

2 On the journal page below, prepare adjusting and closing entries using the information contained in the work sheet prepared in Exercise **1**.

General Journal

19___		**Adjusting Entries**		
		a		
June	30			
		b		
	30			
		c		
	30			
		d		
	30			
		e		
	30			
		f		
	30			
		Closing Entries		
	30			

5

ACCOUNTING FOR PURCHASES AND SALES OF MERCHANDISE

HIGHLIGHTS OF THE CHAPTER

1 A merchandising company is one whose principal activity is buying and selling merchandise. It uses the same accounting concepts and methods as the service-type business we studied in Chapters 1 to 4. The merchandising company, however, requires some other accounts and techniques to control and record the purchase and sale of merchandise.

2 The principal source of revenue for a merchandising company is from the sale of goods. To succeed, it must sell its goods at prices higher than the prices paid in acquiring those goods from manufacturers or other suppliers. The selling price of goods in a retail store must cover both (a) the cost of the goods to the store and (b) the operating expenses, such as rent and advertising, and still leave a reasonable profit (net income).

3 The *revenue* of a merchandising company comes from *selling goods to customers*. A sale of merchandise is recorded by debiting Cash or Accounts Receivable and crediting a revenue account called *Sales*.

4 The customers of the merchandising company concern may occasionally find that the goods they bought are unsatisfactory, and return them to the store. This is called a *sales return*. Sales returns are recorded by debiting *Sales Returns and Allowances* and crediting either the customer's account or Cash.

5 Credit terms may vary between companies and industries. Some common credit terms are *n/30*, which is read "net 30 days," and

n/60. Net 30 days means the customer must make payment in full within 30 days of the date of the invoice.

6 The seller may offer a *cash discount* to encourage customers to pay invoices early. Thus, credit terms of *2/10, n/30* would mean the customers may take a deduction of 2% of their invoices if they pay within 10 days. Otherwise, they have 30 days to pay the full amount of the invoices. A cash discount is called a *sales discount* by the seller and a *purchase discount* by the buyer.

7 The seller records a sales discount by debiting an account called Sales Discounts and crediting Accounts Receivable. In the income statement, both the Sales Discounts and the Sales Returns and Allowances accounts are deducted from Sales to show a *net sales* figure.

8 In a multiple-step income statement (see Highlight **29**), the *cost of goods sold* is deducted from the net sales figure to determine the amount of *gross profit*. Gross profit is the *excess* of the sales price of goods sold over the seller's cost for those goods. Gross profit often is expressed as a *percentage of net sales* which is called the *gross profit rate*.

9 An *inventory* of merchandise consists of the stock of goods on hand and *available for sale* to customers. There arc two alternative approaches to determine the amount of inventory and the cost of goods sold: (a) the *perpetual inventory method* and (b) the *periodic inventory method*.

10 For articles of high unit value, such as automobiles, the *perpetual inventory method*

is appropriate. Under this method, the *Inventory* account is debited when merchandise is purchased. As each unit is sold, its cost is transferred from the Inventory account to an account called *Cost of Goods Sold*. Thus we have a perpetual or running record of the cost of goods sold during the period and the cost of goods on hand. In this chapter we will concentrate on the *periodic inventory method*, which is very widely used.

 11 Under the *periodic inventory system*, the cost of merchandise acquired is debited to an account entitled *Purchases*, instead of being debited to Inventory. As units are sold, *no entry is made to record the cost of the goods sold*. Thus, the accounting records do not show from day to day the cost of the goods on hand (inventory) or the cost of goods sold during the period. Instead, the value of the inventory is determined *at the end of each accounting period* by taking a *physical count* of the merchandise in stock.

12 The *cost of goods sold* is computed by the following steps:

a Add the goods on hand at the beginning of the period (the ending inventory from last period) plus any additional goods acquired during the period (purchases) to get the *cost of goods available for sale*.

b From the cost of goods available for sale, subtract the goods which were not sold (namely, the inventory on hand at the end of the current period) to get the *cost of goods sold* during the period.

13 The cost of goods sold section of the income statement of a merchandising company using the *periodic inventory method* would appear as follows for the month of May:

Cost of goods sold:	
Inventory (Apr. 30)	$ 5,100
Purchases	6,300
Cost of goods available for sale	$11,400
Less: Inventory (May 31)	5,400
Cost of goods sold	$ 6,000

14 Several other factors may have to be considered in computing the cost of goods sold. For example, when merchandise purchased is found to be unsatisfactory and returned to the supplier, the return is recorded by debiting Accounts Payable and crediting *Purchase Returns and Allowances*. Purchase Returns and Allowances must then be *deducted* from Purchases in the cost of goods sold section of the income statement because the cost of goods that were returned to the supplier should not be included in the cost of goods available for sale.

15 If merchandise is paid for within the discount period, the buyer may take advantage of the cash discount. For example, if $1,000 of merchandise is purchased on terms of 2/10, n/30, the buyer may take a 2% purchase discount ($20) if payment is made within 10 days. The buyer records a purchase discount by debiting Accounts Payable and crediting Purchase Discounts. Since a purchase discount reduces the cost of purchased merchandise, the Purchase Discounts account is deducted from Purchases in arriving at the cost of goods available for sale.

16 The freight charges on goods acquired during the period are a legitimate part of the cost of goods available for sale. Freight charges on *inbound* shipments of merchandise are recorded by debiting an account called *Transportation-in*. Transportation-in must then be added to Purchases to determine the total cost of goods acquired during the period. *Note*: Do not confuse Transportation-in with the freight expense on *outbound* shipments. Freight on outbound shipments is a selling expense, not part of the cost of goods being acquired.

17 Look at an expanded cost of goods sold section, including Purchase Returns and Allowances, Purchase Discounts, and Transportation-in, in your textbook (page 193).

18 In a work sheet for a merchandising business, the ending inventory does not appear in the trial balance. It is written on a line below the trial balance and the adjustments. The amount of the ending inventory is placed in the Income Statement credit column and in the Balance Sheet debit column. This treatment results in reporting the ending inventory in the income statement (cost of goods sold section) and in the balance sheet among the assets.

19 Closing entries for a merchandising business include entries to (a) eliminate the beginning inventory, (b) record the ending inventory, and (c) close the accounts relating to the sales and purchases of merchandise.

20 The beginning inventory is cleared out of the Inventory account by a debit to Income Summary and a credit to Inventory. The

ending inventory is brought on the books by a debit to Inventory and a credit to Income Summary.

21 Purchases, Transportation-in, Sales Returns and Allowances, and Sales Discounts have *debit* balances and are closed in the same entry that closes the *expense* accounts. Purchase Returns and Allowances, and Purchase Discounts have *credit* balances and are closed with the *revenue* accounts.

22 The financial statements of a single proprietorship include a *statement of owner's equity*, which shows all of the changes in owner's equity during the period. The statement starts with the beginning balance in the owner's capital account and then shows any increases in equity (net income and additional investments and decreases in equity (net loss or withdrawals) for the period. The resulting total is the owner's equity at the end of the period, which will appear in the balance sheet. A statement of owner's equity is illustrated on page 198 of your textbook.

23 Standard classifications generally are used in balance sheets and income statements to make these statements easier to read and more informative. These standard classifications help investors to make comparisons between companies.

24 On the balance sheet, assets are usually classified into three groups: current assets, plant and equipment, and other assets. *Current assets* consist of cash and items capable of being *converted into cash* within a short period without interfering with normal business operations. Examples are marketable securities, receivables, inventories, and prepaid expenses.

25 Liabilities are divided between current and long-term. Those debts which must be paid within one year or the *operating cycle* (whichever is longer) are called *current liabilities*. Those maturing at more distant dates are long-term. Accounts payable and accrued wages payable are examples of current liabilities.

26 The operating cycle is the period of time a business usually takes to perform its function of buying (or making) inventory, selling that inventory, and collecting the accounts receivable generated by those sales. This may be described as the period of time a business takes to convert cash into inventory, into accounts receivable, and then back into cash,

as illustrated by the following diagram of the operating cycle.

(buy inventory) (sell inventory)   (collect receivables)

Cash→Inventory→Accounts Receivable→Cash

27 Current assets and liabilities are used to measure a firm's *solvency*, or debt-paying ability. One measure of solvency is the *current ratio*. The current ratio is computed by dividing the total of current assets by total current liabilities. A current ratio of about 2 to 1 is generally considered indicative of reasonable debt-paying ability.

28 Another measure of solvency is the amount of *working capital*. Working capital is the *excess* of current assets over current liabilities (current assets *minus* current liabilities).

29 The extent of classification within an income statement depends upon whether the statement is organized in the multiple-step or the single-step format. In a *multiple-step* income statement, costs and expenses are deducted from revenue in a series of steps. First, the cost of goods sold is deducted to arrive at gross profit. Next, operating expenses are deducted to determine Income from Operations. Operating expenses are usually subdivided between selling expenses and general and administrative expenses. Items of revenue and expense *not related* to selling and administrative functions (such as interest earned on investments) are deducted to arrive at net income. A multiple-step income statement is illustrated on page 206 of your textbook.

30 In a *single-step* income statement, all costs and expenses are deducted from total revenue in one single step. An illustration appears on page 207 of your text.

TEST YOURSELF ON ACCOUNTING FOR PURCHASES AND SALES OF MERCHANDISE

True or False

For each of the following statements, circle the T or the F to indicate whether the statement is true or false.

T F   1 The accounting concepts and methods presented in Chapters 1 to 4 for a service-type business are not applicable to a merchandising business.

T F   2 Gross profit is the profit the business

would have made if all of the goods available for sale had been sold during the period.

T F 3 If the gross profit rate is 40%, this means that the cost of goods sold is 60% of the sales price.

T F 4 Salary to the owner and interest on the owner's investment are not deducted as expenses in determining the net income of a business.

T F 5 When a cash sale is made by a merchandising business, the transaction is described by a debit to Cash and a credit to Sales, whether or not the sales price exceeded the cost of the goods sold.

T F 6 The purchase of either merchandise or office equipment by a merchandising concern would be recorded as a debit to Purchases and a credit to either Cash or Accounts Payable.

T F 7 The perpetual inventory method will reflect from day to day the cost of goods sold so far during the period and the current balance of goods on hand.

T F 8 The perpetual inventory system is appropriate for businesses handling high unit-cost goods, such as automobiles or fur coats, but is less practical for stores handling a large quantity of low-priced items.

T F 9 When the periodic inventory method is used, the Inventory account is debited when merchandise is purchased and credited when goods are sold.

T F 10 The Transportation-in account contains the freight charges paid on inbound shipments of merchandise and is added to the Purchases account as a step toward finding the cost of goods available for sale.

T F 11 When a periodic inventory system is in use, the cost of goods sold section contains two amounts for Inventory: a beginning inventory which is added in arriving at the cost of goods available for sale, and an ending inventory which is subtracted to determine the cost of goods sold.

T F 12 At the end of the period, the beginning inventory is eliminated by debiting Income Summary and crediting Inventory.

T F 13 2/10, n/30 means that a customer is entitled to a 10% discount if the in-

voice is paid within two days, or the whole amount may be paid within 30 days.

T F 14 The beginning inventory figure on this period's income statement was the ending inventory figure on last period's income statement.

T F 15 The entry to place the ending inventory on the books consists of a debit to Inventory and a credit to Accounts Payable.

T F 16 In the work sheet the ending inventory amount will appear in the Income Statement credit column and the Balance Sheet debit column but will not appear in the Trial Balance columns.

T F 17 When a customer pays an amount which includes sales tax, part of the total receipts represent a liability account rather than revenue.

T F 18 A subtotal showing gross profit appears in a multiple-step income statement, but not in a single-step income statement.

T F 19 The operating cycle of a business is the period of time between payroll dates.

T F 20 The current ratio is used to measure the relative profitability of two or more companies.

Completion Statements

Fill in the necessary words to complete the following statements:

1 The inventory account is debited when goods are acquired and credited when they are sold according to the _perpetual_ inventory method. Inventory is determined by a _physical count_ when the _periodic_ inventory method is used.

2 Adding net purchases to the beginning inventory gives the _cost of goods available for sale_. Subtracting _ending inventory_ from this figure leaves the _cost of goods sold_.

3 The excess of sales revenue over the cost of goods sold is called _gross profit_.

4 The return of merchandise to Cougar Company by a customer would be recorded on Cougar Company's books as a debit to

<u>Sales return and allowances</u>
and a credit to either __cash__ or __accounts__
__receivable__.

5 Glass Maker sells merchandise to Kay, Inc., for $2,000, at terms of 2/10, n/30. Kay, Inc., makes payments one week after the date of invoice by sending a check for $ __1960__ . The entry to be made by Glass Maker upon receipt of the check would consist of a debit to cash for $ __1940__ , a __debit__ to __sales__ __discount__ for $ __40__ , and a credit to __Accounts__ __receivable__ for $ __2000__ .

6 There are two ways to account for state sales taxes: either (a) credit a __liability__ account for the amount of the tax at the time of sale or (b) wait until the end of the period and transfer the total tax owed out of the __sales__ account and into an account called __Sales tax payable__ .

7 In a classified balance sheet, the three groups of assets are: (a) __Current asset__, (b) __plant and equipment__, and (c) __other assets__ .

8 The amount by which current assets exceed current liabilities is called __working capital__ . Current assets divided by current liabilities is called the __current ratio__ . These two computations are made to measure the __solvency__ of a business enterprise.

9 The period of time a business usually takes to convert cash into inventory, then into receivables, and finally back into cash is called the __operating cycle__ .

10 An income statement which shows subtotals for such items as gross profit, total operating expenses, and income from operations is called a __multi__ - __step__ income statement.

Multiple Choice

Choose the best answer for each of the following questions and enter the identifying letter in the space provided.

_____ 1 Which of the following list of accounts is used to compute the cost of goods sold?

a Purchases, Inventory, and Sales Returns and Allowances.
b Gross Profit, Purchase Returns and Allowances, and Transportation-in.
c Inventory, Net Sales, and Purchases.
d None of the above.

_____ 2 By adding the net purchases during the period to the beginning inventory and deducting the ending inventory, we obtain an amount called the:
a Cost of goods available for sale.
b Cost of goods sold.
c Gross profit on sales.
d Operating expenses.

_____ 3 The ending inventory of Bar Marine was $42,000. If the beginning inventory had been $50,000 and the cost of goods available for sale during the period totaled $104,000, the cost of goods sold must have been:
a $196,000
b $112,000
c $ 62,000
d None of the above.

_____ 4 The beginning inventory is removed from the books by a closing entry which:
a Debits Inventory and credits Income Summary.
b Debits Income Summary and credits Inventory.
c Debits Inventory and credits Cost of Goods Sold.
d Debits Cost of Goods Sold and credits Inventory.

_____ 5 Gourmet Groceries purchased canned goods at an invoice price of $1,000 and terms of 2/10, n/30. Half of the goods were mislabeled and therefore were returned immediately to the supplier. If Gourmet Groceries pays the invoice within the discount period, the amount paid will be:
a $1,000
b $980
c $480
d $490

_____ 6 The Toy Castle, a retail toy store, had current assets of $72,000 and a current ratio of 2 to 1. The amount of working capital must have been:
a $144,000
b $108,000
c $72,000
d $36,000

_____ **7** The net sales of Regent Musical Supply in October were $20,000. If the cost of goods available for sale during the month was $18,000 and the gross profit amounted to $8,000, the ending inventory must have been:

a $4,800
b $6,000
c $10,000
d Some other amount.

Exercises

1 Insert the missing figures in the following income statement. Gross profit is 40% of net sales and net income is 10% of net sales.

Sales			$ *161,000*
Sales returns & allowances		$ 4,500	
Sales discounts		1,500	*6,000*
Net sales			$155,000
Cost of goods sold:			
Inventory, Jan 1		$ 22,000	
Purchases	$ 98,500		
Less: Purchase returns and allowances	$3,100		
Purchase discounts	2,000	*5,100*	
Net purchases		*$93,400*	
Add: Transportation-in		3,600	
Cost of goods purchased		*97,000*	
Cost of goods available for sale		$ *119,000*	
Inventory, Dec. 31		26,000	
Cost of goods sold			*93,000*
Gross profit on sales			$ *62,000*
Operating expenses			*46,500*
Net income			$ *15,500*

2 Each of the following four horizontal lines represents data taken from a separate multiple-step income statement. Insert the missing amounts in the spaces provided. Indicate a net loss by placing brackets around the amount, as for example, in line a, (20,000)

	Net Sales	Cost of Goods Available for Sale	Ending Inventory	Cost of Goods Sold	Gross Profit	Operating Expenses	Net Income or (Loss)
a	400,000	325,000	*75K*	250,000	*150K*	*170K*	(20,000)
b	700,000	*500K*	90,000	*410K*	290,000	235,000	*55K*
c	250,000	210,000	*32K*	*178K*	72,000	105,000	*(33K)*
d	*550K*	*412K*	82,000	330,000	*220K*	185,000	35,000

6
INTERNAL CONTROL

HIGHLIGHTS OF THE CHAPTER

1 To many people, "internal control" means the precautions a business takes to protect itself against fraud. Actually, such precautions are only a small part of a system of internal control. The basic purpose of internal control is to *promote the efficient operation of a business*.

2 A system of internal control consists of all steps taken to (a) safeguard assets against waste, fraud, or inefficient use; (b) ensure reliability in accounting data; (c) promote compliance with company policies; and (d) evaluate the level of performance in all divisions of the business. In short, a system of internal control consists of all measures taken by management to provide assurance that everything goes according to plan.

3 Internal controls may be classified into two categories:

a *Accounting controls* These are the internal controls which have a direct bearing upon the reliability of the financial statements. Accounting controls include the measures concerned with safeguarding assets, authorizing and approving transactions, and the reliability of accounting data. An example of an accounting control is the requirement that a person whose duties include handling cash shall not be responsible for maintaining accounting records.

b *Administrative controls* These are internal controls that apply primarily to operational efficiency and compliance with company policies but have *no* direct bearing upon the reliability of the financial statements. Exam-ples of administrative controls include rules that no employees be required to work more than a specified number of consecutive hours and policies regarding refunds and exchanges of merchandise by customers.

4 The strength of internal accounting controls in force determines the reliability of the accounting records. When CPAs conduct an audit of a company, they always study and evaluate the system of internal control as a step toward forming an opinion on the fairness of the financial statements. For this purpose, the CPAs are primarily concerned with accounting controls rather than administrative controls. A weakness in internal accounting control does not mean that the accounting records are erroneous but does suggest to the CPAs the *possibility* that errors may exist.

5 The Foreign Corrupt Practices Act requires large corporations to maintain a system of internal control which provides assurance that transactions are executed only with the knowledge and authorization of management. Also, the act requires periodic comparisons of accounting records for assets with assets actually on hand. The purpose of these requirements is to prevent the creation of secret "slush funds" or other misuses of corporate assets. Thus, a strong system of internal control is now required by federal law.

6 No "standard" system of internal control can be designed to fit all businesses; each system must be "tailor-made" to fit the needs of the organization. However, there are several basic concepts of internal con-

trol which apply to most businesses. These include:

a *A logical organization plan* This should clearly indicate the departments or persons responsible for such functions as purchasing, receiving incoming shipments, maintaining accounting records, handling cash, and approving customers' credit. A separate person (or department) should be responsible for each function. Lines of responsibility and authority can be shown by an *organization chart*.

b *Adequate subdivision of duties* No one person should handle all aspects of a transaction from beginning to end. When several people are involved in each transaction, the work of one employee tends to serve as a check upon the work of another. Each transaction should go through four steps: it should be *authorized, approved, executed,* and *recorded*. Internal control is strengthened when each of these steps is handled by a different employee (or department).

c *Use of serially numbered documents* Most business documents, such as invoices, checks, and sales tickets, are serially numbered. The serial numbers are used to keep track of all documents. Without serial numbers on the documents, no one would know how many had been written or whether some had been lost or concealed.

d *Personnel with competence and integrity* No system of internal control will work unless the people assigned to operate it are competent.

e *Preparation of financial forecasts* Internal control is strengthened by the use of financial forecasts because errors or irregularities which cause actual results to differ from planned results will be identified and investigated.

f *An internal audit staff* Internal auditors have as their objective improving the operational efficiency of the business. They continuously study and evaluate both accounting and administrative controls and make recommendations to management for improving the system. All large businesses have an internal audit staff.

7 Strong internal control is more difficult to achieve in a small business than in a large one, because with only a few employees it is not possible to have extensive subdivision of duties. Even the smallest businesses, however, should follow such control procedures as using serially numbered documents and separating the responsibility for maintaining accounting records from responsibility for handling cash. Active participation by the owner in the key control procedures also strengthens internal control in a small business.

8 Although strong internal control is highly effective in protecting assets and increasing the reliability of accounting data, no system of internal control is foolproof. *Collusion* between two or more employees can defeat the system. Carelessness or misunderstandings can cause breakdowns in the system. Also, a system of internal control should not be so elaborate that its cost exceeds the value of the protection gained.

9 Since no system of internal control is foolproof, many companies require that employees who handle cash be *bonded*. A *fidelity bond* is a type of insurance in which a bonding company agrees to reimburse an employer, up to an agreed dollar limit, for losses caused by fraud or embezzlement by bonded employees. Fidelity bonds are not a substitute for strong internal control; they do nothing to assure the reliability of accounting data or prevent inefficient use of company assets.

10 While strong internal control calls for the division of duties between departments, it is necessary for these departments to know what the others are doing so that they may work efficiently together. Carefully designed business documents are used to coordinate the efforts of the departments and ensure that all transactions are properly authorized, approved, executed, and recorded.

11 A *purchase order* should always be prepared by the purchasing department whenever goods are ordered. One copy of the purchase order is sent to the supplier; this is the supplier's authorization to send the goods. Carbon copies of the purchase order go to the receiving department and the accounting department of the purchasing company.

12 The seller of the goods prepares an *invoice* when a purchase order is received. The invoice describes the quantities and prices of goods which will be sent to the buyer. From the viewpoint of the seller an invoice is a *sales invoice*; from the buyer's viewpoint it is a *purchase invoice*.

13 The seller mails the invoice to the buyer at the same time the goods are shipped. At the

time the invoice is issued the seller of the goods will record the sale.

14 The goods will arrive at the receiving department of the buyer. The receiving department will inspect the goods as to quality, condition, and quantities received. A *receiving report* is then prepared and sent to the accounting department.

15 The accounting department will then verify the invoice to see if payment should be made. Verifying an invoice consists of three basic steps:

a Comparing the invoice with the purchase order to see that the goods were actually ordered at the terms stated on the invoice.

b Comparing the receiving report with the purchase order and invoice to see that all the goods were received in satisfactory condition.

c Verifying the arithmetic extensions and footings of the invoice.

16 When the verification procedures are completed, the buyer will record the purchase of the goods.

17 If any discrepancy exists between the amount the buyer is willing to pay and the amount of the invoice, the buyer may send a *debit* or *credit memorandum* to the seller. This is notice to the seller that the buyer is debiting (reducing) or crediting (increasing) the *account payable on the buyer's books*. The seller may respond with a debit or credit memorandum to show that he or she is debiting (increasing) or crediting (decreasing) the corresponding *account receivable on the selling company's books*.

18 Most companies follow a policy of taking all available purchase discounts. The buyer may record purchases involving a purchase discount by using either (a) the gross price method or (b) the net price method.

19 Under the *gross price method*, the buyer records an account payable at the full invoice price and records payment within the discount period by debiting Accounts Payable and crediting Cash and Purchase Discounts. This method was discussed in Chapter 5.

20 Under the alternative *net price method*, the buyer records the account payable at the invoice price *minus the discount*, which is called the *net price*. Payment within the discount period is then recorded merely by debiting Accounts Payable and crediting

Cash for the amount paid. However, when the buyer fails to pay within the discount period, he or she will have to pay an amount *greater* than the balance of the account payable. When this occurs, the buyer should debit Accounts Payable for the net price, debit *Purchase Discounts Lost* for the amount of the discount not taken, and credit Cash for the amount of the payment.

21 The gross price method results in recording purchase discounts *taken*, which is deducted from Purchases in the income statement, just like Purchase Returns and Allowances. If the net price method is used, Purchase Discounts Lost shows the discounts *not taken* and appears in the income statement as an operating expense. The net price method has the advantage of directing management's attention to the company's failure to follow the policy of taking all purchase discounts.

22 Once invoices are approved for payment, they are put in a *tickler file* under the date on which the invoice is to be paid. Each day the invoices currently due for payment are removed from the tickler file and sent to the cashier for payment.

TEST YOURSELF ON INTERNAL CONTROL

True or False

For each of the following statements, circle the T or the F to indicate whether the statement is true or false.

T (F) 1 Sound internal control would call for the same employee to keep all the accounting records and handle all cash transactions so that responsibility for cash shortages could be attached to one person.

(T) F 2 Measures taken to ensure employees' compliance with company policies are part of the system of internal control.

(T) F 3 In conducting an audit of a company's financial statements, CPAs always study and evaluate the system of internal accounting controls.

T (F) 4 When internal control is weak, the financial statements are always in error.

T F   5 Internal auditors study and evaluate both administrative and accounting internal controls and make recommendations to management for improving the system.

T F   6 Subdivision of duties to achieve strong internal control means that many employees should be authorized to make purchases or payment for purchases.

T F   7 Internal control is strengthened when the four steps of authorizing, approving, executing, and recording transactions are performed by different persons.

T F   8 In a strong system of internal control, losses from fraud or embezzlement are impossible.

T F   9 Collusion between two or more employees can cause a breakdown in internal control.

T F   10 When all employees are bonded, there is no need for internal control procedures.

T F   11 It is easier to achieve strong internal control in a large business than in a small one.

T F   12 One reason for serially numbering purchase orders is that a missing document will quickly come to the attention of management.

T F   13 Comparing the purchase invoice with the purchase order provides assurance that all goods ordered have been received in satisfactory condition.

T F   14 A purchase order usually includes the quantity of items being ordered, a description of the items, the unit cost per item, and the total amount the buyer expects to pay.

T F   15 The invoice is prepared by the buyer of the goods, and a copy is sent to the seller.

T F   16 Comparing the purchase order with the receiving report will show that all the goods ordered actually arrived and that all goods that arrived were actually ordered.

T F   17 The employee who authorized the purchase of merchandise should inspect the merchandise on arrival and prepare a receiving report.

T F   18 A debit memorandum issued by the buyer of merchandise means the buyer has debited his or her liability

account to the seller and expects to pay less than the amount of the invoice.

T F   19 If the seller receives a debit memorandum from a customer and agrees the memorandum is valid, the seller will credit the account receivable from that customer.

T F   20 When the net price method is used to record purchases of merchandise, the buyer's accounting records will show the amount of purchase discounts lost, rather than the amount of purchase discounts taken.

Completion Statements

Fill in the necessary words or amounts to complete the following statements:

1 Internal controls which have no direct bearing upon the reliability of the financial statements are called _administrative_ controls, and internal controls which relate to safeguarding assets and promoting the reliability of accounting data are called _accounting_ controls.

2 _Collusion_ between two or more employees may cause a breakdown in a system of internal control.

3 Factors contributing to strong internal control include adequate _subdivision_ of duties, a logical _forecasting_ plan, use of _serial numbering_ documents, _competent_ personnel, and an _internal auditing_ staff.

4 Comparison of the _purchase order_ with the _receiving report_ shows whether the same quantity and quality of goods were received as had been ordered.

5 The seller of goods prepares a _sales_ invoice and mails one copy to the buyer. The buyer refers to this document as a _purchase_ invoice and compares it with the _purchase order_ to see that the seller is providing the same goods at the same terms the buyer has agreed to pay.

6 When returning some damaged merchandise to the seller, the buyer will send the seller a _debit memorandum_. If the seller accepts

the returned goods as partial settlement of the buyer's account, the seller will send a *credit memorandum* to the buyer.

7 Jade Company uses the net price method to record the purchase of merchandise with an invoice price of $5,000, at terms of 2/10, n/30. If payment is not made until *after* the discount period, the issuance of the check should be recorded by a debit to Accounts Payable for $ *4900* , a *debit* to *cash discounts lost* for $ *100* , and a credit to Cash for $ *5000* .

Multiple Choice

Choose the best answer for each of the following questions and enter the identifying letter in the space provided.

_____ **1** Which of the following measures would be most effective in creating a strong system of internal control in a merchandising business?
a Require two signatures of responsible officials on all purchase orders, receiving reports, and sales invoices.
b Delegate full responsibility to an appropriate employee or supervisor for all aspects of transactions with a designated group of customers or suppliers.
c Arrange for an annual audit by a firm of certified public accountants.
d Establish an organization structure that will provide separate departments for such functions as purchasing, receiving, selling, accounting, and credit and collection, so that the work of one organizational unit tends to verify that of another.

_____ **2** Internal control over purchases is strengthened when the functions of ordering and receiving merchandise are performed:
a By two separate departments.
b By the accounting department.
c By a department which has no responsibilities other than purchasing and receiving merchandise.
d By serially numbered employees.

_____ **3** The company receiving a shipment of goods might send a credit memorandum to the supplier if:
a Some of the goods were damaged.
b The purchase invoice was understated.

c The shipment was late.
d The purchase invoice was overstated.

_____ **4** On July 1, Sea Marine Company received a purchase order dated June 28 from Bayshore Boat Sales. Sea Marine shipped the merchandise and mailed a sales invoice on July 6. The merchandise and invoice reached Bayshore on July 8. Sea Marine Company should record the sale on:
a July 1.
b July 6.
c July 8.
d Some other date.

_____ **5** If the seller ships goods to a customer but charges more than the customer had expected to pay, the discrepancy should come to light when:
a The purchase order is compared with the purchase invoice.
b The receiving report is compared with the purchase invoice.
c The receiving report is compared with the purchase order.
d The purchase invoice is compared with the sales invoice.

_____ **6** The principal advantage of using the net price method in recording purchases is that:
a The goods cost less.
b The accounting records will draw attention to the failure to take available discounts.
c The buyer's accounting records will agree with those of the seller.
d It is not necessary to pay within the discount period in order to take advantage of the discount.

_____ **7** The net price method of recording invoices may be used in the records of:
a The seller only.
b The buyer only.
c Both the buyer and the seller.
d Neither the buyer nor the seller.

Exercises

1 Listed below are several problems that might occur in a merchandising business. Also shown is a list of internal control procedures. In the spaces provided, indicate the letter of the control procedure that would be most effective in preventing each problem from occurring. If none of the control procedures would effectively prevent a particular problem, enter an x in the space provided.

Problem Situations

_e_ Paid a supplier for goods that were never ordered.

_f_ Sales department makes credit sales to customers who do not meet the company's minimum credit standards.

_c_ Paid a supplier for goods that were never received.

_x_ Sales clerk makes an error in giving change to a cash customer.

(a) _d_ Accounts receivable department is unaware that receivables from several customers were never recorded because copies of the sales invoices were misplaced before being sent to the accounts receivable department.

_d_ An inventory clerk conceals a shortage of merchandise by understating the balance of the Purchases account.

_e_ Prices charged by a supplier exceed the amount that the company had agreed to pay.

_b_ Management is unaware that the company often fails to pay its bills in time to qualify for the cash discounts offered by suppliers.

Internal Control Procedures

a   Use of serially numbered documents

b   Use of the net price method of recording purchases

c   Comparison of purchase invoice with receiving report

d   Separation of the accounting function from custody of assets

e   Comparison of purchase invoice with purchase order

f   Separation of responsibilities for executing and approving transactions

x   None of the above control procedures would effectively prevent this situation from occurring

2   Several steps involved in the purchase of merchandise are listed below in random order. In the column headed *Sequence*, number the steps in the order of their normal occurrence (the first step is already labeled as an example). Next, in the column headed *Department*, insert the letter designating the department in which the step is performed.

Sequence	Department	Procedure
8	a	File paid invoice.
1	c e	Prepare purchase requisition.
7	b	Send check to vendor.
3 / 4	d	Count and inspect goods upon arrival.
4 / 3	d a	Perform steps to verify purchase invoice.
6	a	Record purchase and liability to vendor.
2	c	Issue purchase order.
5	e a	Initial the invoice approval form.

Departments involved:

a. Accounting Department

b. Finance Department

c. Purchasing Department

d. Receiving Department

e. Sales Department or Inventory Control Department

7

ACCOUNTING SYSTEMS: MANUAL AND EDP

HIGHLIGHTS OF THE CHAPTER

1 In the preceding chapters we have used the general journal entry as a tool for analyzing the effects of various financial transactions upon business entities. Although the general journal entry is an effective analytical tool, it is not the fastest way to record a large number of transactions. Every general journal entry requires writing at least two account titles and an explanation of the transaction, as well as posting at least two amounts to the ledger. Since many businesses engage in thousands of individual transactions every day, it is often necessary to streamline the recording process to save time and labor.

2 A *manual data processing system* is a means of providing increased speed and economy in the accounting process without using costly business machines or computers. This type of system *groups transactions* into like classes and uses a *special journal* for each class. This permits division of labor and specialization because each special journal can be maintained by a different employee. Time is also saved because special journals are designed to handle transactions with much less writing and posting than is necessary in the general journal.

3 About 80 or 90% of all transactions fall into four types. These four types and the corresponding special journals are shown at the top of the next column.

Type of Transaction	Name of Special Journal
Sales of merchandise	
on credit	Sales journal
Purchase of merchandise	
on credit	Purchases journal
Receipts of cash	Cash receipts journal
Payments of cash	Cash payments journal

Any transaction not falling into one of the above four types will be recorded in the *general journal*.

4 The *sales journal* is used to record all transactions which are a debit to Accounts Receivable and a credit to Sales (sales on credit). Columns are provided for the date, customer's name, invoice number, and amount of sale. At the end of the month the amount column is totaled and the *total* posted as a debit to Accounts Receivable and a credit to Sales. Detailed postings are made throughout the month to accounts of individual customers in the *accounts receivable subsidiary ledger*.

5 In prior chapters we have assumed that all sales on credit to customers were posted as debits to a single account called Accounts Receivable. Now, with our revised assumption of large volume (perhaps hundreds of customers), we divide the ledger into three separate ledgers: (a) an *accounts receivable subsidiary ledger* with a page for each customer, (b) an *accounts payable subsidiary ledger* with a page for each creditor, and (c) a *general ledger* containing all accounts

except those with individual customers and creditors.

6 When the accounts with individual customers are placed in a separate ledger, a single account with the title of Accounts Receivable continues to be maintained in the general ledger. This **controlling account** represents the *sum* of all the customers' accounts in the subsidiary ledger. A controlling account called Accounts Payable is also maintained in the general ledger representing all the accounts with creditors which form the accounts payable subsidiary ledger. The general ledger still is in balance since all the individual receivable and payable accounts are represented by these two controlling accounts.

7 The *purchases journal* is used to record all purchases of merchandise *on credit*. At the end of the month the journal is totaled and the total is posted to the general ledger as a debit to Purchases and a credit to Accounts Payable. During the month individual postings are made on a current basis to accounts with individual creditors in the *accounts payable subsidiary ledger*.

8 The *cash receipts journal* is used to record *all transactions involving the receipt of cash*. Separate columns are established for cash and for other accounts frequently debited or credited in this type of transaction, such as Sales Discounts and Accounts Receivable. Debit and credit columns are provided for Other Accounts; we write in the name of any other account affected in these columns, and at the end of the month we make an individual posting to that account in the general ledger. The totals of the columns for Cash, Sales Discounts, Accounts Receivable, and Sales are posted to the general ledger at the end of the month.

9 The *cash payments journal* is used to record all transactions involving a cash payment. Separate columns are established for Cash and for accounts such as Purchase Discounts, Accounts Payable, and Purchases, which are frequently affected by a cash payment. Debit and credit columns are also provided for Other Accounts so that any account title required may be written in. The posting of the cash payments journal parallels that described for the cash receipts journal in paragraph 8 above.

10 Most transactions will be recorded in the four special journals we have described. Any transactions which do not affect cash or the purchase or sale of merchandise on credit will be entered in the general journal. Double posting will be required if a general journal entry affects accounts receivable or accounts payable. For example, when a customer returns merchandise for credit to his or her account, we post the credit to the accounts receivable controlling account in the general ledger and also to the individual customer's account in the accounts receivable subsidiary ledger.

11 Accounts with customers and creditors in the subsidiary ledgers are usually of the three-column, running balance type. The right-hand column shows the new balance after each debit or credit entry. Many companies also prefer this form of account for the general ledger.

12 *Posting references* provide a cross reference between ledgers and journals. We use the following symbols: *S*, sales journal; *P*, purchases journal; *CR*, cash receipts journal; *CP*, cash payments journal; and *J*, general journal. The symbol is combined with a number, so that in looking at any debit or credit entry in any ledger, we can identify the journal from which it came and the page number of that journal. (For example, *S7* as a posting reference in the accounts receivable subsidiary ledger would tell us that the debit to a customer's account came from page 7 of the sales journal.)

13 To prove that all ledgers are in balance at the end of the period, a trial balance of the general ledger is prepared, and in addition a list of the balances in each subsidiary ledger is prepared to prove that the total agrees with the related controlling account.

14 Many variations in special journals are possible. For example, a special column can be added for any account which is frequently debited or credited. An additional special journal can be created for any type of transaction which *occurs frequently*, such as sales returns by credit customers of a retail store.

15 Some businesses keep a file of invoices and post directly from these to the ledger accounts rather than copying data from invoices into a sales journal or a purchases

journal. This system is called *direct posting from invoices*. At the end of the month the file of invoices is totaled and a general journal entry is used to post the total to the controlling account in the general ledger.

16 Although a manual system of processing accounting data, strictly defined, would call for handwritten records, such machines as cash registers, multicopy forms, desk calculators, and other machines are used in many small businesses.

17 Computers can perform routine tasks, such as posting, arithmetic computations, and the preparation of schedules, with incredible speed and accuracy. The basic concepts of data processing, however, are the same in EDP systems as in manual systems.

18 Although EDP equipment is highly reliable, errors may still occur in computer output. Errors in input data, failure to record transactions, fraudulent human intervention, improper programming, and operator errors may all lead to errors in computer output.

19 A strong system of internal control is necessary to ensure the reliability of computer output. These internal controls should include *input controls* and *program controls*.

  a *Input controls* are the precautions taken to ensure that input data entered into the computer are correct. Two common input controls are the use of *control totals* and a *verifier key punch*.

  b *Program controls* (or processing controls) are error-detecting routines built into the computer program. An *item count* and a *limit* (or *reasonableness*) *test* are examples of program controls.

TEST YOURSELF ON DATA PROCESSING SYSTEMS

True or False

For each of the following statements, circle the T or the F to indicate whether the statement is true or false.

  T F 1 Sale on credit of old office equipment no longer needed in the business would be recorded in the sales journal.

T F 2 The total of the Accounts Payable column in the cash payments journal is posted at the end of the month as a debit to Accounts Payable and a credit to Cash.

 T F 3 The purchase of office supplies on credit is recorded in the purchases journal.

 T F 4 Purchases of merchandise on credit are recorded in the purchases journal.

  T F 5 The Accounts Receivable column in the cash receipts journal is intended for credit entries.

 T F 6 When customers are permitted to return merchandise for credit to their accounts, the transactions are usually recorded in the general journal.

 T F 7 The sale of merchandise for cash is recorded in the sales journal.

 T F 8 The total of the Other Accounts column in the debit section of the cash receipts journal is not posted to the ledger.

 T F 9 If a trial balance of the general ledger is in balance, this proves that each controlling account is in agreement with the related subsidiary ledger.

T F 10 A subsidiary ledger for accounts receivable is usually arranged in alphabetical order of customers' names.

T F 11 *Double posting* of a general journal entry crediting Accounts Receivable means posting the credit to the controlling account in the general ledger and to a customer's account in the subsidiary ledger.

 T F 12 When special journals, controlling accounts, and subsidiary ledgers are used, no posting to any ledger is performed until the end of the month.

 T F 13 The basic concepts of data processing are similar in both EDP systems and manual systems.

 T F 14 The use of EDP equipment virtually eliminates the need to maintain a strong system of internal control.

 T F 15 Computer output will always be correct unless the computer malfunctions.

 T F 16 One input control is to have the computer add up the dollar total of items being processed and compare this sum with a predetermined control total.

 T F 17 A *limit test* is a program control which will detect if any of the input data are missing.

 T F 18 Computers are used to post accounts receivable and prepare payrolls but not to maintain journals and ledgers and prepare financial statements.

 T F 19 A *limit test* and an *item count* would both be appropriate program controls in the preparation of weekly pay-checks by computer.

Completion Statements

Fill in the necessary words to complete the following statements:

1 Special journals have the advantage of saving much time in journalizing and _posting_.

2 When merchandise is purchased on credit, the transaction is recorded in the _purchase_ _____ journal. If a portion of the merchandise is returned for credit to the supplier, the return is recorded in the _general_ journal and the _debit_ side of the entry is double-posted.

3 The column total of the sales journal is posted at the end of the month as a _debit_ to _accounts_ _receivable_ and as a _credit_ to _sales_.

4 Some companies do not use a sales journal but instead post directly from the _sales_ _invoices_ to the customers' accounts in the accounts receivable ledger. When this is done, the _invoices_ are totaled and an entry is made in the _general_ journal debiting the Accounts Receivable _Controlling_ _____ account and crediting Sales.

5 Measures taken to assure the reliability of data entered into a computer system are termed _input_ controls. Error detecting routines written into the computer program are called _program_ controls.

6 The symbol (X) placed below a column total in the cash receipts journal or cash payments journal means the column total should _not_ _be_ _posted_.

7 A business will usually benefit by establishing a special journal for any type of transaction that _occurs_ _frequently_.

8 The amount of an employee's salary was accidentally keypunched as $8,000 instead of $800. A verifier key punch is not used. A computer preparing paychecks should detect this error because the total payroll will not agree with the _control_ _total_ _____, and a _limit_ _test_ should prevent an $8,000 item from being processed.

Multiple Choice

Choose the best answer for each of the following questions and enter the identifying letter in the space provided.

_____ 1 The total of a single-column purchases journal is posted at the end of the month:

a As a debit to Accounts Payable and a credit to Purchases.

b To the Purchases account, Cash account, and Sales account.

c To the Purchases account only.

d As a debit to Purchases and a credit to Accounts Payable.

_____ 2 The Rex Company records all transactions in a two-column general journal but is considering the installation of special journals. The number of sales on credit during January was 325 and the number of sales for cash was 275. Therefore:

a The use of a sales journal in January would have saved 324 postings to the Sales account.

b The use of a cash receipts journal would have reduced the number of postings to the Cash account but would not have affected the number of postings to the Sales account.

c The total number of transactions recorded in the sales journal (if one had been used in January) would have been 600, but only two postings would have been necessary from that journal.

d If special journals were installed, the entry to close the Sales and Purchases accounts at the end of the period would be made in the sales journal and the purchases journal, respectively.

_____ 3 The purchases journal is a book of original entry used to record:

a Purchase of any asset on credit.

b Purchase of merchandise for cash or on credit.

c Purchase of merchandise on credit only.

d Purchases and purchase returns and allowances.

_____ 4 A major advantage of controlling accounts is that their use makes it possible:

a To reduce the number of accounts in the general ledger.

b To determine on a daily basis the total amount due from customers and total amount owing to creditors.

c To reduce the number of entries in subsidiary ledgers.

d To increase the number of columns in special journals.

_____ 5 When a general journal and four special journals are in use, the entries in the Cash account will come:

a From all of the books of original entry.

b From the four special journals.

(c) From only two of the four special journals.

d Principally at month-end from adjusting and closing entries.

_____ 6 The cash receipts journal is used:

a For transactions involving a debit to Cash and debits or credits to other balance sheet accounts.

(b) For all transactions involving the receipt of cash, regardless of the number of other accounts involved.

c For transactions involving not more than two accounts.

d For transactions involving the receipt of cash but not affecting subsidiary ledgers.

_____ 7 Which of the following is *not* an advantage that can be achieved by an EDP system?

a Operating data can be made available to managers faster than with a manual system.

(b) The accuracy of EDP equipment eliminates the need for internal control.

c Sales transactions can be recorded instantaneously in the accounting records as the sales clerk rings up the sale on an electronic cash register.

d The need for manual labor to perform the posting function can virtually be eliminated.

_____ 8 Posting of accounts receivable with individual customers is done by computer. Credit sales totaling $19,742 were made to 809 customers. A key-punch operator made a keypunching error and recorded a $35 sale to Roger Jones at $53. Two controls which could detect this error are:

a An item count and a limit test.

(b) A limit test and a control total.

(c) A control total and a verifier key punch.

d A verifier key punch and an item count.

Exercises

1 For each of the following transactions, indicate the journal which should be used by placing the appropriate symbol in the space provided.

S = sales journal, P = purchase journal, CR = cash receipts journal, CP = cash payments journal, J = general journal

a	Sold merchandise on credit	S
b	Purchased merchandise for cash	CP
c	Purchased truck for cash for use in business	✓ CP
d	Collected account receivable and allowed a cash discount	CR
e	Recorded depreciation for the period	✓
f	Made entry to close the expense accounts at end of period	✓
g	Accepted note receivable from customer in settlement of account receivable	CR ✓
h	Paid employee salaries	CP
i	Made entry to accrue salaries at end of year	✓ CR
j	Sold merchandise for cash	CR
k	Purchased merchandise on credit	P
l	Returned merchandise to supplier for credit	✓
m	Purchased office equipment on credit	✓/P
n	Allowed customer to return merchandise for credit	✓

2 For each of the following general ledger accounts indicate the source of debit and credit postings by entering a symbol representing the proper journal. Use the same code as in Exercise 1.

		Debit	Credit
a	Purchases	P	✓
b	Purchase Returns and Allowances	✓	✓, CR
c	Purchase Discounts	✓	CP
d	Sales	✓	S, CR
e	Sales Returns and Allowances	✓, CP	✓
f	Sales Discounts	CR	✓
g	Accounts Payable	✓ CP	P, ✓
h	Accounts Receivable	S	CR ✓
i	Cash	CR	CP
j	Depreciation Expense	✓	✓

THE CONTROL OF CASH TRANSACTIONS

HIGHLIGHTS OF THE CHAPTER

1 The term *cash* includes currency, coin, checks, money orders, and money on deposit with banks. Items which a bank will *not* accept for deposit, such as notes receivable and postdated checks, are *not* included in cash. Cash is a current asset and the most liquid of all assets. A company may have numerous bank accounts plus cash on hand, but these will be lumped together to show a single figure for cash in the balance sheet.

2 Management's job with respect to cash includes (a) preventing loss from fraud or theft; (b) accounting for cash receipts, cash payments, and cash balances; and (c) always having enough cash to make necessary payments, but not excessive cash deposits which produce no revenue. To meet these objectives, management needs a strong system of internal control.

3 Cash offers the greatest temptation to theft, and this makes the problem of internal control especially important. Basic rules to achieve strong internal control over cash include:

a Separating the handling of cash from the maintenance of accounting records.

b Establishing specific and separate routines to be followed in handling cash receipts, making cash payments, and recording cash transactions.

c Depositing all cash receipts in the bank daily and making all payments by check.

d Requiring that every expenditure be verified and approved before payment is made.

e Separating the function of signing checks from the functions of approving expenditures and recording cash transactions.

4 *Cash receipts* may be received over the counter from customers or through the mail. All cash received over the counter should be promptly recorded on a cash register in plain view of the customer. Prenumbered sales tickets should be prepared in duplicate whenever possible. The participation of two employees in each cash receipts transaction is desirable. For example, one person opens the mail, prepares a list of checks received, and forwards one copy of the list to the accounting department and another copy with the checks to the cashier who will deposit them.

5 Good internal control over *cash disbursements* requires that all payments (except those from petty cash) be made by prenumbered checks. The officials authorized to sign checks should not have authority to approve invoices for payment or to make entries in the accounting records. Before an official signs a check, he should require that supporting documents justifying the payment be presented to him. These documents should be stamped "Paid," and the checks should be mailed without going back to the person who prepared them.

6 One widely used means of controlling cash disbursements is the *voucher system*. A *voucher* (a serially numbered form) is prepared for each expenditure. Approval signatures are placed on the voucher to show that the expenditure was authorized, the goods or services received, the invoice

prices verified, and the proper accounts debited and credited. A completed voucher must accompany every check submitted for signature. Before signing the check, the official authorized to make cash disbursements will review the voucher to determine that the expenditure has been approved.

7   Internal control is strong in a voucher system, because each expenditure must be verified and approved before a check is issued, and because the function of signing checks is separated from the functions of approving expenditures and recording cash transactions.

8   In a voucher system, a *voucher register* replaces the purchases journal but is expanded to record all types of expenditures. The typical voucher register has numerous columns: columns for the voucher number, date of entry, name of creditor, and date and number of check issued in payment; a credit column for Vouchers Payable; and numerous other money columns for accounts frequently used. Since every approved voucher is entered in the voucher register, the column for the liability account *Vouchers Payable* is credited for the amount of every voucher.

9   At the end of the month the totals of the money columns in the voucher register are posted to the various accounts indicated, except for the column for Other General Ledger Accounts. Items in this column are posted individually.

10 Each line of a voucher register represents a liability to a creditor. When a voucher is paid, the check number and date are entered on that line to show the liability is ended. A list of the "open" items (lines without check numbers and dates) is the equivalent of a subsidiary ledger of vouchers payable.

11 When a voucher is due to be paid, it is removed from the unpaid vouchers file, a check is prepared (but not signed), and the issuance of the check is recorded in the *check register*. The voucher, check, and all supporting documents are then sent to the designated official in the finance department.

12 In the finance department, an official will review the voucher and supporting documents to determine that the expenditure has been properly verified and approved. The official then signs the check and mails it directly to the payee. The voucher and supporting documents are *perforated to prevent reuse* and filed in a paid voucher file in the accounting department.

13 The *check register* used in a voucher system is a simplified form of cash payments journal. Since checks are issued only in payment of approved and recorded vouchers, every check issued is recorded by a debit to Vouchers Payable and a credit to Cash. The only other money column is for credits to Purchase Discounts.

14 The use of bank checking accounts provides assurance that all cash transactions are recorded. Each month the bank will provide the depositor with a *statement* of his or her account, showing the beginning balance, dates and amounts of deposits, deductions for checks paid, any other charges, and the ending balance. All paid checks are returned to the depositor with the bank statement. When numerous checks are being deposited daily, it is inevitable that occasionally one will *bounce*; that is, the drawer of the check will have insufficient funds on deposit to cover it. The check will be marked *NSF* (not sufficient funds), charged back against the depositor's account, and returned to the depositor. An NSF check should be regarded as a receivable rather than cash, until it is collected directly from the drawer, redeposited, or determined to be worthless.

15 The amount of cash which appears on the balance sheet of a business should be the correct amount of cash owned at the close of business on that date. To determine this amount, it is necessary to *reconcile* the monthly bank statement with the balance of cash as shown by the depositor's accounting records. The balance shown on the bank statement will usually not agree with that shown on the depositor's books because certain transactions will have been recorded by one party but not by the other. Examples are outstanding checks, deposits in transit, service charges, NSF checks, and errors by the bank or by the depositor.

16 The *bank reconciliation* will identify the items which cause the balance of cash per the books to differ from the balance shown on the bank statement, and it will show the adjusted or correct amount of cash. Those reconciling items which have not yet been recorded by the depositor (or which reflect errors on the depositor's part) must be

entered on the books to make the accounting records correct and up-to-date at the end of the period.

17 *Electronic funds transfer systems* involve the use of computer terminals rather than checks to transfer funds to and from bank accounts. The use of such systems may lead eventually to a "checkless society," in which credit cards and computer terminals take the place of the traditional paper check.

18 In every business some small expenditures are necessary for which it is not practicable to issue checks. Taxi fares, and small purchases of office supplies or postage stamps are common examples. To control these small payments not being made by check, almost every business establishes a *petty cash fund*. A check is written for perhaps $200 or $300 and is cashed, and the cash is kept on hand for use in making small expenditures. A receipt or *petty cash voucher* should be obtained and placed in the fund to replace each cash payment. Therefore the fund always contains a constant amount of cash and vouchers. The expenses are recorded in the accounts when the fund is replenished, perhaps every two or three weeks. The entry for the replenishment check will consist of debits to the proper expense accounts and a credit to Cash.

TEST YOURSELF ON THE CONTROL OF CASH TRANSACTIONS

True or False

For each of the following statements, circle the T or the F to indicate whether the statement is true or false.

T F **1** The balance sheet item of Cash includes amounts on deposit with banks, and also currency, money orders, and customers' checks on hand.

T F **2** Reconciling a bank account means determining that all deductions shown on the bank statement represent checks issued by the depositor in the current period.

T F **3** No entry is made in the accounting records at the time a small payment is made from the petty cash fund.

T F **4** Internal control over cash should include measures to prevent fraud or loss, to provide accurate records of cash transactions, and to ensure the maintenance of adequate but not excessive cash balances.

T F **5** Internal control over cash receipts is most effective when one person is made solely responsible for receiving and depositing cash and making related entries in the accounting records.

T F **6** All cash receipts should be deposited intact in the bank daily, and all cash payments should be made by check.

T F **7** The purpose of preparing a bank reconciliation is to identify those items which cause the balance of cash per the bank statement to differ from the balance of cash per the ledger, and thereby to determine the correct cash balance.

T F **8** In preparing a bank reconciliation, outstanding checks should be deducted from the balance shown on the bank statement, and deposits in transit (or undeposited receipts) should be added to the bank balance.

T F **9** James Company deposited a check from a customer, Ray Prince, but the bank returned the check with the notation NSF and deducted it on James Company's bank statement. A telephone call to Prince's office indicated that he would be out of town for some weeks. James Company decided to hold the check until Prince returned. The check should be included in the figure for Cash on the balance sheet of James Company.

T F **10** The Petty Cash account should be debited when the fund runs low and a check is drawn to replenish it.

T F **11** The principal advantage of a *voucher system* is that it provides strong internal control over the making of expenditures and the payment of liabilities.

T F **12** The voucher register is a substitute for a sales journal.

T F **13** A voucher register is used to record all expenditures, whereas a purchases journal is usually limited to recording purchases of merchandise on credit.

(T) (F) **14** In a company using a voucher system, the replenishment of the petty cash fund would call for an entry in both the voucher register and the check register.

(T) F **15** A voucher is a document which shows that the necessary steps to verify the propriety of an expenditure have been performed and that a cash disbursement is justified.

Completion Statements

Fill in the necessary words to complete the following statements.

1 The term *cash* includes not only currency, coin, and money orders, but also _checks_ and the balances of _account receivable_.

2 An adequate system of internal control over cash should include separating the function of handling cash from the _recording of accounting transactions_.

3 Cash frauds often begin with temporary unauthorized "borrowing" by employees of cash received from customers. One effective step in preventing such irregularities is to insist that each day's cash receipts be _daily deposited_ in the bank.

4 If duties relating to cash handling and the maintenance of accounting records are sufficiently subdivided so that the work of one person or department serves to verify that of another, then the permanent concealment of fraud is possible only through the _collusion of 2 or more_.

5 Among the most common reconciling items in a bank reconciliation are _outstanding checks_, which should be deducted from the balance shown by the bank, and _deposits in transit_, which should be added to the balance shown by the bank statement.

6 The abbreviation *NSF* applied to a check returned by a bank means _non sufficient fund_ and calls for an entry on the depositor's books debiting _accounts receivable_.

7 In the preparation of a bank reconciliation, various reconciling items are added to or deducted from the balance per the bank statement or the balance per the depositor's records. Outstanding checks should be _deducted from_ the balance per the _bank statement_. Deposits in transit should be _added to_ the balance per the _bank statement_. Bank service charges should be _deducted from_ the balance per the _depositor records_. Collections made by the bank in behalf of the depositor should be _added to_ the balance per the _depositors records_.

8 When a voucher system is in use, the recording and payment of the monthly telephone bill would require two entries: (a) an entry in the _voucher system_ debiting _telephone expense_ and crediting _voucher payable_ and (b) an entry in the _check register_ debiting _voucher payable_ and crediting _cash_.

9 In a voucher system, every cash disbursement must be authorized by personnel of the _accounting_ department but the related check must be signed by an officer of the _finance_ department. After a check is signed, it should be mailed directly to the _payee_; the related voucher should be _perforated_ and returned to the _accounting_ department.

Multiple Choice

Choose the best answer for each of the following questions and enter the identifying letter in the space provided.

_____ **1** Which of the following practices is undesirable from the standpoint of maintaining adequate internal control over cash?

a Recording overages and shortages from errors in handling over-the-counter cash receipts in a ledger account, Cash Over and Short.

b Authorizing the cashier to make bank deposits.

(c) Authorizing the official who approved invoices for payment to sign checks.

d Appointing as custodian of a petty cash fund

an employee who has no responsibility with respect to maintenance of accounting records.

_____ **2** Checks received through the mail should be:
a Transmitted to the accounts receivable department without delay.
b Deposited by the mail-room employee.
c Listed by the mail-room employee and forwarded to the cashier; a copy of the list should be sent to the accounts receivable department.
d Handled first by the accounts receivable department, which after making appropriate entries in the accounts should turn over the checks to the cashier to be made part of the daily bank deposit.

_____ **3** When a bank reconciliation has been satisfactorily completed, the only related entries to be made on the depositor's books are:
a To correct errors existing in the accounts.
b To record outstanding checks and bank service charges.
c To record items which explain the difference between the balance per the books and the adjusted cash balance.
d To reconcile items which explain the difference between the balance per the books and the balance per the bank statement.

_____ **4** In establishing and maintaining a petty cash fund:
a The Petty Cash account is debited only when the fund is first established or subsequently changed in size.
b The Petty Cash account is debited whenever the fund is replenished.
c The contents of the fund should at all times be limited to currency, coin, and checks.
d The contents of the fund should at all times be limited to currency, coin, checks, money orders, undeposited cash receipts, petty cash vouchers, and notes receivables from employees.

_____ **5** An NSF check held by the payee should be carried on its records as:
a An element of cash on hand.
b Notes receivable.
c Accounts receivable.
d Cash over and short.

_____ **6** Which of the following is *not* a significant element of internal control over cash disbursements?
a Perforating or stamping "Paid" on supporting invoices and vouchers.

b Using serially numbered checks and accounting for all numbers in the series.
c Use of a Cash Over and Short account.
d Establishment of a petty cash fund.

_____ **7** Which of the following is not a significant element of internal control over cash receipts?
a Prelisting customers' remittances received in the mail.
b Establishing a petty cash fund.
c Depositing each day's cash receipts intact in the bank.
d Prenumbering sales tickets.

_____ **8** The adoption of a voucher system makes it unnecessary to use:
a An imprest system of handling petty cash expenditures.
b A purchases journal.
c Any subsidiary ledgers.
d A separate journal for recording cash disbursements.

_____ **9** Which of the following statements describes an advantage of the use of a voucher system?
a Assures that every expenditure is reviewed and verified before payment is made.
b Provides automatically a comprehensive record of business done with particular suppliers.
c Provides a highly flexible system for handling unusual transactions.
d Reduces the number of checks that will be written during any given period.

_____ **10** At the end of the month the *column totals* of a voucher register are:
a Used to determine whether an equality of debits and credits exists, but they are not posted.
b Posted to general ledger accounts only.
c Posted to subsidiary ledger accounts only.
d Posted to both general ledger and subsidiary ledger accounts.

Exercises

1 Indicate the proper sequence of the following events in the operation of a voucher system by numbering the steps in order of their normal occurrence.

_____ Voucher reviewed by treasurer and check signed and mailed.

_____ Preparation of voucher, including verification of prices, quantities, terms, and other data on vendor's invoice.

_____ Receipt of goods and preparation of receiving report.

_____ Issuance of purchase order.

_____ Purchase and related liability recorded in voucher register.

_____ Voucher filed in paid voucher file.

_____ Voucher filed in unpaid voucher file by payment date.

_____ Voucher and supporting documents perforated to prevent reuse.

_____ Preparation of check for signature and payment recorded in check register.

2 You are to fill in the missing portions of the bank reconciliation shown on this page for the Hunter Corporation at July 31, 19__, using the following additional information:

a Outstanding checks: no. 301, $2,500; no. 303, $600; no. 304, $1,800; no. 306, $1,282.

b Service charge by bank, $6.

c Deposit made after banking hours on July 31, $1,950.

d A $264 NSF check drawn by our customer Jay Kline, deducted from our account by bank and returned to us.

e An $1,800 note receivable left by us with bank for collection was collected and credited to our account. No interest involved.

f Our check no. 295, issued in payment of $580 for office supplies, was erroneously written as $688 but was recorded in our accounts as $580.

HUNTER CORPORATION
Bank Reconciliation
July 31, 19__

Balance per depositor's records, July 31, 19__. $11,364
Add: _Note Receivable_   1,800
     check error   13,064

Deduct: _Service Charge 6.00_   270
     NSF 264   12,894
            270   108
                 12,786

Adjusted balance . . . . $

Balance per bank statement, July 31, 19__. $17,018
Add: _Deposits_   1,950
                 18,968

Deduct: 6,182
   _301_   2500
   _303_   600   12,786
   _304_   1800
   _306_   1282
               6,182

Adjusted balance (as above) . . . . $

3 The following entries, in general journal form, concern the establishment and operation of a petty cash fund. You are to use the information contained in the explanation portions of the entries to complete the journal entries in proper form.

		Debit	Credit
Sept. 11	_Petty Cash_	300	
	cash		300
	To record the establishment of a $300 petty cash fund.		
Sept. 30	_Postage Exp_	48	
	Travel Exp	26	
	Miscell Exp	55	
	Cash		129

To replenish the petty cash fund for the following: postage, $48; travel, $26; and miscellaneous expense, $55.

Subtract
high to low
add
low to high

9

RECEIVABLES AND PAYABLES

HIGHLIGHTS OF THE CHAPTER

1 An important factor in the growth of the American economy has been the increasing tendency to sell goods on credit. In most large businesses, the major portion of total sales is actually sales on credit. Since every credit sale creates some sort of receivable from the customer, it follows that accounts receivable and/or notes receivable will be large and important assets on the balance sheets of most businesses.

2 A business can increase sales by giving its customers easy credit terms. But no business wants to sell on credit to customers who will be unable to pay their accounts. Consequently, many businesses have a credit department which investigates the credit records of new customers to see if they are acceptable credit risks.

3 A few accounts receivable will prove to be uncollectible. As long as the portion of uncollectible accounts is relatively small, it is to the advantage of the business to go ahead and incur these losses because the extension of credit to customers is also bringing in a lot of profitable business. The losses from accounts that do prove uncollectible are an *expense* resulting from the use of credit to increase sales.

4 A most fundamental accounting principle is that *revenue must be matched with the expenses incurred in securing that revenue.* Uncollectible Accounts Expense is caused by selling goods or services to customers who fail to pay their bills. The expense is therefore incurred in the *period the sale is made* even though the receivable is not determined to be uncollectible until some following period. At the end of each accounting period before preparing financial statements, we must therefore *estimate* the amount of uncollectible accounts expense. This estimate is brought on the books by an adjusting entry debiting *Uncollectible Accounts Expense* and crediting *Allowance for Doubtful Accounts.* The allowance for Doubtful Accounts is a *contra-asset account*; it appears in the balance sheet as a deduction from Accounts Receivable and thus leads to an *estimated realizable value* for receivables.

5 Allowance for Doubtful Accounts is sometimes called *Allowance for Bad Debts.* Uncollectible Accounts Expense is sometimes referred to as *Bad Debts Expense.*

6 Since the allowance for doubtful accounts is necessarily an estimate rather than a precise calculation, there is a fairly wide range of reasonableness within which the amount may be set. The factor of *conservatism* which historically has been of considerable influence on accounting practice implies a tendency to state assets at their minimum values rather than in a purely objective manner. Establishing a relatively large allowance for doubtful accounts also means recording a relatively large amount of uncollectible accounts expense, thus tending to minimize net income for the current period.

7 Two methods of estimating uncollectible accounts expense are in wide use. The first method, which we call the *balance sheet approach*, relies on aging the *accounts receiv-*

able and thereby arriving at the total amount estimated to be uncollectible. The allowance for uncollectible accounts is then adjusted (usually increased) to this estimated uncollectible amount, after *giving consideration to the existing balance* in the allowance account.

8 The alternative method of estimating uncollectible accounts expense stresses that the *expense* is usually a fairly constant *percentage of sales* (or of sales on credit). Therefore the amount of the adjustment is computed as a percentage of the period's sales *without regard to any existing balance* in the allowance account. This method is often called the *income statement approach* to estimating uncollectible accounts expense.

9 An *aging schedule* for accounts receivable is a list of the balances due from all customers, with each amount placed in a column indicating its age. Thus, we might use columns with headings such as Not Yet Due, Past Due 1 to 30 Days, Past Due 31 to 60 Days, etc. Each column total should be computed as a percentage of total receivables. Changes in the percentages from month to month indicate whether the quality of receivables is improving or deteriorating.

10 When a customer's account is determined to be uncollectible, it should immediately be written off. The write-off consists of a debit to the Allowance for Doubtful Accounts and a credit to Accounts Receivable. The credit will be posted to the customer's account in the subsidiary ledger as well as to the controlling account in the general ledger. Since the write-off reduces both the asset Accounts Receivable and the contra-asset Allowance for Doubtful Accounts, *there is no change in the net carrying value of receivables*. Neither is there any recognition of expense at the time of the write-off. The write-off merely confirms the validity of our earlier estimate in recording uncollectible accounts expense in the period the sale was made.

11 The *direct charge-off method* of recognizing uncollectible accounts expense does not recognize any expense until a particular account receivable is determined to be uncollectible. At that point the receivable is written off with an offsetting debit to Uncollectible Accounts Expense. An allowance account is not used. There is little theoretical support for the direct charge-off method because it makes no attempt to match revenue with the expenses associated with that revenue. This method is not widely used.

12 Making credit sales to customers who use major credit cards avoids the risk of uncollectible accounts because the account receivable is paid promptly by the credit card company. Making sales through credit card companies also has the advantages of eliminating the work of credit investigations, billing, and maintaining an accounts receivable subsidiary ledger. However, credit card companies charge a fee equal to a percentage (usually 1 to 5%) of each credit sale.

13 In analyzing financial statements it is common practice to consider the relationship between average receivables and annual credit sales. For example, if annual credit sales were $2,400,000 and average receivables were $600,000, receivables would represent one-fourth of a year's sales (90 day's sales). If the credit terms are, say, 30 days, it is apparent that many receivables are past due, that the *turnover* of receivables is too slow, and that corrective action is needed.

14 *Installment sales* typically require a small down payment and a long series of monthly payments, perhaps extending over several years. For income tax purposes, a business is permitted to spread the profit on an installment sale over the period of collection in proportion to the cash received. For financial statements, however, the installment basis of measuring income is not permissible. The principle of matching revenue with related expenses is best achieved by recognizing the entire gross profit in the period of the sale and by establishing an allowance for doubtful accounts.

15 A promissory note is an unconditional promise in writing to pay on demand or at a future date a definite sum of money. Most notes are for periods of a year or less and are therefore classified as current assets by the payee and as current liabilities by the maker of the note. Most notes bear interest (a charge made for the use of money). Interest rates are stated on an annual basis, and a 360-day year is usually assumed. The formula is: *Principal* $\times$ *rate of interest* $\times$ *time* = *interest*. (*Prt = i*.)

16 The face amount of each note receivable is debited to the Notes Receivable account in the general ledger. The notes themselves when properly filed are the equivalent of a subsidiary ledger. An adjusting entry for interest accrued on notes receivable is neces-

sary at the end of the period. The entry will debit Accrued Interest Receivable and will credit Interest Revenue. If reversing entries are not used, the entry in the following period when the note is collected will be a debit to Cash offset by a credit to Notes Receivable for the face amount of the note, a credit to Accrued Interest Receivable for the amount of the accrual, and a credit to Interest Revenue for the remainder of the interest collected.

17 If the maker of the note defaults (fails to pay as agreed), an entry should be made to transfer the note and any interest earned to an account receivable. If both parties agree that a note should be renewed rather than paid at maturity, an entry should be made debiting and crediting the Notes Receivable account and explaining the terms of the new note.

18 Notes receivable are often *discounted*, that is, sold to a financial institution, with the seller endorsing the note and thereby agreeing to make payment if the maker defaults. The purpose is to obtain cash quickly.

19 When a company endorses a note and discounts it to a bank, the company promises to pay the bank if the maker of the note fails to do so. This liability of the endorser is known as a *contingent liability*. A contingent liability is a potential liability which will either develop into a real liability or be eliminated, depending upon some future event. Contingent liabilities are disclosed in *footnotes* to the balance sheet and are not included in the regular liability section.

20 To compute the amount of cash obtainable by discounting a note receivable, first compute the maturity value of the note (principal plus interest due at maturity). Then, deduct from the maturity value the discount or interest charged by the bank. This discount is calculated by multiplying the bank's rate of interest times the maturity value for the number of days between the date of discounting and the date of maturity.

21 *Current liabilities* are amounts payable to creditors within one year or the operating cycle, whichever is longer. A company's debt-paying ability is judged, in part, by the relationship of its current assets to its current liabilities. Some examples of current liabilities are notes payable, accounts payable, cash dividends payable, and various types of accured liabilities.

22 A note payable may be issued as evidence of indebtedness to banks or to other creditors. When money is borrowed from the bank, two approaches may be used in drawing up the note: (a) the note may be drawn for the *principal amount*, and interest stated separately, to be paid at maturity, or (b) the note may be drawn for the *amount borrowed plus the interest to be paid at maturity*. When the latter procedure is followed, the rate of interest (or the amount of interest) is not separately listed on the note.

23 When the note is drawn for the principal amount, Cash is debited and Notes Payable is credited at the time the note is issued. The entry to record the payment of principal and interest requires a debit to Notes Payable for the amount of principal, a debit to Interest Expense for the interest paid, and a credit to Cash.

24 When the note is drawn for the *amount being borrowed plus the interest*, the note is for an amount larger than the immediate liability because the note includes interest *not yet owed* to the creditor. When such a note is drawn, Cash is debited for the amount received, *Discount on Notes Payable* is debited for the interest not yet owed, and Notes Payable is credited for the face amount of the note. Discount on Notes Payable is a *contra-liability* account and is subtracted from Notes Payable on the balance sheet, so that the net liability reflects only the amount owed at present.

25 When the note is paid, the interest has been earned by the creditor. The balance of the Discount on Notes Payable account is therefore recognized as interest expense (debit Interest Expense; credit Discount on Notes Payable). Notes Payable is debited and Cash is credited to record the payment of the note.

26 If a note is not repaid in the same period it was issued, it will be necessary to recognize the interest which has accrued (become owed) on the note during each period. If the note is drawn only for the principal amount, the interest which has accrued during the period is recognized by a debit to Interest Expense and a credit to the liability account Accrued Interest Payable. If the interest was included in the face of the note, the interest which accrues each period is transferred from Discount on Notes Payable (interest not yet owed) to Interest Expense. This

entry would debit Interest Expense and credit (reduce) the contra-liability account Discount on Notes Payable.

27   When a *note receivable* is drawn to include future interest charges in the face amount of the note, the amount of the unearned interest should be credited to a *contra-asset* account entitled *Discount on Notes Receivable*. The interest which is earned each period is then transferred from Discount on Notes Receivable (representing the unearned interest) to the revenue account, Interest Revenue. The journal entry will debit (reduce) the contra-asset account Discount on Notes Receivable and credit Interest Revenue.

28   The concept of *present value* is based on the time value of money. You would probably prefer to receive $1,000 today rather than $1,000 one year from today. If you invested $1,000 today, it would grow to a larger amount during the next year. The concept of present value applies to those long-term notes receivable and notes payable which do not bear any stated rate of interest or which bear an unrealistically low rate of interest. A portion of such long-term notes should be *assumed to represent an interest charge*.

29   If a business buys equipment by issuing a long-term note payable bearing no interest, the present value concept should be used. This will require a debit to Equipment for the present value of the note and a debit to Discount on Notes Payable for the excess of the face amount of the note over its present value. These two debits are offset by a credit to Notes Payable for the face amount of the note. The amount in the Discount on Notes Payable account will be transferred to Interest Expense over the life of the note.

30   A company selling an asset and receiving a long-term, non-interest-bearing note in payment should also use the present value concept in recording the transaction. A contra-asset account, Discount on Notes Receivable, is credited with the difference between the face amount of the note and its present value. The amount of the discount will be transferred to Interest Revenue over the life of the note.

31   A great deal of merchandise is sold on the installment plan, calling for regular payments over many months. Substantial interest charges are usually included in the installment contract signed by the customer. The transaction is recorded by a debit to Installment Contracts Receivable for the face amount of the contract. This debit is offset by a credit to Sales for the *present value* of the future payments and by a credit to Discount on Installment Receivables for the unearned finance charges. The amount credited to this contra-asset account will be transferred to Interest Revenue over the collection period. Thus the interest charges in a contract calling for 36 monthly payments will be earned over a period of 36 months.

TEST YOURSELF ON RECEIVABLES AND PAYABLES

True or False

For each of the following statements, circle the T or the F to indicate whether the statement is true or false.

T F   1   The practice of estimating uncollectible accounts expense at the end of each accounting period is designed to match revenue and expenses so that all expenses associated with the revenue earned in the period are recognized as expense in that same period.

T F   2   During the first year of its existence, Cross Company made most of its sales on credit but made no provision for uncollectible accounts. The result would be an overstatement of assets and owner's equity, an understatement of expense, and an overstatement of net income.

T F   3   Conservatism in the valuation of accounts receivable would call for holding the amount entered in Allowance for Doubtful Accounts to a bare minimum.

T F   4   The *balance sheet* approach to estimating uncollectible accounts expense emphasizes the aging of accounts receivable and the adjustment of the allowance account to the level of the estimated uncollectible amount.

T F   5   The *income statement* approach to estimating uncollectible accounts expense does not require the use of an allowance account.

T F   6   When the year-end provision for uncollectible accounts expense is estimated as a percentage of sales, the estimate is recorded without regard for the existing balance in the allowance account.

T F 7 The *direct charge-off* method does not cause receivables to be stated in the balance sheet at their estimated realizable value.

T F 8 When a given account receivable is determined to be worthless, it should be written off the books by an entry debiting Uncollectible Accounts Expense and crediting the Allowance for Doubtful Accounts.

Allow Doubtful A/R

T F 9 When a company collects an account receivable previously written off as worthless, an entry should be made debiting Accounts Receivable and crediting Allowance for Doubtful Accounts. A separate entry is then made to record collection of the account.

T F 10 The write-off of an account receivable determined to be worthless by debiting the Allowance for Doubtful Accounts will not affect the net carrying value of the receivables in the balance sheet.

T F 11 Annual credit sales divided by the amount of average accounts receivable indicates how long it takes to convert receivables into cash.

T F 12 X Co. sells merchandise on 30-day accounts and also on a 36-month installment plan. Under both methods, the amount debited to a receivable account will be equal to the amount credited to the sales revenue account.

T F 13 A retailer who sells to a customer using a national credit card will have an uncollectible account if the customer never pays the credit card company.

T F 14 When a company accepts an interest-bearing note from a customer, the accounting entry should include a debit for the principal plus the interest specified in the note.

T F 15 When a non-interest-bearing note receivable is discounted with a bank, the cash proceeds will usually be equal to the maturity value of the note.

T F 16 Interest may be stated separately or included in the face amount of a note payable.

T F 17 In reporting notes payable in the bal-

ance sheet, the Discount on Notes Payable account should be subtracted from the balance in the Notes Payable account.

T F 18 If the interest is not included in the face amount of a note payable, accrued interest at the end of a period should be recognized in a separate liability account; if the interest is included in the face amount, accrued interest should be recognized by decreasing the Discount on Notes Payable account.

T F 19 Contingent liabilities may not become real liabilities and need not be disclosed in the financial statements or footnotes to the statements.

T F 20 When a retail store sells merchandise to a customer who uses a bank credit card (such as Visa or MasterCard), the account to be debited is Cash rather than Accounts Receivable.

T F 21 When a company discounts a note receivable at its bank, the amount of cash received may be either more or less than the face value of the note.

T F 22 The concept of present value is applied to long-term notes receivable and payable rather than to short-term notes.

T F 23 The present value of a sum of money due several years in the future is always larger than the future amount.

T F 24 When a company sells goods in exchange for a long-term non-interest-bearing note receivable, the valuation of the note at its present value is necessary to avoid an overstatement of assets, net income, and owner's equity.

Completion Statements

Fill in the necessary words or amounts to complete the following statements:

1 The accounting principle which underlies the practice of estimating uncollectible accounts expense each period is known as _____ .

This process is essential to the periodic determination of _____ _____ .

2 If the Allowance for Doubtful Accounts is understated, the net realizable value of accounts receivable will be _____ ,

owner's equity will be _____ , and net income will be _____ .

3 The income statement approach to uncollectible accounts emphasizes estimating _____ _____ _____ for the period, while the balance sheet approach emphasizes estimating the proper level for the _____ _____ _____ .

4 Bitterroot Company obtained a $16,000 note receivable from a customer and discounted it at the bank the same day, receiving a sum of $15,940. The entry to record the discounting would be a debit to Cash for $ _____ , a _____ to _____ _____ for $ ____ , and a credit to Notes Receivable for $_____ .

5 If the interest on a 60-day note with a face value of $10,000 amounts to $250, the rate of interest is ____ % per annum.

6 The entry to record interest accrued on notes receivable at the year-end consists of a debit to _____ _____ _____ _____ and a credit to _____ _____ . Of these accounts, the one to be closed into the Income Summary is _____ _____ .

7 The Inn Place made credit sales of $4,200 to customers using Global Express credit cards. Global Express charges retailers a fee of 4%. The entry to record collecting the cash from these credit sales would be a debit to Cash for $____ , a _____ to _____ _____ _____ _____ for $___ , and a _____ to _____ _____ for $_____ .

8 Discount on Notes Payable is a _____ _____ account which should be _____ from the face value of notes payable in the liability section of the balance sheet. The amount of the Discount on Notes Payable will eventually be recognized as _____ _____ .

9 Discount on Notes Receivable is a _____ _____ account which should be _____ _____ from the face value of _____ _____ . The amount of the Discount

on Notes Receivable will eventually be recognized as _____ _____ .

10 Company A borrows $10,000 cash and signs a note for $10,150, due in 60 days. On the same day, Company B borrows $10,000 cash and signs a note for $10,000 plus 9% interest, due in 60 days. Both companies prepared financial statements 30 days after borrowing the money. The liability relating to the loan for Company A (Note Payable less remaining Discount on Notes Payable) would be $_____ ; the liability for Company B (Notes Payable plus Accrued Interest Payable) would be $_____ . At the maturity of the notes, Company A must pay $_____ and Company B must pay $_____ to the lender.

Multiple Choice

Choose the best answer for each of the following questions and enter the identifying letter in the space provided.

_____ 1 When an allowance for the estimating of uncollectible accounts is in use, the writing off of an individual account receivable as worthless will:

a Be recorded by a debit to Uncollectible Accounts Expense.
b Increase the balance in the allowance account.
c Decrease the debit balance in the allowance account.
d Have no effect on the working capital of the company.

_____ 2 Bryan Company, after aging its accounts receivable, estimated that $3,500 of the $125,000 of receivables on hand would probably prove uncollectible. The Allowance for Doubtful Accounts contained a credit balance of $2,300 prior to adjustments. The appropriate accounting entry is:

a A debit to Uncollectible Accounts Expense and a credit to Allowance for Doubtful Accounts for $1,200.
b A debit to Uncollectible Accounts Expense and a credit to Allowance for Doubtful Accounts for $3,500.
c A debit to Uncollectible Accounts Expense and a credit to Allowance for Doubtful Accounts for $5,800.
d A debit to Allowance for Doubtful Accounts and a credit to Accounts Receivable for $3,500.

_____ **3** Pine Company uses the income statement approach in estimating uncollectible accounts expense and has found that such expense has consistently approximated 1% of net sales. At December 31 of the current year receivables total $150,000 and the Allowance for Doubtful Accounts has a credit balance of $400 prior to adjustment. Net sales for the current year were $600,000. The adjusting entry should be:

a A debit to Uncollectible Accounts Expense and a credit to Allowance for Doubtful Accounts for $5,600.

b A debit to Uncollectible Accounts Expense and a credit to Allowance for Doubtful Accounts for $6,400.

c A debit to Allowance for Doubtful Accounts and a credit to Accounts Receivable for $6,000.

d A debit to Uncollectible Accounts Expense and a credit to Allowance for Doubtful Accounts for $6,000.

_____ **4** The presence of the account Discount on Notes Payable indicates that:

a Money was borrowed on a short-term basis at a rate in excess of the going market rate.

b Assets were increased at the time of borrowing by an amount in excess of the cash received.

c Interest has been paid in advance of the due date.

d A note payable has been issued for an amount equal to the sum of the principal and interest payable on the maturity date of the note.

_____ **5** The presence of the account Discount on Notes Receivable indicates that:

a A contingent liability exists.

b The face amount of a note receivable includes the interest receivable at the maturity date.

c Interest expense will be incurred in future periods.

d Total liabilities are less than if the discount had not been recorded.

_____ **6** Mann Company accepts numerous notes receivable from its customers. When the maker of a note defaults, Mann Company should:

a Transfer the principal of the note to Accounts Receivable and write off the accrued interest as a loss.

b Make no accounting entry if the maker of the defaulted note will sign a renewal note on equally favorable terms.

c Debit Accounts Receivable for the principal of the note plus interest earned, offset by credits to Notes Receivable and Interest Revenue.

d Record a contingent liability for the maturity value of the note.

_____ **7** Carl sold equipment today and received in payment a 10-year note receivable bearing interest at 1% a year. If Carl's accounting for this transaction follows the concept of *present value*:

a Discount on Notes Receivable will be debited for the difference between the present value the note and its maturity value.

b The note will be recorded at its face value or its maturity value, whichever is lower.

c The Notes Receivable account will increase each year by 1% through use of an annual adjusting entry.

d An amount will be recorded as Discount on Notes Receivable at the date of acquiring the note and transferred gradually to Interest Revenue over the 10-year life of the note.

_____ **8** Ace Company is arranging to borrow $50,000 from its bank for a period of 6 months at an annual interest rate of 12%. The bank has agreed that Ace Company may sign either of two forms of promissory note: a note for $50,000 with interest stated separately or a note with interest included in the face amount.

a The cost of borrowing will be the same with either form of note, but Ace Company's balance sheet will show a large total amount of liabilities if interest is included in the face amount of the note.

b The cost of borrowing will be less if the interest is stated separately.

c An account for Discount on Notes Payable should be used regardless of which form of note is selected.

d The amount of interest expense will be the same and the total liability related to the bank loan will be the same regardless of which form of note is chosen.

Exercises

1 A list of account titles, each preceded by a code letter, appears below. Using this code, indicate the accounts to be debited and credited in properly recording the 10 transactions described. In some cases more than one account may be debited or credited.

(Note that *X designates any account not specified in the list.*)

A Cash
B Notes Receivable

C Accounts Receivable
D Allowance for Doubtful Accounts
E Notes Payable
F Discount on Notes Payable
G Accrued Interest Payable
H Uncollectible Accounts Expense
I Interest Expense
J Credit Card Discount Expense
X Any account not listed

2 Compute the interest on the following amounts using the assumption of a 360-day year.

a $12,000 at 14% for 60 days: $ _____

b $ 8,400 at 18% for 75 days: $ _____

c $ 4,000 at 12% for 90 days: $ _____

d $ 9,000 at 12½% for 120 days: $ _____

e $13,000 at 15% for 180 days: $ _____

Transactions	Account(s) Debited	Account(s) Credited
Example: Sold merchandise, receiving part cash and the balance on account.	A, C	X
1 Wrote off the account of J. Smith as uncollectible.		
2 Borrowed $5,000 from a bank, signing a note for the amount of $5,000, with interest stated at 16%.		
3 Collected cash from a national credit card company (not a bank) for credit card sales made this week.		
4 Discounted at bank a non-interest-bearing note receivable on same day note was received.		
5 Reinstated the account of J. Smith, written off in **1** above, when Smith promised to make payment.		
6 Recognized interest expense for the period relating to $5,000 note payable in **2** above. Note not yet due.		
7 Borrowed from a bank, signing a note in which the face amount included the interest.		
8 Collected the J. Smith account in full.		
9 Paid the $5,000 note originating in **2** above and all interest due, 20 days after making the adjusting entry in **6** above.		
10 Recognized interest expense for the period relating to note originating in **7** above. Note not yet due.		

10
INVENTORIES

HIGHLIGHTS OF THE CHAPTER

1   In previous chapters you have become familiar with the use of a dollar amount for inventory in both the balance sheet and the income statement; however, the amount for inventory has been given without much discussion as to its source.

2   In this chapter we consider what goods are properly included in inventory, how the cost of the ending inventory is computed, and what the advantages and disadvantages are of several alternative methods of valuing inventory.

3   In a retail or wholesale business, inventory consists of *all goods owned and held for sale* in the regular course of business.

4   The *cost of goods available for sale* minus the *ending inventory* equals the *cost of goods sold*. When we assign a value to the ending inventory, we are thereby also determining the *cost of goods sold* and therefore the *gross profit on sales*.

5   The ending inventory of one year is the beginning inventory of the next year. Therefore an error in the valuation of ending inventory will cause the income statements of two successive years to be in error by the full amount of the error in inventory valuation.

6   a   When *ending* inventory is understated, net income will be understated.
    b   When *ending* inventory is overstated, net income will be overstated.
    c   When *beginning* inventory is understated, net income will be overstated.
    d   When *beginning* inventory is overstated,

net income will be understated.

7   In other words, an inventory error is *counterbalancing* over a two-year period. If ending inventory is overstated, the income for the current year will be overstated, but income for the following year will be understated by the same amount. The reverse is also true: if ending inventory is understated, the income for the current year will be understated but income for the following year will be overstated.

8   An error in inventory valuation will cause several parts of the financial statements to be in error. On the income statement, the cost of goods sold, the gross profit on sales, and the net income will all be wrong by the full amount of the inventory error. On the balance sheet of the year in which the inventory error occurs, the owner's equity, the total current assets, and the balance sheet totals will also be in error.

9   Since an error in inventory has a counterbalancing effect on income over a two-year period, the owner's equity and the balance sheet totals will be correct at the end of the second year.

10   Taking a physical inventory is common practice at the end of each year. This means counting the merchandise owned, multiplying the quantity of each item by the unit cost to get a dollar value, and adding these values together to arrive at a total dollar figure for inventory.

11   Inventory includes all goods owned regardless of location. Title passes from seller to buyer when delivery is made. For goods in

transit at year-end, we must consider the terms of shipment. If the terms of shipment are *F.O.B. shipping point*, the goods in transit are the property of the buyer. If the terms are *F.O.B. destination*, the goods remain the property of the seller while in transit.

12   The primary basis of accounting for inventory is *cost*, which includes transportation-in (the cost incurred in bringing the merchandise to the point where it is to be offered for sale).

13   When several lots of identical merchandise are purchased at different prices during the year, which price should be considered as the cost of the units remaining in the year-end inventory? We shall consider four alternative valuation methods: (a) specific identification, (b) average cost, (c) first-in, first-out, and (d) last-in, first-out.

14   The specific identification method *may* be used if the units in the ending inventory can be identified as having come from specific purchases.

15   The average-cost method is computed by dividing the total *cost* of units available for sale by the number of units available for sale. This *weighted-average unit cost* is then multiplied by the number of units in the ending inventory.

16   The first-in, first-out method (*fifo*) is based on the assumption that the first merchandise acquired is the first sold. Therefore, ending inventory consists of the most recently acquired goods and is valued at the prices paid in the more recent purchases.

17   The last-in, first-out method (*lifo*) assumes that the most recently acquired goods are sold first and that the ending inventory consists of the "old" merchandise acquired in the earliest purchases. Thus, the prices applied in valuing the ending inventory are the prices paid on the earliest purchases. The more recent prices are considered to apply to the cost of the goods sold.

18   During a period of changing prices, each of these four alternative inventory methods will lead to different figures for cost of goods, gross profit on sales, net income, and owner's equity. However, all are acceptable because they are merely alternative methods of measuring *cost*.

19   During a period of rising prices, the *lifo* method will lead to the smallest inventory value, the lowest net income, and the lowest income tax. This is because the more recent (and higher) costs are considered to be the cost of the units sold and the earlier (and lower) purchase prices are considered to be the cost of the unsold units comprising the ending inventory. Supporters of lifo argue that income is most accurately measured by *matching* the *current* cost of merchandise against *current* sales prices regardless of which physical units of merchandise are actually delivered to customers.

20   The *fifo* method produces a realistic balance sheet amount for inventory close to current replacement cost, whereas the *lifo* method produces a balance sheet value for inventory reflecting prices in the distant past.

21   *Inflation complicates the measurement of net income.* During a period of rising prices, the cost of replacing goods sold exceeds the historical cost of goods sold as reported in the income statement. Many accountants and business executives believe that the use of historical costs tends to *overstate* net income because the business must pay a higher cost (the replacement cost) than is deducted from revenue (the historical cost) with respect to goods sold.

22   The excess of the replacement cost of goods sold over their historical cost is termed *inventory profit*. Inventory profit is a restricted type of income, since it must be reinvested in inventory just to maintain inventory levels and therefore is not available for withdrawal by the owners. During a period of inflation, fifo results in a lower historical cost of goods sold than does lifo. Thus, fifo causes a larger amount of inventory profit to be included in reported net income.

23   To show the effects of inflation, the FASB requires large corporations to disclose what it would cost to replace their inventories at current prices and what their cost of sales would be if computed by using the replacement cost of the goods sold. When we consider the cost of replacing goods sold to customers, it appears that many companies have been much less profitable than their financial statements (based on historical costs) have indicated.

24   Continuing inflation and high income tax rates have led to increased interest by business managers in lifo. The lifo method causes reported net income to reflect the increasing

cost of replacing the goods sold during the year and also tends to avoid basing income tax payments on an exaggerated measurement of taxable income.

25 If the utility of inventory falls below cost because of deterioration, price-level declines, or other reasons, it may be valued at the *lower-of-cost-or-market*. The word *market* in this context means *replacement* cost. The justification is prompt recognition of any loss which may have occurred. In no case should inventory be carried at more than its *net realizable value*.

26 The lower-of-cost-or-market rule may be applied to each item in the inventory, or to each category of inventory, or to the inventory as a whole.

27 The retail method may be used to estimate the cost of the ending inventory, as follows:
a Determine the retail price of goods available for sale by adding the retail value of the beginning inventory to the retail price of goods purchased during the period.
b Compute the *cost percentage* by dividing the cost of goods available for sale by the retail price of these goods.
c Estimate the *retail value* of the ending inventory by subtracting net sales from the retail value of the goods available for sale.
d Convert the ending inventory valuation to *cost* by multiplying the ending inventory at retail prices by the cost percentage determined in b, above.

28 The retail method also may be used to simplify the pricing of the annual physical inventory taken at a retail store. The inventory would be counted and priced as follows:
a Take a physical inventory, pricing the goods at *retail prices*. This is easier than pricing the goods at cost, because the goods have price tags showing their retail price.
b Determine the cost percentage (see steps a and b in Highlight 27).
c Use the cost percentage to reduce the valuation of the ending inventory from retail to cost.

29 The *gross profit method* of estimating inventories is useful when inventory is lost by fire or theft, or when it is desired to prepare monthly financial statements without incurring the expense of taking a physical inventory.

30 An assumption underlying the gross profit method is that the gross profit rate does not change from period to period. Thus, we may determine the current cost percentage from the income statement of the last period. The cost percentage is found by dividing the cost of goods sold by net sales. (The cost percentage also is equal to 100% minus the gross profit rate.)

31 Once the cost percentage is known, the gross profit method is applied as follows:
a Determine the cost of goods available for sale from the general ledger records of beginning inventory and net purchases.
b Estimate the cost of goods sold by multiplying net sales for the period by the cost percentage.
c Deduct the estimated cost of goods sold from the cost of goods available for sale to find the ending inventory.

32 Whatever method of inventory is selected, it should be followed consistently from period to period to avoid distorting reported income merely because of changes in accounting method.

33 Up to this point, we have emphasized the *periodic inventory system* in which inventory is not known from day to day but determined by taking a physical inventory periodically. The alternative is a *perpetual inventory system* which provides a continuous running balance of inventory.

34 In a perpetual inventory system, purchases are debited directly to the Inventory account rather than to a Purchases account. A sale of merchandise requires two entries: (a) a debit to Cash (or Accounts Receivable) and a credit to Sales for the sales price and (b) a debit to Cost of Goods Sold and a credit to Inventory for the *cost* of the merchandise. To avoid making a large number of entries in the general journal, we can enter a special column in the sales journal to show the cost of the goods sold in each transaction. At the end of each month the total of this "cost" column can be posted as a debit to Cost of Goods Sold and a credit to Inventory.

35 There are several advantages to a perpetual inventory system. Internal control is strengthened because management will become aware of any shortages when the physical count of inventory is compared with the perpetual inventory records. Since the perpetual inventory records always show

the amount which should be on hand, a physical inventory may be taken at dates other than year-end. Also, monthly or quarterly financial statements can readily be prepared from the perpetual inventory records without the need for a physical inventory. Although more costly to operate, the perpetual inventory system is appropriate for a business dealing in goods of high unit value.

TEST YOURSELF ON INVENTORIES

True or False

For each of the following statements, circle the T or the F to indicate whether the statement is true or false.

T F   1 A major objective of accounting for inventories is proper measurement of net income.

T F   2 An error in the valuation of inventory at the end of the period will cause errors in net income for two periods.

T F   3 Taking the inventory refers to the physical count to determine the quantity of inventory on hand; pricing the inventory means determining the cost of the inventory on hand.

T F   4 If the terms of shipment are F.O.B. shipping point, the goods in transit should normally belong to the seller.

T F   5 Errors in the valuation of inventory are counterbalancing; an error which causes an overstatement of net income this period will cause an understatement next period.

T F   6 Inventories are usually valued at cost, but the cost figure for an inventory can differ significantly depending upon what inventory method is used.

T F   7 The recording of a sale in the wrong period will have no effect on the net income for each period if the goods are excluded from inventory in the period in which the sale is recorded.

T F   8 An overstatement of ending inventory will cause an understatement of net income.

T F   9 The specific identification method of inventory valuation is particularly appropriate for low-priced, high-volume articles.

T F 10 The average-cost method places more weight on the prices at which large purchases were made than on the prices at which small purchases were made.

T F 11 Using the first-in, first-out (fifo) method during a period of rising prices implies that the cheaper goods have been sold and the more costly goods are still on hand.

T F 12 If we consider the "true" cost of sales to be the replacement cost of goods sold, income statements using historical costs tend to understate net income during periods of inflation.

T F 13 During a period of rapid inflation, using lifo will maximize reported net income.

T F 14 Using the lifo method implies that the ending inventory consists of the most recently acquired goods.

T F 15 Inventory profits result from increasing the selling price of merchandise.

T F 16 The use of the lower-of-cost-or-market rule produces a conservative inventory valuation because unrealized losses are treated as actually incurred.

T F 17 The gross profit method permits a business to estimate ending inventory without actually taking a physical count of the goods on hand.

T F 18 The retail method of inventory valuation permits us to take and price the physical inventory at current retail prices rather than look up invoices to determine the cost of goods on hand.

T F 19 Consistency in the valuation of inventories requires that a method once adopted cannot be changed unless the company is sold.

T F 20 A perpetual inventory system is easier and less expensive to operate than is a periodic inventory system.

T F 21 In a perpetual inventory system, ledger accounts for inventory and the cost of goods sold are continuously updated for purchases and sales of merchandise.

Completion Statements

Fill in the necessary words or amounts to complete the following statements:

1 If goods are shipped F.O.B. destination, the _____ to the goods while in transit belongs to the _____ and the goods should be excluded from the inventory of the _____ .

2 Ending inventories are *overstated* as follows:

Year 1 by $20,000; Year 2 by $8,000; and Year 3 by $15,000. Net income for each of the three years was computed at $25,000. The corrected net income figure (ignoring the effect of income taxes) for each of the three years is: Year 1, $ _____; Year 2, $ _____ ; Year 3, $ _____ .

3 The four most commonly used inventory valuation methods are: _____ _____ _____ , _____ _____ _____ , _____ _____ , and _____ _____ .

4 One of the most significant recent developments in accounting practice is the requirement by the FASB that large corporations disclose the _____ cost of their inventories and their cost of sales computed by using the _____ cost of goods sold. This disclosure indicates that income statements using _____ cost may have been (overstating, understating) _____ _____ the profitability of many companies during periods of inflation.

5 Inventory profits represent the difference between the historical cost of goods sold and the _____ _____ of goods sold. Inventory profits are a restricted type of income because they must be _____ in _____ and because they are not available for distribution to owners or to finance expansion. During a period of rising prices, companies using the _____ inventory method might be expected to have the largest inventory profits.

6 The lower-of-cost-or-market rule results in the recognition of a _____ in the _____ cost of inventory. However, an _____ in the _____ _____ cost would not be recognized.

7 During a period of rising prices, using the _____ method implies that the cheaper goods are still on hand while the more expensive ones were sold.

8 The method of inventory valuation frequently used by retail stores is first to value the inventory at _____ and then to convert this amount to a _____ figure by applying the _____ of cost to selling prices during the current period.

9 In a perpetual inventory system, purchases are recorded by a debit to _____ and a credit to Accounts Payable. Sales are recorded by two entries: (a) a debit to Accounts Receivable and a credit to _____ for the _____ price of the merchandise and (b) a debit to _____ _____ _____ _____ and a credit to _____ for the _____ of the goods.

Multiple Choice

Choose the best answer for each of the following questions and enter the identifying letter in the space provided.

____ **1** Which of the following items would *not* be included in inventories on the balance sheet?
a Raw materials used in manufacture of chemicals.
b Building materials used in construction.
c Cars left by customers at an auto repair shop.
d Goods purchased but not yet delivered to premises (title passed).

____ **2** An overstatement of $1,000 in the inventory at the end of Year 4 would:
a Understate the beginning inventory of Year 5.
b Have no effect on net income of Year 3.
c Overstate purchases for Year 5.
d Have no effect on net income of Year 4.

____ **3** Which of the following is *not* an acceptable inventory method?
a Lower of cost or market.
b Sales value.
c Specific identification.
d First-in, first-out.

____ **4** During a period of rising prices, which inventory pricing method might be expected to give the lowest valuation for inventory on the balance sheet and the lowest net income figure?
a Cost on a lifo basis.
b Cost on a fifo basis.
c Weighted-average cost.
d Fifo, lower of cost or market.

____ **5** The gross profit method of estimating inventories:
a Is a useful means of determining the rate of gross profit without taking a physical inventory.
b Is a useful means of verifying the reasonableness of a physical inventory count.
c Provides information about the number of units in the ending inventory.

d Provides information about changes in the rate of gross profit.

_____ 6 *Net realizable value*, as the term is used in relation to inventory valuation, means:

a Replacement cost of the goods in inventory.

b Cost of the goods on a fifo basis increased by anticipated selling expenses.

c Selling price of the goods minus anticipated selling expenses.

d Sales price of the goods minus anticipated selling expenses and profit margin.

_____ 7 Goods costing $750 are sold for $1,000 at the end of Year 1, but the sale is recorded in Year 2. The goods *were* included in the ending inventory at the end of Year 1. The most likely effect of this error is:

a Net income for Year 1 was understated by $1,000.

b Net income for Year 2 was overstated by $250.

c Beginning inventory for Year 2 is understated by $750.

d Net income for Year 1 was overstated by $250.

Exercises

1 In each of the situations described below, indicate the effect of the error on the various elements of financial statements prepared at the end of the current year, using the following code:

O = overstated, U = understated, NE = no effect

Situation	Revenues	Costs and/or Expenses	Net Income	Assets	Liabilities	Owner's Equity
a No record made of goods purchased on credit and received on Dec. 31. Goods omitted from inventory.						
b Made sale in late December; goods were delivered on Dec. 31 but were also included in inventory on Dec. 31.						
c In taking the physical inventory, some goods in a warehouse were overlooked.						
d A purchase made late in year was recorded properly on the books, but the goods were not included in the ending inventory.						

2 The following inventory information is available for the month of May:

	Units	Total Cost
Beginning inventory, May 1	500	$5,000
Purchase, May 3	400	4,400
Purchase, May 10	800	9,600
Purchase, May 21	300	3,900

The replacement cost of each unit on May 31 is $12.50. Sales amounted to 1,500 units at an average price of $16.10.

Compute the cost of the ending inventory of 500 units and the cost of goods sold under each of the following inventory methods:

	Inventory	Cost of Goods Sold
a Fifo—cost	$ _6300_	$ _6600_
b Fifo—cost or market, whichever is lower .	$ _____	$ _____
c Lifo—cost	$ _5000_	$ _17900_
d Average—cost	$ _575_	$ _17175_

3 On March 8, Crown Jewelry store was robbed of its entire inventory. The following information is available from the company's accounting records:

Inventory, January 1	$60,000
Purchases, January 1 through March 8	39,600
Net sales, January 1 through March 8	81,000

The gross profit of Crown Jewelry over the past several years has consistently averaged 40% of net sales. Using the gross profit method, estimate the cost of the inventory stolen on March 8.

4 ToyMart uses the retail method to estimate its inventory at the end of each month. The following information is available at July 31:

	Cost	Retail
Inventory, June 30	$292,500	$450,000
Purchases during July	187,500	300,000
Goods available for sale during July	$480,000	$750,000

Net sales during July amounted to $350,000. Compute the following:

a The cost percentage that would be used in applying the retail method for the month of July ___64___ %

b The estimated inventory at July 31, stated in retail prices $ __400,000__

c The estimated inventory at July 31, stated at cost $ __256,000__

11
PLANT AND EQUIPMENT: DEPRECIATION

HIGHLIGHTS OF THE CHAPTER

1 The term *plant and equipment* is used to describe long-lived assets used in the operation of the business and not held for sale to customers. The term *fixed assets* has been used to describe plant assets but is now used less frequently.

2 A plant asset is a *stream of services* to be received by the owner over a long period of time. As the services are received, a portion of the asset is consumed and should be recognized as an expense (depreciation).

3 The major categories of plant and equipment include:

a Tangible plant assets, such as land, buildings, and machinery. Most of these assets are *subject to depreciation*, whereas land, for example, is generally *not subject to depreciation*.

b Intangible assets, such as patents, copyrights, trademarks, franchises, organization costs, leaseholds, and goodwill. The term *intangible assets* is used to describe noncurrent assets which have *no physical form*. The cost of intangible assets is subject to *amortization*.

4 The major accounting problems relating to plant and equipment are:

a Determining the cost of the plant asset.

b Procedures for allocating the cost of a plant asset to accounting periods.

c Recording costs (such as repairs) incurred in using plant assets.

d Recording the disposal of plant assets.

5 All *reasonable* and *necessary* expenditures incurred in acquiring a plant asset and placing it in use should be recorded in an asset account. The cost may include the list price, sales or use taxes paid, freight and handling costs, installation costs, and insurance prior to the time that the asset is placed in service.

6 Cash discounts reduce the net cost of the asset. Interest paid when an asset is purchased on the installment plan should be recorded as an expense rather than as part of the cost of acquiring the asset.

7 The cost of land may include real estate commissions, escrow fees, title insurance fees, delinquent taxes (including penalties and interest), etc. Separate ledger accounts are always maintained for land and buildings. Certain land-improvement cost, such as fences, driveways, parking lots, sprinkler systems, and landscaping, have a limited life and should be recorded in a separate account and depreciated.

8 When a building is purchased, the total cost includes the price paid plus all incidental costs, such as termite inspection fees, legal fees, and major repairs necessary before the building is occupied. When a building is constructed by the owner, the total cost of the building includes all direct expenditures (labor, materials, building permit, etc.) plus a reasonable estimate of indirect costs (overhead).

9 A *capital expenditure* is one that will benefit many accounting periods; a *revenue expenditure* is one that will benefit only the current

accounting period. Capital expenditures are recorded in asset accounts and are deducted from revenue through the process of depreciation; revenue expenditures are recorded in expense accounts as incurred.

10 If a capital expenditure is erroneously recorded as a revenue expenditure, the current period's net income will be understated and future periods' net income will be overstated because no depreciation expense will be recognized. If we erroneously record a revenue expenditure as a capital expenditure, the current period's net income will be overstated and future periods' net income will be understated.

11 *Depreciation* is the process of *allocating the cost of plant assets* to the periods in which services are received from the assets. A separate depreciation expense account should be maintained for each major group of depreciable assets, and the total amount of depreciation expense for the fiscal period should be disclosed in the income statement.

12 Depreciation is *not* a process of assigning a market value (or realizable value) to plant assets, nor is it a process of accumulating a fund for the replacement of assets when they become worn out or obsolete. Depreciation is an *allocation process*: The cost of an asset, less residual value, is allocated to the years that are benefited from the use of the asset.

13 The balance in the Accumulated Depreciation account represents the portion of the historical cost of plant assets which has expired to date; this account does *not* represent a fund of cash accumulated to replace plant assets.

14 The two major causes of depreciation are:
a Physical deterioration from use.
b Obsolescence due to technological changes or changing needs of the company.

15 The methods of computing periodic depreciation are:
a Straight-line:
$$\frac{\text{Cost} - \text{residual value}}{\text{Estimated years of useful life}}$$
b Units of output:
$$\frac{\text{Cost} - \text{residual value}}{\text{Total estimated units of output}} \times \text{units produced}$$
c Fixed-percentage-on-declining balance: Book value of the asset multiplied by a rate which

is usually twice the straight-line rate.
d Sum-of-the-years'-digits: Cost minus residual value multiplied by a fraction, of which the numerator is the remaining years of useful life and the denominator is the sum of the years of useful life.

16 The *straight-line method* is the simplest and the most widely used method of computing depreciation. Under this method an *equal portion* of the cost of the asset (less residual value) is allocated to each period of use. This method is most appropriate when usage of an asset is fairly uniform from period to period.

17 When the usage of an asset fluctuates and output can be estimated in terms of some unit (such as tons produced or miles driven), a more equitable allocation of a plant asset can be obtained by computing depreciation on the basis of output. Cost (less residual value) is divided by estimated output to obtain a depreciation *rate per unit*. Depreciation for a period is computed by multiplying the rate per unit by the number of units produced.

18 Under *accelerated depreciation* methods, larger amounts of depreciation are recorded in the early years of use and reduced amounts in later years. Accelerated methods are particularly appropriate when obsolescence is more significant than physical deterioration in rendering the asset less useful or productive. In some cases the use of an accelerated depreciation method tends to equalize the total expense of using an asset because decreasing periodic depreciation charges are offset by increasing repair outlays as the asset gets older.

19 A business need not use the same method of depreciation for all its assets. Also, different methods may be used for tax purposes than are being used in the accounting records and financial statements.

20 For income tax purposes, assets acquired after January 1, 1981, may be depreciated by a special method called the Accelerated Cost Recovery System (ACRS). ACRS is an accelerated method for three reasons: (1) the rate table published by the IRS allows for writing-off higher percentages in the early years, (2) ACRS makes no provision for a salvage value, and (3) assets generally may be written off over a period shorter than their actual useful lives.

21 ACRS is used for income tax purposes only; it generally *is not* acceptable for financial reporting purposes.

22 Depreciation rates are based on estimates of useful life. If the estimate of useful service life is found to be in error, the estimate should be revised, and the *undepreciated cost of the asset should be allocated over the years of remaining useful life*. A change in annual depreciation expense may also result from a change in the *estimate of residual value* or from a change in the *method* of computing depreciation.

23 In an economy characterized by inflation, the current replacement cost of plant assets may be much greater than their historical cost. Supporters of *replacement cost accounting* argue that income is *overstated* when depreciation expense is based upon historical cost because these costs are less than the *current value* of the asset services being used up.

24 The criticism of historical cost is a convincing one. For this reason, the SEC now requires large corporations to *disclose* the estimated replacement cost of their plant assets and the depreciation expense computed using these costs. This rule does *not* mean that replacement cost is used *instead* of historical cost; rather, the current replacement cost data are presented in a footnote as *additional supplementary information*.

25 The use of current replacement cost is a very controversial issue in accounting practice throughout the world. Great Britain has recently changed from historical cost to current value as the basis for financial reporting. If the current value concept of income measurement becomes widely accepted, there may be important changes in the level of profits reported by businesses, in income tax policies, and in all types of business decisions.

TEST YOURSELF ON PLANT AND EQUIPMENT; DEPRECIATION

True or False

For each of the following statements, circle the T or the F to indicate whether the statement is true or false.

T F 1 In a broad sense, the cost of a machine or a building may be viewed as a long-term prepaid expense.

T F 2 An auto owned by a glass manufacturer would be reported under Plant and Equipment, while glass owned by an auto manufacturer would be classified as Inventory.

T F 3 The cost of land that is entered in the books should not include any transaction costs, such as real estate commissions paid.

T F 4 *Capital expenditures* are those disbursements which are allocated to several accounting periods; *revenue expenditures* are charged off as current expenses.

T F 5 The cost of a plant asset should include all costs necessary to get the asset ready for use, including the cost of the units spoiled in production while the asset was being adjusted and tested.

T F 6 A small expenditure, such as $20 for a set of spark plugs, may reasonably be charged to expense even though the expenditure may benefit several periods.

T F 7 Obsolescence may be a more significant factor than wear and tear through use in putting an end to the usefulness of many depreciable assets.

T F 8 Depreciation expense for a period should be a reasonably good estimate of the change in the fair market value of an asset during the period.

T F 9 If the price of construction goes up by 25% during Year 1, the amount of depreciation on a building already owned will be increased, but not necessarily by 25%.

T F 10 In practice, the residual value of an asset is often ignored in estimating annual depreciation expense.

T F 11 The units-of-output method of depreciation yields similar results to *accelerated* methods of depreciation when the rate of output increases steadily over a period of years.

T F 12 The Accumulated Depreciation account is a fund established for the replacement of assets, but it will not be large enough to cover the cost of replacement during a period of inflation.

T F 13 The fixed-percentage-on-declining-balance method of depreciation has a "built-in" residual value and can never allocate 100% of the original cost of an asset to expense.

T F 14 The sum-of-the-years'-digits method and the units-of-output method are called accelerated depreciation methods.

T F 15 The same method of depreciation must be used for all assets owned by the same company.

T F 16 A company organized after January 1, 1981 should use the ACRS method of depreciation in its financial statements even if another method is used for income tax purposes.

T F 17 When it becomes evident that a plant asset will have a useful life longer than had been originally estimated, the depreciation rate will be revised according to the new estimate of useful life.

T F 18 If depreciation were based upon current replacement costs rather than historical costs, most companies would report lower net income.

Completion Statements

Fill in the necessary words or amounts to complete the following statements:

1 The process of _____depreciation_____ allocates the _____cost_____ of a plant asset to the periods in which services are received from the asset.

2 Four methods of computing depreciation are: _____Straight line_____ , _____Sum of years_____ , _____declining balance method_____ , and _____acrs method_____ .

3 The two causes of depreciation are: (a) _____physical deterioration_____ and (b) _____obsolescence_____ .

4 If a _____capital_____ expenditure is erroneously recorded as a _____revenue_____ expenditure, net income will be _____understated_____ in the current period, and overstated in every future period in which depreciation should have been recognized.

5 Net income for three consecutive years was reported as follows:

Year 1	$30,000
Year 2	$39,000
Year 3	$40,000

At the beginning of Year 1 a capital expenditure of $15,000 for a new machine, which should have been depreciated over a five-

year life using the sum-of-the-years'-digits method, was erroneously charged to repair expense. The correct net income for the three years should have been as follows:

Year 1, $_____ ; Year 2, $_____ ; Year 3, $_____ .

6 The ACRS method of depreciation is used on assets acquired after January 1, _____1981_____ . This method is allowable for _____income tax_____ purposes and is (widely used, not acceptable) _____not acceptable_____ for use in financial statements.

7 Supporters of replacement cost accounting argue that net income is the excess of revenue over the _____current value_____ of the resources used up in producing that revenue. This argument suggests that the current practice of basing depreciation expense upon _____historical_____ cost tends to (overstate, understate) _____overstate_____ net income.

Multiple Choice

Choose the best answer for each of the following questions and enter the identifying letter in the space provided.

_____ 1 *Depreciation*, as the term is used in accounting, means:
a The systematic write-off of the cost of a natural resource over its productive life.
b The allocation of the cost of a plant asset to expense to reflect the use of asset services.
c The physical deterioration of an asset.
d The decrease in the market value of an asset.

_____ 2 The book value of a depreciable asset is best defined as:
a The undepreciated cost of the asset.
b The price that the asset would bring if offered for sale.
c Accumulated depreciation on the asset since acquisition.
d The original cost of the asset.

_____ 3 The straight-line method of depreciation:
a Generally gives best results because it is easy to apply.
b Assumes that the asset provides equal benefits in each accounting period.
c Should be used in a period of inflation because it accumulates, at a uniform rate, the fund for the replacement of the asset.

d Is the best method to use for income tax purposes.

_____ **4** *Accumulated depreciation*, as used in accounting, may be defined as:

a Earnings retained in the business that will be used to purchase another asset when the present asset is depreciated.

b Funds (or cash) set aside to replace the asset being depreciated.

c The portion of the cost of a plant asset recognized as expense since the asset was acquired.

d An expense of doing business.

_____ **5** A and B Companies purchase identical equipment having an estimated service life of 10 years. A Company uses the straight-line method of depreciation, and B Company uses the sum-of-the-years'-digits method. Assuming the companies are identical in all other respec

a B Company will record more depreciation on this asset over the entire 10 years than will A Company.

b At the end of the third year, the book value of the asset will be lower on A Company's books than on B Company's.

c A Company's depreciation expense will be greater in the first year than B Company's.

d A Company's net income will be lower in the ninth year than B Company's.

_____ **6** Big Company purchased land for $80,000 subject to delinquent property taxes of $4,000. These taxes were paid immediately by Big Company, along with interest of $320 on the delinquent taxes. The cost of this land should be recorded by Big Company at:

a $80,000
b $84,000
c $84,320
d Some other amount.

Exercises

1 A truck with an estimated life of four years was acquired on March 31, Year 1, for $11,000. The estimated residual value of the truck is $1,000, and the service life is estimated at 100,000 miles. Depreciation for fractional periods is computed to the nearest full month. Compute depreciation for Year 1 and Year 2 using the following methods:

		Year 1	Year 2
a	Straight-line	$ _1375_	$ _2500_
b	Output (miles driven: Year 1, 20,000; Year 2, 40,000)	$ _2000_	$ _4000_
c	Sum-of-the-years'-digits .	$ _3000_	$ _3250_
d	Fixed-percentage-on declining-balance (twice the straight-line rate) . . .	$ _4125_	$ _3437.5_

$$a\quad \frac{11K-1K}{4}\times\frac{9}{12}\qquad \frac{11K-1K}{4}$$

$$b.\quad 11K-1K\times\frac{20,000}{100,000}$$

$$11K-1K\times\frac{40,000}{100,000}$$

$$c\quad 11K-1K\times\frac{4}{10}\times\frac{9}{12}$$

$$11K-1K\times\frac{4}{10}\times\frac{3}{12}+11K-1K\times\frac{3}{10}\times\frac{9}{12}$$

$$d\quad 11K\times50\%\times\frac{9}{12}$$

$$11K-4125\times50\%$$

2 In the space provided below, record the following transactions completed during 19___ relating to a machine:

Jan. 4 Acquired a machine for $4,000, paying $1,000 cash and signing a note payable for $3,000 at 8% interest per annum due in 90 days.

Jan. 6 Paid moving and installation costs of $250 on the machine.

Apr. 4 Paid balance due on purchase of machine.

June 30 Recorded depreciation for six months for fiscal year ended on this date. Estimated life of the machine is 10 years with a residual value of $650. Use straight-line depreciation.

19___	General Journal		
Jan. 4	Machine	4000	
	Note Payable		3000
	Cash		1000
6	Machine	250	
	Cash		250
April 4	Note Payable	3000	
	Interest Expense	60	
	Cash		3060
June 30	Depreciation Expense : Machine	180	
	Accumulated Depreciation : Machine		180

10 yrs × 12 months = 120 mo

4250 − 650 × 6/120

12
PLANT AND EQUIPMENT, NATURAL RESOURCES, AND INTANGIBLES

HIGHLIGHTS OF THE CHAPTER

1 When units of plant and equipment wear out or become obsolete they must be discarded, sold, or traded in. To record the disposal of a depreciable asset, the cost of the asset must be removed from the asset account, *and the accumulated depreciation* (on that asset) *must be removed* from the contra-asset account.

2 Sometimes an asset remains in service after it has been fully depreciated. The asset and the accumulated depreciation remain on the books until the asset is disposed of. But since all the cost of the asset has been allocated to expense, *no more depreciation should be recorded.*

3 The *book value* of a depreciable asset is its cost minus accumulated depreciation. If the asset is sold for a price above book value, there is a *gain* on the sale. If the asset is sold for less than book value, there is a *loss.*

4 When a depreciable asset is sold, the amount of the gain or loss is determined by comparing the book value of the asset sold with the amount received from the sale. The amount of a gain would be *credited* to a *Gain on Disposal of Plant Assets* account, and a loss would be *debited* to *Loss on Disposal of Plant Assets.*

5 As a result of using different depreciation methods, an asset's basis for income tax purposes may differ from its book value. In this event, the gain or loss on disposal of the asset computed for tax purposes will differ from that reported in the financial statements.

6 When plant assets are disposed of at a date other than the end of the year, depreciation is recorded for the fractional period preceding disposal. As discussed in Chapter 11, depreciation for fractional periods may be computed by the half-year convention or by rounding to the nearest full month.

7 For purposes of determining taxable income, no gain or loss is recognized when a depreciable asset is *traded in* on a similar asset. The cost of the new asset is recorded as the sum of the *book value of the old asset plus any additional amount paid* (or to be paid) for the new asset.

8 The *trade-in allowance* and the *list price* of the new asset are *not recorded in the accounts*; their only function is in determining the amount the purchaser must pay in addition to trading in the old asset.

9 Income tax regulations and financial accounting rules are alike in not recognizing a gain on an exchange of similar plant assets, but they differ when the exchange results in a loss. A loss on an exchange of similar plant assets may not be deducted for tax purposes, but it *should be recognized* in the financial statements. An exchange results in a loss when the trade-in allowance for the old asset is less than its book value.

10 Control accounts and subsidiary ledgers may be an important internal control device over accounting for plant and equipment assets. A subsidiary ledger, with a card for each specific asset, is established for each major classification of plant assets (such as land, buildings, and office equipment) maintained in the general ledger. Each general ledger

account for a type of plant asset, and the related general ledger accumulated depreciation account, become *controlling accounts* representing one of the subsidiary ledgers.

11 Each card in the subsidiary ledgers has an identification number which is also attached to the related asset. This permits a physical inventory of plant and equipment to be taken to prove whether all units shown in the records are actually on hand.

12 Natural resources, such as mines or timber stands, are physically extracted and converted into inventory. These assets are recorded at cost and reported separately in the balance sheet.

13 *Depletion* is the process of *allocating the cost* of a natural resource to the units removed. The depletion rate is computed by dividing the cost of the natural resource by the estimated number of units available to be removed. The rate is then multiplied by the number of units removed during a period to determine the total depletion charge.

14 For tax purposes, the IRS permits companies in some industries to take a deduction for depletion expense equal to a specified percentage of revenue from production of mineral deposits. This *percentage depletion* is used *only for tax purposes* and is not acceptable in financial statements.

15 *Intangible assets* are those noncurrent assets which do not have physical substance but which contribute to the process of earning revenue. Intangibles are recorded at cost and should be *amortized* over their useful lives. It is often difficult to estimate the useful life of an intangible asset, but the maximum amortization period *may not exceed 40 years*. Intangible assets generally are amortized by the straight-line method.

16 *Goodwill* is the market value of a going business *in excess of* the fair market value of the other identifiable assets of the business. It represents the *present value* of expected future earnings in excess of the normal return on the net identifiable assets of the business. The term *net identifiable assets* refers to all assets, except goodwill, minus liabilities.

17 The existence of the intangible asset goodwill is indicated when an entire business is sold for a price in excess of the fair market value of the other assets. The willingness of the purchaser to pay this higher price indi-

cates he or she is paying for an expected excess earning capability of the going business over the earning capability of similar businesses. These above-average earnings may arise from favorable customer relations, superior management, or other intangible factors.

18 Goodwill may exist in many businesses, but it should be recorded in the accounts *only when it is purchased*.

19 The following three methods may be used in *estimating* the value of goodwill owned by a business unit:

a Negotiated agreement between buyer and seller. If a business with net assets (at market value) of $80,000 is sold for $100,000, this suggests that goodwill of $20,000 is identified with this business.

b A multiple of the amount by which the average annual earnings exceed normal earnings. If the normal earnings are estimated at $20,000 and average annual earnings are $22,500, goodwill may be estimated at, say, 5 times excess earnings ($22,500 − $20,000), or $12,500.

c The capitalized value of excess earning power. For example, if excess earnings amount to $5,000 and the capitalization rate agreed upon is 20%, the goodwill would be estimated at $25,000 ($5,000 ÷ .20).

20 A *patent* is an exclusive right to manufacture a particular product. Patents are intangible assets which should be recorded at cost and amortized over the useful life of the patent.

21 *Trademarks* are the exclusive right to use a trademark, brand name, or commercial symbol. The cost of trademarks often is so small that such costs are charged directly to expense.

22 *Franchises* are rights granted by companies or governmental units to conduct a certain type of business in a specific geographic area. An example is the right to operate a McDonald's restaurant in a specific neighborhood. The cost of a franchise should be amortized over the life of the franchise agreement (but not to exceed 40 years).

23 *Copyrights* are exclusive rights to protect the production and sale of literary or artistic materials for the life of the creator plus 50 years. Only if a copyright is purchased will the expenditure be material enough to be amortized over the useful life.

24 *Deferred charges* are expenditures expected to yield benefits in future accounting

periods, which should be amortized over their useful lives. Deferred charges, such as plant rearrangement costs, are another type of intangible asset.

25 Some accountants believe that spending money for research and development creates an intangible asset. However, it is usually very difficult to determine at the time of the expenditures whether any future benefit exists. For this reason, the FASB has ruled that all research and development expenditures should be *charged to expense* rather than recorded as intangible assets. (This rule does not apply to the development costs incurred by companies developing natural resources.)

TEST YOURSELF ON PLANT AND EQUIPMENT, NATURAL RESOURCES, AND INTANGIBLES

True or False

For each of the following statements, circle the T or the F to indicate whether the statement is true or false.

T F   1 Whenever a depreciable asset is sold, both the cost of the asset and the accumulated depreciation must be removed from the accounts.

T F   2 If a plant asset is sold at a price different from its book value, a gain or loss on the sale will occur.

T F   3 When the ACRS depreciation method is used for income tax purposes, the tax basis of an asset usually is greater than the asset's book value in the financial statements.

T F   4 For both tax purposes and preparing financial statements, no gain is recognized when the trade-in allowance on a plant asset exceeds its book value.

T F   5 For both tax purposes and preparing financial statements, no loss is recognized when the trade-in allowance on a plant asset is less than its book value.

T F   6 Depreciation should never be recorded for fractional periods, even when an asset is disposed of in the middle of a fiscal year.

T F   7 A subsidiary ledger may be maintained for plant assets to help ensure that all plant assets in the records are actually owned.

T F   8 Depletion refers to the allocation of the cost of an intangible asset over the periods that benefits are received.

T F   9 The rate at which depletion is recognized depends upon an estimate of the number of units of a resource that may be removed.

T F   10 Percentage depletion is a technique used in the preparation of financial statements but is not an acceptable method for income tax purposes.

T F   11 Intangible assets are assets that cannot be sold.

T F   12 Often, intangible assets are written off to expense immediately because determining the periods in which benefits will be received may be nearly impossible.

T F   13 The systematic write-off of intangible assets to expense is known as *amortization*.

T F   14 Goodwill is the present value of future earnings in excess of the normal return on net identifiable assets.

T F   15 When a business has superior earnings for many years, goodwill probably exists and should be recorded on the books.

T F   16 If a buyer of a business pays a price for the business in excess of the fair market value of the net identifiable assets, the buyer may record goodwill as one of the assets being acquired.

T F   17 Goodwill, trademarks, patents, and copyrights are all examples of intangible assets.

T F   18 Expenditures for research and development may be charged to either an asset account or an expense account, depending upon whether or not the expenditure is expected to produce future economic benefit.

Completion Statements

Fill in the necessary words or amounts to complete the following statements:

1 The entry to record the disposal of a depreciable asset will always include a credit to the asset account for the ___original cost___ of the asset and a debit to the ___accumulated___ ___depreciation___ account.

2 The term ___basis___ describes the book value of an asset for income tax purposes.

3 Tax regulations provide that the cost of new equipment shall be the sum of the _book value_ of any old equipment traded in plus any _additional_ _cost_ paid or to be paid in acquiring the new equipment.

4 Each card in a _subsidiary ledger_ for plant assets shows an _identification_ _number_ which should also appear on a metal tag attached to the asset itself. Thus, a physical _inventory_ of plant and equipment may be taken to prove whether all units shown in the records are actually on hand.

5 The cost of intangible assets should be _amortized_ by the _straight line_ method over a period not to exceed _40_ years.

6 Goodwill is the _present value_ of estimated future earnings in _excess_ of a normal return on net identifiable assets. Goodwill is recorded in the accounts only when it is _purchased_ .

Multiple Choice

Choose the best answer for each of the following questions and enter the identifying letter in the space provided.

_____ 1 Assume that an asset is depreciated as 5-year property by the ACRS method for income tax purposes and over 8 years by the straight-line method in the financial statements. If the asset is sold after 3 years, which of the following situations might result?
a A gain for tax purposes and a loss in the financial statements.
b A gain for tax purposes and a larger gain in the financial statements.
c A loss for tax purposes and a smaller loss in the financial statements.
d A loss of equal amount both for tax and financial statement purposes.

_____ 2 Morgan Company has traded in a machine on a similar asset, paying cash for the difference between list price and the trade-in allowance. The trade-in allowance on the old machine was greater than its book value. The cost of the new asset should be recorded as:
a The list price of the new asset.
b The estimated fair value of the old asset plus the cash paid.
c The book value of the old asset plus the cash paid.
d The trade-in allowance on the old asset plus the cash paid.

_____ 3 The best evidence of goodwill existing in a business is:
a The appearance of goodwill on the balance sheet.
b Numerous contributions to charitable organizations.
c A long-standing reputation for manufacturing a high-quality product.
d A long record of earnings greater than those of like-size firms in the same industry.

_____ 4 Which of the following assets would not be subject to the process of depletion?
a The cost of developing a producing mine.
b The cost of buying a producing oil well.
c The cost of a patent on a new mining process.
d The cost of geological surveys to locate oil.

_____ 5 Which of the following is not an intangible asset?
a A patent.
b A copyright.
c A note receivable.
d Goodwill.

_____ 6 Lucky Strike Mines recognizes $2 of depletion for each ton of ore mined. This year 750,000 tons of ore were mined, but only 700,000 tons were sold. The amount of depletion that should be deducted from revenue this year is:
a $2,900,000
b $1,500,000
c $1,400,000
d $ 100,000

Exercises

1 A machine which cost $6,000 had an estimated useful life of six years and an estimated salvage value of $600. Straight-line depreciation was used. In the space provided, prepare the journal entry (omitting explanation) to record the disposal of the machine under each of the following assumptions:

a The machine was sold for $4,000 cash after two years' use.

b After three years' use, the machine was sold for $3,500 cash.

c After four years' use, the machine was traded in on a similar machine with a list price of $8,000. The trade-in allowance was $3,100.

2 The Golden Calf, a Las Vegas gambling casino, had net identifiable assets of $12,000,000 and earned an average net income of $3,120,000 per year. Other Las Vegas casinos averaged a net income equal to 20% of their net identifiable assets. An investment group negotiating to buy the Golden Calf offers to pay $12,000,000 for the casino's net identifiable assets, plus an amount for goodwill. The investment group determined the amount to be paid for goodwill by capitalizing the Golden Calf's annual earnings in excess of the industry average earnings at a rate of 25%. Compute the *total price* the investment group is offering to pay for the Golden Calf.

Computations:

normal
earnings
$$12,000,000$$
$$\times .20$$
$$2,400,000$$

excess earn 3,120,000 − 2,400,000 = 720,000

Goodwill 720,000 ÷ .25 = 2,880,000

price offered 12,000,000 + 2,880,000 = 14,880,000

Answer: $ _____

General Journal			
a	Cash (sold)		4000	
	Accum Depreciation		1800	
	Loss on disposal of asset		200	
	Machine			6000
	To remove from accounts			
b	Cash (sold)		3500	
	Accum Depreciation		2700	
	Gain on disposal of asset			200
	Machine			6000
	To record sale			
c	Machine (new) (trade in)		7300	
	Accum Depreciation		3600	
	Machine (old)			6000
	Cash			4900
	Trade in			

13
PAYROLL
ACCOUNTING

HIGHLIGHTS OF THE CHAPTER

1 Payroll involves a large share of total costs, sometimes 50% or more. Federal and state laws require detailed payroll records for each employee, and regular reports to be filed with government agencies, along with payment of amounts withheld from employees and payroll taxes on the employer.

2 The input data to the payroll accounting system include employees' names, social security numbers, regular hours worked, overtime, pay rates, and taxes. The output data include paychecks, payroll records, withholding statements, and reports to government agencies.

3 Strong internal controls over payrolls are necessary because of the large expenditures involved, the necessity for prompt, accurate payment of employees, and the required filing of detailed reports to government.

4 Payroll fraud (such as "padding the payroll" with fictitious names) has been made more difficult by the required frequent filing of payroll data with the government and the maintenance of individual earnings' records for each employee identified by a social security number.

5 Payroll accounting is a repetitive process quite adaptable to the use of computers. Automation of payroll accounting does *not* eliminate the danger of payroll fraud or the need for subdivision of duties as a basis for internal control.

6 Payroll activities should be separated into the functions of (a) employing workers, (b) timekeeping, (c) payroll preparations and record keeping, and (d) distribution of paychecks or pay envelopes to employees. When each of these functions is handled by a separate department, internal controls tend to be strong, the records reliable, and the opportunity for fraud held to a minimum.

7 Detailed payroll records are required by law; they also serve other purposes such as helping to determine eligibility for vacations, sick leave, and retirement pay.

8 A clear distinction must be made between *employees* and *independent contractors*. Employees are subject to payroll taxes and reports, but independent contractors are not. If the person or business receiving the service has a right to control and direct the methods used by the person rendering the service, an employer-employee relationship exists. Examples of independent contractors (nonemployees) would be the CPA who audits a business or typists who use their own typewriters on their own premises to type term papers for students. Payment to independent contractors is called a *fee* rather than salary or wages and is not part of the payroll.

9 Employers engaged in interstate commerce are required by the Federal Fair Labor Standards Act (also known as the Wages and Hours Law) to pay overtime at a minimum rate of $1\frac{1}{2}$ times the regular rate for hours worked in excess of 40 per week.

10 FICA (Federal Insurance Contributions Act) taxes, or simply *social security taxes*, are withheld from the employee's pay to help pay for retirement payments and Medicare.

A separate FICA tax of the same amount is levied on the *employer*. The rate of tax and the base (amount to pay to which the rate applies) have been increased many times, and more increases are scheduled for future years. For convenience in all problems in this study guide, we assume the rate of FICA tax to be 7% on both the employer and employee applicable to a base of $40,000 (the first $40,000 of wages earned in each calendar year).

11 For example, assume that in January an employee earns $1,000. The employer will withhold $70 ($1,000 × .07) from the employee's paycheck. The employer will then pay the government $140, consisting of the $70 withheld from the employee plus an additional $70 tax on the employer.

12 Employers are also required to withhold federal income tax from employees' pay. Each employee files a *Withholding Allowance Certificate* (Form W-4), showing the number of exemptions claimed (one for the employee and one for each dependent). This enables the employer to compute the proper amount of tax to withhold. The objective is to make the amount of income tax withheld closely approximate the individual's tax liability at the end of the year.

13 The following journal entry illustrates recording of a payroll and deductions from employees' pay. It does not show the payroll tax on the employer, this will be illustrated in paragraph 19.

Sales Salaries Expense	11,000	
Office Salaries Expense	9,000	
FICA Taxes Payable		
($20,000 × .07)		1,400
Liability for Income Taxes		
Withheld		4,150
Accrued Payroll		14,450

To record the payroll and related deductions for period ending Jan. 31.

14 Some companies pay employees in cash (when banking or check-cashing facilities are not convenient). A statement of gross earnings, deductions, and net pay is usually printed on the pay envelope. Payment of employees in cash does not provide as good internal control as the use of checks.

15 By January 31 each year, employers are required to furnish every employee with a *Wage and Tax Statement* (Form W-2) in duplicate. It shows gross earnings for the preceding calendar year and amounts withheld for FICA tax and income tax. The employer must also send a copy to the Internal Revenue Service. The employee must attach a copy to his or her federal income tax return.

16 The employer must maintain a detailed earnings record for each employee, showing for each pay period the gross earnings, the deduction for FICA tax, the income tax withheld, any other deductions authorized by the employee, and the net pay. These records show when the employee's gross earnings for the calendar year exceed the $40,000 base for FICA tax and thus put an end to that particular deduction. These records also provide the information for the quarterly reports which the employer must file with federal and state authorities.

17 Every business must use a calendar year in accounting for payroll taxes, even though it uses a fiscal year for other purposes. The employer must file reports on amounts withheld from employees at the end of each quarter. Payments must be made at much more frequent intervals to a designated bank unless the amounts are quite small (less than $200 a quarter).

18 Thus far we have concentrated on payroll taxes on employees. Payroll taxes are also levied on the *employer*, and these are expenses of the business. Payroll taxes levied upon the employer include social security tax (already mentioned), federal unemployment insurance tax (FUTA), and state unemployment tax (SUTA). In this study guide we assume the rate of FUTA tax to be .8% and SUTA tax to be 2.7%, both applied to a base of $7,000 (the first $7,000 earned by each employee in a calendar year).

19 To illustrate recording the *employer's* payroll taxes, assume the same $20,000 payroll for January used in paragraph 13. The journal entry would be:

Payroll Taxes Expense	2,100	
FICA Taxes Payable		
($20,000 × .07)		1,400
State Unemployment taxes Payable ($20,000 × .027)		540
Federal Unemployment Taxes Payable ($20,000 × .008)		160

To record payroll taxes on employer for period ended Jan. 31.

Since this payroll is for January, we have assumed that none of the employees has as yet reached the $7,000 level of cumulative earnings at which FUTA taxes cease.

20 Payroll taxes become a legal liability when wages are paid, not when wages are earned. In accruing unpaid wages at year-end, it would be logical to accrue payroll taxes levied on the employee. However, the Internal Revenue Service will not permit an expense deduction for payroll tax expense in computing taxable income until the period the wages are paid. Rather than handle the payroll tax expense one way on the books and another way on the income tax return, most companies choose not to accrue payroll taxes on the employer.

21 All taxes withheld from employees are owed by the employer to the government and are classified as current liabilities on the balance sheet. Payroll tax *expense* appears in the income statement, often divided between selling expenses and general expenses.

TEST YOURSELF ON PAYROLL ACCOUNTING

True or False

For each of the following statements, circle the T or the F to indicate whether the statement is true or false.

T F 1 The separation and subdivision of duties cease to be essential to strong internal control over payrolls if payroll activities are performed by a computer.

T F 2 For strong internal control, paychecks should be distributed to employees by an official of the personnel department, not the payroll department or the finance department.

T F 3 FICA taxes are levied on both employer and employee.

T F 4 FUTA taxes are levied on both employer and employee.

T F 5 Federal income taxes withheld from employees' wages appear in the accounting records of the employer as part of the Payroll Taxes Expense account.

T F 6 Every employer is subject to FUTA (unemployment tax) regardless of how many or how few employees he or she has.

T F 7 Participation in the social security program provided by the Federal Insurance Contributions Act is a voluntary decision of the individual employee.

T F 8 All persons who perform services for a business for remuneration are subject to income tax withholding.

T F 9 Employees as well as employers are required to contribute to most state unemployment compensation programs.

T F 10 The base to which FICA taxes are applicable is higher than the base for FUTA taxes.

T F 11 The payment by a company to a CPA for performing an annual audit is not subject to income tax withholding or payroll taxes.

T F 12 The function of a paymaster is to prepare paychecks and deliver them to employees or to a departmental supervisor if the employee is absent on payday.

T F 13 In determining whether an employee's accumulated earnings have reached the maximum amount subject to FICA tax, the employer must use a calendar year even if the business maintains its accounts on a fiscal year ending June 30.

T F 14 Payroll taxes are usually not accrued at year-end as are salaries and wages because payroll taxes expense is not a deductible item for income tax purposes until the period in which the wages are paid.

T F 15 The Employee's Withholding Allowance Certificate (Form W-4) is required of all employees but is not actually used by the employer until the time arrives for filing the quarterly report with the government.

T F 16 The part of unemployment compensation tax going to the state is larger than the part going to the federal government.

T F 17 The repetitive nature of payroll activities makes them particularly suitable for processing by a computer.

T F 18 If an employee earns $50,000 a year

and the FICA tax rate is 7%, the government will receive a total of $7,000 representing the employee's and employer's FICA contribution for the year.

Completion Statements

Fill in the necessary words or amounts to complete the following statements:

1 An attorney, a CPA, or a management consultant who performs services for a business entity and has numerous other clients is referred to as an independent _contractor_ rather than as an _employee_.

2 When an employer withholds income tax from an employee, the amount withheld will be credited to a _liability_ account.

3 The contractual amount which an employee earns during a pay period is referred to as _gross earnings_. This amount minus _deductions_ equals the amount of the check or cash received by the employee, which is often termed the _take home pay_.

4 An employee earns $4,000 per month, and tax rates are as follows: FICA, 7%; FUTA, .8%; and SUTA, 2.7%. The *total* cost to the employer during January of having this employee on the payroll would be $ _4420_ . During December of the same year, assuming no change in salary, the cost to the employer would be $ _4000_ .

5 Form _W-2_ is a withholding statement, furnished by the employer to employees and to the _Internal Revenue Service_.

6 The typical deductions from an employee's gross earnings include _FICA_, _federal income taxes_ , and _insurance etc_.

7 Payroll taxes levied on the employer usually consist of _FICA taxes_, _federal unemployment taxes_ , and _State unemployment taxes_ .

8 The employer is obligated to maintain an _employee earnings record_

for each employee, which will provide among other things the amount of cumulative earnings for the calendar year.

9 A type of payroll fraud which involves the inclusion on the payroll of fictitious names and/or names of former employees is called _padding the payroll_.

Multiple Choice

Choose the best answer for each of the following questions and enter the identifying letter in the space provided.

_____ 1 Federal unemployment taxes are levied on:
a Employees at the rate of 2.7% of the first $7,000 of wages earned.
b Employers and employees at the same rate.
c Employers of one or more persons.
d None of the above.

_____ 2 The amounts withheld from an employee's gross earnings are recorded by the employer as:
a Payroll expense.
b Current assets.
c Contra-asset accounts.
d Current liabilities.

_____ 3 A tax which is levied on employers and not withheld from employees' pay is:
a FUTA tax.
b FICA tax.
c Federal income tax.
d State income tax.

_____ 4 The use of computers for processing payrolls:
a Practically eliminates the danger of payroll fraud.
b Has not eliminated the need for separation and subdivision of duties to maintain strong internal control.
c Eliminates the need for the employee's individual earnings record.
d Is less common than for preparation of general journal entries.

_____ 5 The FICA tax deducted from an employee's pay should be:
a Debited to an expense account.
b Credited to a liability account.
c Classified as payroll tax expense.
d Applied against the employee's income tax liability at the end of the year.

Exercises

1 For each employee listed below, compute the payroll taxes *on the employer* for the current pay period. Assume an FICA rate of 7% on a base of $40,000, a state unemployment tax of 2.7% on a base of $7,000, and a federal unemployment tax of .8% on a base of $7,000.

Employee	Cumulative Earnings for Year up to Current Period	Payroll for Current Period	FICA Taxes	FUTA Taxes		Total Taxes on Employer
				State	Federal	
Adams	$ 45,000	$ 5,000	$ ―	$ ―	$ ―	$ ―
Barnes	37,800	4,200	294	―	―	294
Corey	4,800	1,200	84	32.4	9.6	126
Daniel	18,900	2,100	147	―	―	147
Eliot	5,400	1,800	126	48.6	14.4	189
Ford	11,250	1,250	87.50	―	―	87.5
Gray	—0—	1,900	133	51.3	15.2	199.5
Totals	$123,150	$17,450	871.5	132.3	39.2	1043

2 For the payroll period ended January 15, the payroll records for office salaries of Bend Company showed $30,000 of gross earnings and income tax withholding of $5,700. The payroll is subject to an FICA rate of 7% on a $40,000 base, to state unemployment tax of 2.7% on a $7,000 base, and federal unemployment tax of .8% on a $7,000 base. Complete the two separate journal entries to record (a) the accrued payroll and deductions from employees' pay and (b) the payroll taxes on the employer resulting from this payroll.

19	General Journal		
Jan. 15 (a)	Office Salaries Expense	30,000	
	FICA		2100
	Fed income tax		5700
	Accrued Payroll		22,200
	To record payroll and related deductions for pay		
	period ended Jan. 15.		
15 (b)	Payroll Taxes Expense		
	FICA		2100
	State unemployment tax		189
	Fed unemployment tax		56
	To record payroll taxes on employer for pay		
	period ended Jan. 15.		

14

ACCOUNTING PRINCIPLES AND CONCEPTS; EFFECTS OF INFLATION

HIGHLIGHTS OF THE CHAPTER

1 *Generally accepted accounting principles* are the ground rules for financial reporting. The financial statements of all publicly owned corporations are prepared in conformity with these principles.

2 In order to qualify as "generally accepted," an accounting principle should be widely used and should be supported by one or more of the following groups:

a The *AICPA* (the professional association of licensed CPAs), through its research efforts and the pronouncements of the *Accounting Principles Board* (APB). (The APB has been replaced by the Financial Accounting Standards Board.)

b The *Financial Accounting Standards Board* (an organization with representatives from public accounting, industry, government, and accounting education), through publication of *Statements of Financial Accounting Standards*.

c The *Securities and Exchange Commission* (an agency of the federal government), through publication of *Accounting Series Releases*.

3 One basic accounting concept is that the information in an accounting report is compiled for a carefully defined *accounting entity*. An accounting entity is any economic unit which controls resources and engages in economic activities. An individual, a division of a corporation, or a whole business enterprise are all examples of possible accounting entities. The important thing is that the entity is clearly defined before the reports

are prepared, and then only the activities of that entity are reported.

4 Another important principle is the *going-concern assumption*. This means that we assume that a business will continue in operation for an indefinite period of time sufficient to carry out all its commitments. The going-concern principle is the reason why all assets are not valued at their liquidating value.

5 The preparation of *periodic* financial reports is another accounting principle. To be useful, financial statements must be timely and available at frequent intervals so that decision makers may observe trends and changes in the economic condition of an accounting entity. However, when the life of a business is divided into specific *fiscal periods* (accounting periods), the results can only be estimates. For instance, the portion of the cost of a building to be deducted from the revenue of the current month is based upon an estimate of how long the building will be used.

6 Another assumption underlying financial statements is the *stability of the measuring unit*. We assume that the dollar is constant and that it does not change in *purchasing power*. This means we ignore changes in the purchasing power of the dollar resulting from inflation or deflation. For example, since 1960 there has been inflation in the United States. A dollar will not buy as much today as it did in 1960. If we bought $15,000 worth of land in 1960, it might cost $50,000 or more to buy a similar piece of land today, just because of inflation. However, assets

are not written up to current dollar values in financial statements: we make the simplifying assumption that the value of the dollar is constant and does not change over time.

7 *Objectivity* is one of the most basic accounting principles. This means that the valuation of assets and liabilities is based on *objective evidence*, such as an actual *exchange price*. An objective value is one that is free from *bias* and can be verified by an independent party. Objectivity is one reason why assets are valued at historical cost (an actual exchange price) rather than at estimated current market value.

8 Even though objectivity is a major goal of accounting, some measurements must still be estimates based on judgment. Depreciation, for example, is not completely objective because it depends upon an estimate of useful life.

9 Both the balance sheet and the income statement are affected by the *cost principle*. Assets are valued at their *cost*, rather than at their current market values. Expenses represent the *cost* of goods and services used up in the effort to generate revenue. The major argument supporting the cost principle is that cost can be determined *more objectively* than can current market value.

10 The timing of revenue recognition is determined by the *realization principle*. Accountants usually do not recognize revenue until it is realized. Revenue is realized when (a) the earning process is essentially complete and (b) objective evidence exists as to the amount of revenue earned.

11 In theory it is possible to recognize revenue:
a As production takes place.
b When production is completed.
c When sale or delivery of the product is made or the services are rendered.
d As cash is collected from customers.
  In most cases, the accountant recognizes revenue at the time of sale of goods or the rendering of services.

12 Under special circumstances, accountants deviate from the realization principle. For example, the *percentage-of-completion* method of accounting for long-term construction projects recognizes revenue during production.

13 Companies selling goods on the installment plan sometimes use the *installment method* of reporting for income tax purposes. Under the installment method, the seller recognizes the gross profit on sales gradually over an extended period of time as the cash is actually collected from customers. The installment method is used primarily for tax purposes; it is seldom used in financial statements.

14 The timing of expense recognition is determined by the *matching principle*. Expenses may be recognized in two major ways: (a) in relation to the product sold or services rendered or (b) in relation to the time period during which revenue is earned.

15 *Consistency* is the principle which means that once an accounting method is selected, it will be constantly used and not changed from period to period. For example, if we used straight-line depreciation on our building last month, we should not switch to fixed percentage on declining balance this month. If we did, there would be a change in net income caused by the change in an accounting method rather than any real economic changes.

16 The principle of *disclosure* means that all *material* (significant) and *relevant* facts concerning financial position and the results of operations must be communicated to the users of financial statements. This disclosure may be made either in the financial statements or in *footnotes* to the financial statements.

17 The concept of *conservatism* may not be an accounting principle, but it plays an important role in financial reporting. Conservatism means that when estimates must be made, the accountant will lean toward *understatement* of asset values and net income rather than toward overstatement.

18 CPAs conduct an audit of financial statements to render their opinion on whether the statements were prepared in accordance with *generally accepted accounting principles*, and whether the statements *present fairly* the financial position and results of operations of the accounting entity. The CPAs *do not guarantee* the accuracy of financial statements, but their *opinion* is highly regarded by users of those statements.

19 Inflation has decreased the usefulness of cost-based financial statements. When costs and expenses are based on historical costs incurred long ago, they *understate the current value* of the resources being consumed in the

production of revenue. As a result, cost-based financial statements tend to *overstate income* and report large, but fictitious, profits during periods of sustained inflation. This is a serious problem when we consider that income tax regulations, resource allocation decisions, and wage demands are based upon the popular misconception that business profits are much larger than they really are. The need to bring financial statements into accord with economic reality is the greatest challenge facing the accounting profession.

20 Two approaches to modifying an income statement to show the effects of inflation have received much attention. These are:

a *Constant-dollar accounting*—an approach in which costs and expenses not already based on the current price level are restated for changes in the *general* price level.

b *Current-cost accounting*—an approach in which costs and expenses are based upon the current value (replacement cost) of the *specific* resources being consumed, rather than upon their historical cost.

21 By combining transactions which take place during a period of rising prices, accountants in effect ignore the "size" of the measuring unit—the dollar. The *purchasing power* (command over goods and services) of the dollar changes over time. A *general price level index* shows the relative purchasing power of the dollar at different times. For example, if the general price level index rises from 100 in Year 1 to 150 in Year 5, it takes $1.50 in Year 5 to have the equivalent purchasing power of $1 in Year 1.

22 In a conventional historical cost income statement, revenue and expenses measured in current dollars are combined with those stated in "old" dollars of greater purchasing power. Revenue and most expenses result from transactions occurring in the current year and are therefore already expressed in current dollars. Depreciation expense, however, is based on "old" dollars, spent when the depreciable asset was acquired. The cost of goods sold also includes some "old" dollars, because the beginning inventory was purchased prior to the current year.

23 In a constant-dollar income statement, costs and expenses based on "old" dollars are *restated* at the number of current dollars representing the *equivalent amount of purchasing power*. The adjustment of historical costs to the equivalent number of current dollars is made using a general price index. When all revenue and expenses are stated in units of similar purchasing power, we can see whether the amount of *purchasing power* controlled by the business is increasing or decreasing as a result of operations.

24 In addition to the increase or decrease in purchasing power resulting from revenue and expense transactions, a business may have a gain or loss in purchasing power from having monetary items during a period of changing prices. *Monetary items* are those assets and liabilities representing claims to a fixed number of dollars. If monetary assets are held while prices rise, a purchasing power *loss* results; if money is owed during a period of inflation, a purchasing power *gain* results.

25 Constant-dollar accounting does not abandon historical cost as the basis of measurement, but simply *restates the historical cost* in terms of the current purchasing power of money. This is quite different from current-cost accounting, in which costs and expenses are based upon the current *replacement costs* of the specific assets being sold or used up.

26 In a *current-cost* income statement, the amounts shown for depreciation expense and for the cost of goods sold are based on the estimated replacement costs of these specific assets and are *not* computed by using a general price-level index. The replacement cost of specific kinds of assets may increase faster or slower than the general price level. In fact, some replacement costs (such as for pocket calculators) may even decline while the general price level rises.

27 An income statement expressed in current costs shows whether a company earns enough revenue to *replace* the goods and services used up in the effort to generate that revenue. The resulting net income figure represents the maximum amount that the business could distribute to its owners and *still maintain the present size and scale of its operations*.

28 The effect of inflation upon the measurement of net income is so important that the FASB now requires large corporations to include with their cost-based financial statements supplementary schedules showing:

a Net income measured in constant dollars.

b The net gain or loss in purchasing power resulting from holding monetary assets or having monetary liabilities during a period of inflation.

c Net income measured in terms of current costs.

Notice that these disclosures are *supplementary information* and do not replace the use of historical costs in the financial statements.

TEST YOURSELF ON ACCOUNTING PRINCIPLES

True or False

For each of the following statements, circle the T or the F to indicate whether the statement is true or false.

T F 1 Financial statements for companies in different industries should be prepared using the same accounting principles.

T F 2 *Generally accepted accounting principles* are well-established and not subject to change.

T F 3 If a meaningful measure of net income is to result, the same definition of accounting entity must be used in the measurement of revenue and of expenses.

T F 4 A single department or a division within a larger business organization can be viewed as a separate accounting entity.

T F 5 The going-concern principle means that a business is assumed to have an indefinite life and will continue to operate until all the firm's commitments have been satisfied.

T F 6 The assumption that the dollar is a stable measuring unit is consistent with economic reality.

T F 7 Estimates of current market values may be more relevant but less reliable than historical costs for decision-making purposes.

T F 8 If a cash offer to buy land owned by a business is received and rejected, objectivity would require that the land be revalued to the amount of the offer.

T F 9 The cost principle and realization principle are both closely related to the need for objectivity.

T F 10 The realization principle states that revenue should not be recognized until the cash has been collected.

T F 11 The percentage-of-completion method recognizes revenue during the production process.

T F 12 *Consistency* means that all companies within a given industry (such as steel or petroleum) must use similar accounting procedures in the preparation of financial statements.

T F 13 Switching in midyear from lifo to fifo as a means of valuing inventory would be a violation of the principle of consistency and would require disclosure in the financial statements.

T F 14 CPAs prepare and guarantee the financial statements of their clients.

T F 15 Gains in the value of plant assets may be recognized as earned prior to sale if the market value of such assets can be objectively determined.

T F 16 If the general price level goes up, the value of money goes down.

T F 17 Owing money during an inflationary period would be advantageous to the borrower.

T F 18 An income statement adjusted for changes in the general price level shows the amount of purchasing power flowing into or out of the business as a result of operations.

T F 19 An income statement based on current costs shows whether a business is earning sufficient revenue to replace the resources being used up in operations.

T F 20 It is possible for a company to report net income under generally accepted accounting principles but to show a net loss when its income statement is adjusted to constant dollars or current costs.

T F 21 The FASB requires large corporations to use current costs rather than historical costs in their financial statements.

T F 22 Unless inflation is severe, constant-dollar accounting and current-cost accounting will result in the same figure for net income.

Completion Statements

Fill in the necessary words to complete the following statements:

1 The most influential authoritative groups that have contributed to the development of generally accepted principles are: _FASB_ _____, _AICPA_ _____, _AAA_ _____, and _SEC_ _____.

2 An underlying assumption that an accounting entity will continue in operation for an indefinite period of time sufficient to carry out its existing commitments is called the _going concern_ assumption.

3 The term _objectivity_ refers to accounting measurements that are unbiased and can be verified; the term _consistency_ assures users of financial statements that when a given accounting method is adopted, it will not be changed without adequate _disclosure_ in the financial statements.

4 The cost principle calls for assets to be valued at _historical_ rather than at current _market_ values.

5 CPAs conduct an _audit_ of the accounting system of a business and render their _opinion_ as to the _fairness_ of the company's financial statements.

6 It would be theoretically possible to recognize the revenue of a business enterprise as realized at one of the following points in time: _in production_, _production completed_, _sale_, or _cash received_.

7 When the general price level increases, the _purchasing power_ of the dollar _decreases_.

8 In a period of inflation, historical cost-based financial statements tend to (overstate, understate) _understate_ the current value of the resources used in producing revenue and (overstate, understate) _overstate_ the profitability of the business.

9 During a period of inflation, holding monetary assets results in a purchasing power _loss_ and having monetary liabilities results in a purchasing power _gain_.

10 In a constant-dollar income statement, costs based on "old" dollars are restated by use of a _general_ _price_ _index_ at the number of _current_ _dollars_ representing the equivalent amount of _purchasing power_. In a current-cost income statement, expenses are based on the estimated cost to _replace_ the specific assets being used up.

Multiple Choice

Choose the best answer for each of the following questions and enter the identifying letter in the space provided.

_d_ 1 Which of the following does *not* represent a generally accepted accounting principle?
a Accounting information is compiled for an accounting entity.
b Consistency in the application of particular accounting methods enables the user of accounting data to interpret changes in income or in financial position from period to period.
c The going-concern assumption justifies ignoring liquidating values in presenting assets in the balance sheet.
d Constant-dollar financial statements are the primary means of financial reporting by large corporations.

_b_ 2 Financial statements prepared by a business firm are most likely to be:
a Fully reliable.
b Tentative in nature.
c Relevant for all types of decisions.
d Always misleading.

_b_ 3 The independent accountants' opinion on a set of financial statements:
a Consists of three parts: a description of the

scope of the audit, an opinion on the fairness of the statements, and a forecast of net income for the coming year.

b Can be issued only when the accountants have performed an audit of the statements and the accounting records.

c Can be issued if the accounting records have been maintained in a consistent manner even though the company has not followed generally accepted accounting principles.

d Guarantees to users that the statements have been prepared in accordance with generally accepted accounting principles and are free from any material error.

____ 4 Revenue is most commonly recognized at the point that:

a Cash is collected.

b The order is received from customers.

c The sale is made.

d The production of manufactured goods is complete.

____ 5 An income statement adjusted for changes in the purchasing power of the dollar:

a Restates historical costs for changes in the general price level.

b Will show a loss from borrowing during a period of rising prices.

c Restates all monetary items (such as cash and receivables) in terms of current-year dollars.

d Will show more net income during periods of inflation than will an income statement based on historical costs.

____ 6 During an inflationary period:

a Holding monetary assets will result in a purchasing power gain.

b The purchasing power which must be sacrificed to repay a liability of fixed amount is constantly decreasing.

c A purchasing power loss results from borrowing.

d The purchasing power of the dollar is constantly increasing.

____ 7 Holding monetary assets of $1 million during an inflationary period results in a:

a Purchasing power gain.

b Purchasing power loss which is deductible for income tax purposes.

c Neither a purchasing power gain nor a purchasing power loss.

d Purchasing power loss, but no tax deduction.

____ 8 Current-value financial statements:

a Restate historical costs for changes in the general price level.

b Are more objective than financial statements based upon historical cost.

c Show the current value of the resources used up or sold during the period.

d Are required by the SEC from all large corporations.

____ 9 One reason that a large steel company probably would show less net income on a current-cost basis than on a historical cost basis is that the current-cost income statement would include:

a Less revenue.

b A purchasing power loss from holding monetary assets.

c Greater depreciation expense.

d An adjustment of depreciation expense and of the cost of goods sold for changes in the general price index.

Exercises

1 Within the current framework of generally accepted accounting principles, show the immediate effect upon total assets, liabilities, and owner's equity that would be recorded for each of the following situations. Revenue and expenses are to be considered changes in owners' equity. Use the following code:

I = Increase, D = Decrease, NE = No effect

Situation	Assets	Liabilities	Owner's Equity
a An item with a long life and a material cost (a machine) is purchased for cash.	NE	NE	NE
b An item with a long life and an immaterial cost (a pencil sharpener) is purchased for cash.	D		D
c An item of merchandise is acquired for cash at a price far below the price it will be sold for.	NE		NE
d The item in **c** is sold for cash at a price above cost.	I		I
e Cash is collected from a customer for a sale made last period.	NE		NE
f Monetary assets are held during a period of inflation.	NE		NE
g A contractor using the percentage-of-completion method of accounting for long-term contracts finds 10% of the costs have been incurred and they total less than 10% of the contract price.	I		I
h The contractor in **g** finds 40% of the costs have been incurred and they exceed 40% of the contract price.	D		D

2 During Year 5, Baxter Company computed the cost of product X sold (historical cost basis—fifo) as follows:

	Units	Cost
Sold from beginning inventory	50,000	$ 70,000
Sold from Year 5 purchases	90,000	153,000
Cost of product X sold during Year 5	140,000	$223,000

The beginning inventory had been acquired when the general price index stood at 140. During Year 5, the average level of the general price index was 155 and the average replacement cost of product X was $1.70 per unit. Using this information, compute the cost of goods sold for product X on:

a A constant-dollar basis.

$$70{,}000 \times \frac{155}{140} + 153{,}000 =$$

Answer ___230500___

b A current-cost basis.

$$140{,}000 \times 1.70 =$$

Answer ___238,000___

15
PARTNERSHIPS

HIGHLIGHTS OF THE CHAPTER

1 Three common forms of business organizations found in the American economy are single proprietorships, partnerships, and corporations.

2 Partnerships resemble single proprietorships, except that there are *two or more owners* of the business. Each owner is called a *partner* and has all the rights that a single owner of a business would have. Partnerships are often formed to bring together various talents or to bring needed capital into a business. A partnership is often referred to as a *firm*.

3 The principal characteristics of the partnership form of organization are:

a Ease of formation.

b Limited life (a partnership is dissolved whenever there is a change in partners).

c Mutual agency (each partner has the right to bind the partnership to a contract).

d Unlimited liability (each partner may be personally liable for all the debits of the partnership).

e Co-ownership of partnership property and profits.

4 *Advantages of the partnership* form of organization are:

a It brings together sufficient capital to carry on a business.

b It combines special skills of the several partners.

c It offers freedom and flexibility of action.

d It may result in income tax advantages to the partners.

5 *Disadvantages of the partnership* form of organization are:

a A partnership may be terminated upon death or withdrawal of a partner.

b Each partner is personally responsible for partnership debts.

c The partnership is bound by the acts of any partner as long as these acts are within the scope of normal operations.

d The partnership is less effective than a corporation for raising large amounts of capital.

6 A *limited partnership* is a special form of organization which has *limited partners* as well as one or more *general partners*. The general partners have unlimited liability and mutual agency. The limited partners are basically investors rather than partners in the traditional sense. They have the right to participate in profits, but their liability for losses is limited to the amount of their investment. Limited partners usually do not participate in management. Limited partnerships are widely used in ventures designed to provide investors with tax shelters, such as real estate syndications.

7 Every partnership should have a written agreement called a *partnership contract* signed by the partners before beginning operations. The most important points covered in such agreements are (a) a plan for sharing the profits and losses among the partners and (b) the capital and services which are to be contributed by each partner.

8 A *capital account* and a *drawing account* are maintained for *each partner*.

9 When a partner contributes assets other than cash to a partnership, his or her capital account should be credited with the *fair mar-*

ket value of these assets at the date they are invested in the firm.

10 A partner's drawing account is debited when a partner (a) withdraws cash or other assets, (b) pays personal debts with partnership funds, or (c) collects accounts receivable belonging to the firm and personally retains the cash collected.

11 The income statement of a partnership often includes a section to show the division of net income between the partners.

12 A *statement of partners' capital* shows the changes in the partners' capital accounts during a fiscal period. Additional investments made by the partners and their shares of net income are added, and withdrawals are deducted from their beginning capital balances in arriving at their ending capital balances.

13 Partnerships are not required to pay income taxes. However, each partner must pay personal income tax on *his or her share* of partnership net income, *regardless of the amount of withdrawals.*

14 Factors that partners might consider in arriving at a plan to divide net income include:
a Amount of time each partner devotes to the business.
b Amount of capital invested by each partner.
c Other contributions by each partner to the success of the firm.

15 Profit- and loss-sharing agreements may be based on a fixed ratio, or they may provide for salaries to partners and/or interest on partners' capital with the remaining profits divided in a fixed ratio. If a profit sharing plan is not established, profits and losses are shared equally among the partners.

16 If the profit- and loss-sharing agreement provides for salary and interest allowances, any *residual* profit or loss must be divided in some ratio. These provisions are followed even if the net income for the year is less than the total of the salary and interest allowances. The excess of the salary and interest allowances over the net income is charged to the partners in the agreed residual profit- and loss-sharing ratio.

17 Salary and interest allowances to partners are merely a *step toward distributing net income.* Such allowances are *not expenses* to be deducted from revenue in arriving at net income.

18 A new partner may be admitted to a partnership by (a) purchasing an existing partner's interest or (b) investing directly in the firm. If a new partner buys an interest from a present member of a partnership, the only entry necessary on the partnership books is the transfer of the balance in the capital account of the retiring partner to a capital account established for the new partner.

19 When investing in an existing firm, a new partner may receive an equity in the firm equal to, greater than, or less than the amount of his or her investment. If the equity is to be equal to the investment, the capital account is credited for the fair market value of the investment.

20 If a partnership is very successful, new partners may be required to invest more than the equity they receive in the net assets of the firm. The excess investment may be regarded as a *bonus to the old partners* and credited to their capital accounts in the established profit-sharing ratio.

21 When a new partner is required to invest *less* than the equity to be received in the net assets, the old partners are in effect giving part of their equity to the new partner as a bonus for joining the firm. The amount of this bonus should be transferred from the capital accounts of the old partners to the capital account of the new partner.

22 A partnership is *dissolved* when *any change* occurs in the membership of the firm. A partnership is *liquidated* only when all operations are stopped, the liabilities are paid, and any remaining assets are distributed to the partners.

23 The gain or loss resulting from the sale of a partnership, or partnership assets, is divided between the partners in their profit- and loss-sharing ratios.

24 The profit- and loss-sharing ratio is used *only* to allocate profits and losses, *not for sharing cash or any other asset.* After all gains and losses are allocated to the partners' capital accounts, the assets of a liquidated firm can be distributed according to the balances in each capital account.

25 If a partner ends up with a debit balance in his or her capital account, that partner is obligated to *pay the firm* the amount of the debit balance.

TEST YOURSELF ON PARTNERSHIPS

True or False

For each of the following statements, circle the T or the F to indicate whether the statement is true or false.

T F 1 A partnership must always have two or more owners.

T F 2 The single proprietorship necessarily has a limited life, whereas a partnership may have an unlimited life.

T F 3 Mutual agency means that each partner has the right to bind the partnership to contracts.

T F 4 In a traditional partnership, each partner's liability for losses is limited to his or her investment in the firm.

T F 5 A partner usually retains title to assets contributed to a partnership, so that certain assets may be identified as belonging to a given partner.

T F 6 A partnership contract should be drawn up at the end of each year, prior to distributing the net income to the partners.

T F 7 When partners invest assets other than cash in a partnership, their capital accounts should be credited with the current fair market value of those assets.

T F 8 In a limited partnership, none of the partners has unlimited liability for the debts of the business.

T F 9 A partnership must file a tax return even though it pays no income taxes.

T F 10 When a profit- and loss-sharing agreement provides for salary and interest allowances to the partners, these salary and interest allowances should be deducted from revenue in arriving at partnership net income.

T F 11 A partner must pay personal income tax on the amount of withdrawals from a partnership, regardless of his or her share of partnership profits or losses.

T F 12 When new partners invest more than the equity they are to receive in the net assets of an existing partnership, part of the entry to record the new partners' investments is an increase in the capital accounts of the old partners.

T F 13 Partner A has a $15,000 credit balance in his capital account in the firm of A and B. If C buys A's interest in the firm for $20,000, the entry on the partnership books to record the transfer would credit C's capital account for $20,000.

T F 14 When a bonus is allowed to a new partner, part of the entry to record his or her admission to a firm reduces the capital accounts of the former partners.

T F 15 A partnership may be dissolved without being liquidated.

T F 16 If F is admitted to the partnership of D and E, the partnership of D and E has been dissolved even though the business continues to operate.

T F 17 The retirement of a partner by payment from partnership assets could cause the other partners' capital accounts to increase.

T F 18 After a partnership has been liquidated and the creditors have been paid, any remaining assets are distributed to the partners in their profit- and loss-sharing ratios.

Completion Statements

Fill in the necessary words or amounts to complete the following statements:

1 The right of each partner to bind the partnership to contracts is called _____

_____ .

2 R has a balance of $20,000 in her capital account in the partnership of R and S. If R sells one-half of her equity in the firm to T for $15,000 in cash, the entry required on the partnership books would _____ R's capital account for $_____ , and _____ T's capital account for $_____ .

3 L offers to buy a one-third interest in the partnership of M and N by contributing $31,000 cash to the firm. M and N each have capital of $25,000 and share profits and losses equally. In recording L's admission to the firm, L's capital account will be credited for $_____ , and M's and N's capital accounts will each be credited for $_____ .

4 Carr and Davis agree to share profits in a 2

to 1 ratio *after* allowing salaries of $30,000 to Carr and $42,000 to Davis. Assuming that they earn only $18,000 *before* taking into account the salary allowances, Carr's share of the $18,000 profit will be $ _____ and Davis's share will be $ _____ .

5 Ryan invested an additional $4,000 in the partnership during Year 1. Her share of partnership net income for Year 1 was $9,000, of which she withdrew only $2,000. The amount of partnership income that Ryan must report on her individual income tax return is $_____ .

6 The partnership of D, E, and F is being liquidated. All assets have been sold for cash, and all creditors have been paid. The balances of the partners' capital accounts are D, $6,000 credit; E, $2,000 debit; and F, $8,000 credit. D, E, and F share profits and losses equally. The available cash of $12,000 should be distributed as follows: $ _____ to D, $ _____ to E, and $ _____ to F.

Multiple Choice

Choose the best answer for each of the following questions and enter the identifying letter in the space provided.

_____ 1 Which of the following is *not* a characteristic of most partnerships?
a Limited liability.
b Mutual agency.
c Limited life.
d Ease of formation.

_____ 2 Jones invests in a partnership a piece of land which cost his father $10,000. The land had a market value of $15,000 when Jones inherited the land five years ago, and it is currently appraised at $25,000 even though Jones insists that he "wouldn't take $50,000 for it." The land should be recorded on the books of the partnership at:
a $10,000
b $15,000
c $25,000
d $50,000

_____ 3 Partners A and B have capital balances of $15,000 and $12,000, respectively. They share profits and losses in a 2-1 ratio. They sell all the partnership assets for $60,000, which results in a $6,000 gain from book value. The

amount that B should receive as her share of cash upon liquidation of the partnership is:
a $12,000
b $20,000
c $14,000
d $23,000

_____ 4 J, K, and L are partners sharing profits and losses equally. The partnership is being liquidated, and after all assets are converted to cash and all debts paid, there remains $52,000 cash available for distribution among the partners. Partners J and K have capital accounts of $40,000 and $30,000, respectively. Partner L has a debit balance of $18,000 in his capital account. If Partner L is personally insolvent, how much cash will be distributed to Partner J?
a $26,000
b $31,000
c $40,000
d Some other amount

_____ 5 Which of the following best describes the nature of salary and interest allowances in a partnership profit- and loss-sharing agreement?
a Expenses of the business, which should be deducted from revenue in determining net income.
b The amount upon which each partner will have to pay personal income tax.
c A means of distributing net income in relation to services rendered and capital invested by partners.
d A means of determining reasonable monthly withdrawals by each partner.

_____ 6 Mills invests $40,000 for a one-third equity in the partnership of Hayes and Bean. Hayes and Bean had total capital of $62,000. Mills's admission to the firm results in a bonus to Hayes and Bean. In recording Mills's investment, Mills's capital account should be credited for:
a $34,000
b $40,000
c $31,000
d Some other amount

Exercises

1 A and B are partners, having capital balances at the beginning of Year 1 of $30,000 and $40,000, respectively. Indicate in the appropriate columns the division of partnership net income between the partners under the specified conditions. If in any case the

division results in a deduction from partner's capital, place brackets around your answer to indicate this.

2 Selected account balances for C and D, who share profits 60% to C and 40% to D, are shown at the end of Year 1:

Account	Amount
Income Summary	$25,000 (Cr)
C, Drawing	11,000 (Dr)
D, Drawing	16,000 (Dr)
C, Capital	18,400 (Cr)
D, Capital	17,750 (Cr)

a In the space provided below, prepare the closing entries required at the end of Year 1. Omit explanations.

First Situation: Net income is $60,000; partnership agreement provides for:

	A's Share	B's Share
a Net income to be divided 40% to A and 60% to B . . .	$	$
b Interest on beginning capitals at 12%; residual profit or loss divided 70% to A, 30% to B	$	$
c Interest on beginning capitals at 12%; salary to A of $24,000 and to B of $18,000; residual profit or loss divided equally	$	$
Second Situation: Net loss is $16,000; partnership agreement:		
a Says nothing about sharing profits or losses	$	$
b Provides salary to A of $28,000, salary to B of $20,000, residual profit or loss divided 40% to A and 60% to B	$	$

	General Journal		
	Income Summary		

b Complete the partially filled-in statement of the partners' capitals shown below for Year 1, assuming that the partners did not invest additional capital in the business during the year.

C&D
Statement of Partners' Capitals
For Year 1

	C	D	Total
Balance, beginning of year	$18,400	$17,750	$36,150
Add: Net income for year	_____	_____	_____
Subtotal	$	$	$
Less: Withdrawals	_____	_____	_____
Balance, end of year	$	$	$

3 M pays $54,000 cash for a one-third interest in the partnership of K and L. K and L share profits and losses equally, and both have capital balances of $48,000 prior to the admission of M. In the space provided below, prepare the journal entry necessary on the partnership books (omitting explanations) to record the admission of M under each of the following assumptions:

a M buys one-third of K's equity for $26,000 and one-third of L's equity for $28,000.

b M invests $54,000 in the firm, and a bonus is allowed to the former partners.

c M invests $39,000 in the firm, and a bonus is allowed to the new partner.

	General Journal		
a			
b			
c			

HIGHLIGHTS OF THE CHAPTER

1 The dominant form of business organization in the United States is the *corporation*. A corporation is an "artificial being" which is regarded as a legal person, having a continuous existence apart from its owners. Literally thousands, or even millions, of individuals may be the owners of a single corporation; thus the corporation is an ideal means of amassing a great deal of investment capital.

2 Ownership in a corporation is evidenced by transferable *shares of stock*, and owners are called *stockholders*.

3 A corporation offers certain advantages not found in other forms of business organizations:

a The liability of individual stockholders for the debts of a corporation is *limited to the amount of their investment*.

b Large amounts of capital may be gathered by issuing stock to many investors.

c Shares of stock are easily transferable.

d Corporations are usually run by professional management.

4 Some *disadvantages of the corporate form* of organization are:

a A corporation is a *taxable entity* and must pay a high rate of tax on its net income.

b Corporations are subject to a considerable degree of regulation and disclosure of their business and financial affairs.

c The separation of ownership and management (effective control of corporate affairs) may result in management practices which are detrimental to stockholders.

5 Corporations are subject to income taxes.

Income taxes are recognized by a debit to Income Tax Expense and a credit to a liability account, Income Taxes Payable.

6 A corporation is organized by filing an application with the appropriate state agency. The application contains the articles of incorporation and the list of stockholders and directors. Costs of organizing a corporation are recorded in an *Organization Costs* account and are generally written off as expense over a five-year period.

7 Corporate stockholders have certain basic rights:

a To vote for directors (voting rights generally are granted only to holders of common stock).

b To share in profits by receiving dividends (distributions of earnings to the stockholders) declared by the board of directors.

c To share in the distribution of assets if the corporation is liquidated.

d To subscribe to additional shares of stock when the corporation decides to increase the amount of stock outstanding. (This right has been relinquished in some corporations.)

Stockholders *do not* have the right to intervene in the management of a corporation or transact corporation business.

8 The primary functions of the *board of directors* are to manage the corporation and protect the interests of the stockholders. The directors formulate general policies, declare dividends, and review the actions of corporate officers. The board of directors is elected by the stockholders and often includes *outside* directors who are not officers of the corporation.

9 The corporate officers are the active, full-time professional managers of a corporation. Corporate officers usually include a president, several vice-presidents, a controller, a treasurer, and a secretary.

10 The owners' equity section of a corporation's balance sheet is called the *stockholders' equity* section. Stockholders' equity includes at least two classifications: (a) capital contributed by stockholders and (b) capital accumulated and retained through profitable operations.

11 Capital contributed by stockholders comes from the sale of shares of stock. In order to appeal to a large number of investors, a corporation may issue more than one class of stock. When only one class of stock is issued, it is generally referred to as *capital stock*; when two or more classes of stock are outstanding, they usually consist of *common stock* and various types of *preferred stock*.

12 The amount of capital accumulated and retained through the profitable operation of a corporation is shown in the stockholders' equity account called *Retained Earnings*. Retained earnings are increased by profitable operations and decreased by net losses and dividends. Thus, the balance of the Retained Earnings account is the accumulated earnings of the corporation since the business began minus any losses and minus all *dividends* distributed to stockholders. Remember, Retained Earnings is an owners' equity account; *it is not an asset and is not a fund of cash*.

13 At year-end, the Income Summary account of a corporation is closed into the Retained Earnings account. This entry parallels the closing of the Income Summary account of a single proprietorship into the owner's capital account.

14 Withdrawals of cash or other assets from the business by stockholders in a corporation are called *dividends*. Dividends are essentially the same thing as an owner's *drawings* in a single proprietorship, except that dividends are usually paid only from capital accumulated through profitable operations.

15 Cash dividends are stated as a specified amount per share. The amount of cash received by each stockholder is proportional to the number of shares owned. Dividends are *discretionary*; a corporation has no obligation to pay a dividend until that dividend has been declared (authorized) by the board of directors.

16 When the board of directors declares a cash dividend, an entry is made debiting Retained Earnings and crediting a current liability account called Dividends Payable. When the dividend is paid, an entry is made debiting Dividends Payable and crediting Cash. Some companies debit a Dividends account instead of Retained Earnings when a dividend is declared and then close the Dividends account into Retained Earnings at the end of the year.

17 In its simplest form the stockholders' equity section of a corporation's balance sheet includes two accounts: Capital Stock (capital contributed by stockholders when only one class of stock is issued) and Retained Earnings (capital accumulated through profitable operations). If capital generated through operations is negative because of losses, a debit balance account called *Deficit* replaces the Retained Earnings account.

18 *Par value* (or stated value) represents *legal capital*—the amount below which stockholders' equity cannot be reduced except by losses. A dividend cannot be declared if it would reduce total stockholders' equity below the par value of the outstanding shares.

19 Capital stock is generally issued for a sum greater than the par (or stated) value; the excess is credited to Paid-in Capital in Excess of Par (or Stated) Value. Stock is almost never issued for less than par value. In the absence of a par or stated value, the entire proceeds are viewed as legal capital and are credited to the Capital Stock account.

20 Most *preferred stocks*: (a) are entitled to full dividends before any dividends are paid on common stock, (b) have preferred claim to assets in case of liquidation, (c) are callable at the option of the corporation, and (d) have no voting power.

21 The dividend preference of most preferred stocks is *cumulative*. This means if any preferred dividends are omitted, these dividends must be *made up* before any dividends can be paid to common stockholders. Omitted dividends on preferred stock are called *dividends in arrears*.

22 Dividends in arrears are not listed as liabilities because no liability to pay a dividend exists unless the dividend has been declared by the directors.

23 A share of *convertible preferred stock* can be exchanged for an agreed number of shares of

common stock. A holder of convertible preferred stock has greater assurance of receiving regular dividends than does a holder of common stock, while at the same time sharing in any increase in the value of the common stock.

24 An *underwriter* may help a corporation sell a large stock issue. The underwriter guarantees the issuing company a specific price for the stock and makes a profit by selling the stock to the public at a higher price.

25 Market value of a share of stock depends on (a) the level of current and projected earnings, (b) the dividend rate per share, (c) the financial condition of the company, and (d) the mood of the stock market.

26 Once stock is issued, most further stock transactions on the open market are between investors and do not affect the corporation which issued the stock.

27 When stock is issued for assets other than cash, the *fair market value* of the noncash asset or the *market value* of the stock should be used as a basis for recording the transaction.

28 Small corporations sometimes allow investors to *subscribe* to stock by agreeing to pay for the stock in installments or at a future date. The issuing corporation debits Subscriptions Receivable and credits Capital Stock Subscribed when the subscription contract is signed.

29 If assets are donated to a corporation, total assets and total stockholders' equity are increased by the fair market value of the assets received. The receipt of the gift is recorded by debiting the appropriate asset accounts and crediting *Donated Capital.* Donated capital appears in the stockholders' equity section as an element of paid-in capital. No profit is recognized when a gift is received.

30 When only a single class of stock is outstanding, the *book value* per share is computed by dividing the total stockholders' equity by the number of shares outstanding. When both preferred and common stock are outstanding, the book value per share of common stock is computed by dividing the number of shares of common stock into the common stockholders' equity (total stockholders' equity less the redemption value of preferred stock and any dividends in arrears).

31 Ownership of stock is evidenced by a *stock certificate* showing the name of the stockholder and the number of shares owned. At the time of issue, the stock certificate is signed by the president and secretary of the issuing corporation and delivered to the stockholder. When the stockholder sells the shares, the certificate is returned to the corporation and canceled. A new certificate is issued to the new owner of the stock.

32 The balance sheet accounts relating to capital stock are actually control accounts. In order to know who the individual stockholders are, the corporation usually maintains a *stockholders' ledger.* This ledger is continually updated for changes in identity of stockholders.

33 For large corporations, a bank or trust company may serve as a *stock transfer agent* and perform the task of updating the stockholders' ledger. Another bank may act as a *stock registrar* who assumes responsibility for issuing stock certificates to stockholders.

TEST YOURSELF ON CORPORATIONS

True or False

For each of the following statements, circle the T or the F to indicate whether the statement is true or false.

T F 1 Any individual stockholder in a corporation may personally be held liable for all debts incurred by the corporation.

T F 2 A corporation has continuity of existence which permits the business to continue regardless of changes in ownership or the death of a stockholder.

T F 3 A stockholder in a corporation does not have the right to transact corporate business or intervene in the management of the business.

T F 4 Like partnerships and single proprietorships, the corporation itself pays no tax on its income.

T F 5 Stockholders of a corporation elect the board of directors, who in turn appoint the top officers of the corporation.

T F   6   Organization costs are usually written off as expense in the period when a corporation is organized.

T F   7   Stockholders do not make withdrawals from the business as do partners or single proprietors, but receive dividends instead.

T F   8   Dividends are a contractual obligation of the corporation, which must be paid at regular time intervals.

T F   9   Retained earnings is a fund of cash accumulated from profitable operation of the business.

T F   10   Dividends usually cannot be paid on common stock unless the regular dividend has been paid to preferred stockholders.

T F   11   Cash dividends are declared by the board of directors, not by the stockholders of a corporation.

T F   12   Dividends in arrears refers to bypassed preferred dividends which must be made up before any dividends may be paid on common stock.

T F   13   In case of liquidation, the claims of the preferred stockholders are given preference over the claims of creditors.

T F   14   Common stock may be issued at a price different from its par value.

T F   15   When capital stock is sold for a price higher than par value, the Capital Stock account is credited only for the par value of the shares sold.

T F   16   In reference to question **15**, any amount received in excess of the par value of the stock sold is recorded as a credit to the Retained Earnings account.

T F   17   An underwriter guarantees the issuing corporation a set price for a new issue of stock and then resells the stock to the investing public at a higher price.

T F   18   Retained earnings represents the total earnings of a corporation since the date of incorporation minus all dividends that have been declared.

T F   19   Subscriptions receivable is a current asset which results from investors subscribing to stock for which they will pay at some future date.

T F   20   The book value of a share of common stock usually approximates the market price of the stock, particularly for growth companies like Apple Computer and IBM.

Completion Statements

Fill in the necessary words to complete the following statements:

1   The owners of a corporation are _____ _____ , and their ownership of shares of stock is evidenced by a stock _____ .

2   The owner's equity section on a corporate balance sheet is entitled _____ _____ .

3   Among the disadvantages of the corporate form of organization are _____ _____ _____ and _____ _____ .

4   The maximum possible loss of the stockholders in a corporation is limited to _____ _____ _____ .

5   The two major sources of *equity* capital in a corporation are (a) the sale of _____ _____ and (b) _____ earnings.

6   Retained earnings are _____ by net income and _____ by net losses and _____ .

7   When common stock is issued at a price above par value, the _____ _____ of the shares issued is _____ to the _____ _____ account, and the excess is _____ to an account called _____ _____ _____ _____ _____ .

8   Par value represents _____ _____ , which cannot be paid as dividends to stockholders.

9   Most preferred stocks are _____ at the option of the corporation at a stipulated price.

10   The conversion of preferred stock into common generally requires a debit to _____ _____ _____ and credits to _____ _____ and _____ _____ .

Multiple Choice

Choose the best answer for each of the following questions and enter the identifying letter in the space provided.

_____ 1 Which of the following is not a feature of a corporation?
a Limited liability for stockholders.
b Mutual agency.
c Centralized authority.
d Continuous existence.

_____ 2 Title to the assets of a corporation is legally held by:
a The stockholders, jointly and severally.
b The corporation, as a legal entity.
c The president of the corporation in trust for the stockholders.
d The board of directors, as trustees.

_____ 3 Which of the following is *not* a characteristic of most preferred stock?
a Preference as to dividends.
b Participating clause.
c Preference as to assets in event of liquidation of the company.
d No voting power.

_____ 4 Which of the following is most relevant in determining the *cost* of assets acquired in exchange for capital stock?
a Par value of the stock.
b Fair market value of the stock.
c Issuance price of stock already outstanding.
d Estimated useful life of the assets.

_____ 5 The Evans Corporation is authorized to issue 100,000 shares of $10 par value capital stock. It issues one-half of the stock for $25 per share, earns $20,000 during the first three months of operation, and declares a cash dividend of $5,000. The total paid-in capital of the Evans Corporation after three months of operation is:
a $1,000,000
b $1,250,000
c $1,020,000
d $1,265,000

_____ 6 Which of the following is *not* an officer of a corporation?
a Stock registrar.
b Controller.
c Secretary.
d Treasurer.

_____ 7 When stock is sold on a subscription basis and the entire subscription price has been collected, the issuance of a stock is recorded by:
a A debit to Cash and a credit to Capital Stock.
b A debit to Subscriptions Receivable and a credit to Capital Stock Subscribed.
c A debit to Capital Stock Subscribed and a credit to Capital Stock.
d A debit to Capital Stock and a credit to Subscriptions Receivable.

_____ 8 A *deficit* appears on the balance sheet:
a Among the assets.
b As a deduction from total paid-in capital.
c As a deduction from Income Taxes Payable.
d Among the liabilities.

Exercises

1 Eastern Corporation has outstanding 10,000 shares each of two classes of $100 par value stock: 5% cumulative preferred stock and common stock. The corporation reported a deficit of $20,000 at the beginning of Year 2, and preferred dividends for Year 1 were in arrears. During Year 2 the corporation earned $180,000. How large a dividend per share did the corporation pay on the common stock if the balance in retained earnings at the end of Year 2 amounted to $25,000? Use the space below for computations.

Dividends per share $ _____

2 Complete the stockholders' equity section from the account balances shown below:

Organization costs	$ 7,000
Retained earnings	128,000
Paid-in capital in excess of par: preferred stock	10,000
Common stock, no-par value, 50,000 shares .	200,000
$9 preferred stock, $100 par, 1,000 shares . .	100,000
Receivable from underwriters (from sale of stock)	$ 40,000
Plant and equipment	315,000
Accumulated depreciation	125,000
Notes payable	100,000
Donated capital	65,000

Stockholder's equity:

$9 preferred stock $100 par value, 1,000 shares issued and outstanding $ _____

_____

_____

_____

Total paid-in capital $ _____

Total stockholders' equity $ _____

17

CORPORATIONS: OPERATIONS, EARNINGS PER SHARE, AND DIVIDENDS

HIGHLIGHTS OF THE CHAPTER

1 To assist users of an income statement in estimating the income likely to occur in future periods, the results of unusual and nonrecurring transactions are shown in a separate section of the income statement after the income or loss from normal business activities has been determined. Current accounting practice recognizes three categories of "unusual" transactions and accords each one a different treatment in the income statement. These categories are: (1) the operating results of a segment of the business which has been discontinued during the current year, (2) extraordinary items, and (3) other nonoperating items.

2 A *segment* of a business is a component of a company whose activities represent a major line of business or class of customer. The assets and operating results of a segment of a business should be clearly identifiable from other assets and operating results of the company.

3 The operating results of a segment discontinued during the current period are reported separately in the income statement *after* developing the subtotal, *Income from Continuing Operations*. This subtotal presumably is a better indicator of the earning power of continuing operations than is the net income figure.

4 The revenue and expenses shown in the income statement for the year in which a segment of a business is eliminated include *only the revenue and expenses from continuing operations*. The net income or loss from discontinued operations is reported separately; the total revenue from the discontinued segment is disclosed in the notes to the financial statements. Any gain or loss on the disposal of a segment should be reported with the results of the discontinued operations.

5 When an income statement includes sections for both continuing and discontinued operations, the company's income tax expense should be *allocated* between these sections. Only the income tax expense applicable to continuing operations should be deducted as an expense in arriving at Income from Continuing Operations. Any income tax expense (or tax savings) related to the discontinued operations should be considered along with other expenses of the discontinued segment in computing the income (or loss) from discontinued operations.

6 *Extraordinary items* are transactions and events that are *both unusual in nature and occur infrequently in the operating environment of a business*. Examples of extraordinary items include:

a Effects of major casualties, such as an earthquake.

b Expropriation (seizure) of assets by foreign governments.

c Effects of prohibition of a product under a newly enacted law or regulation.

7 When a company has an extraordinary gain or loss in its income statement, *Income before Extraordinary Items* is developed as a subtotal before presentation of the extraordinary items. The extraordinary item is then subtracted (or added) to Income before

Extraordinary Items to arrive at net income. Extraordinary items are shown net of any related income tax effects.

8 Items which qualify as extraordinary losses are rare and extraordinary gains are almost nonexistent. Such things as gains and losses from disposal of plant assets and losses from strikes or lawsuits *do not qualify* as extraordinary items because they are not considered both unusual and infrequent in the environment of a business. These items may be separately identified in the income statement to focus attention on their *nonoperating* nature, but they should be included in Income *before* Extraordinary Items.

9 The income or loss from a discontinued segment of the business is *not* an extraordinary item. When discontinued operations and an extraordinary item appear in the same income statement, the income or loss from the discontinued operations is presented *before* the extraordinary item. Thus, Income before Extraordinary Items includes the operating results of any segments of the business which have been discontinued during the year.

10 Perhaps the most widely used of all accounting statistics is *earnings per share* of common stock. To compute earnings per share, the net income *available to the common stock* is divided by the *weighted-average* number of common shares outstanding during the year. Net income available to the common stock is total net income *less the current year's dividends on preferred stock*. Earnings per share is intended to show the claim of each share of *common stock* to the earnings of the company.

11 Convertible preferred stock and other securities convertible into common stock pose a special problem in computing earnings per share. If these securities are converted, more common stock will be outstanding and earnings per share will be *diluted* to a smaller figure. Companies with complex capital structures show two earnings per share figures: (a) *primary earnings per share*, based upon the weighted-average number of common shares *actually* outstanding, and (b) *fully diluted earnings per share*, based on the *maximum potential* number of shares outstanding.

12 Earnings per share based upon reported net income are shown at the bottom of the income statement. If the income statement includes Income before Extraordinary Items or Income from Continuing Operations, these subtotals should also be presented on a per-share basis.

13 A *dividend* is generally understood to mean a pro rata cash distribution by a corporation to its stockholders. Dividends are declared by the board of directors after giving careful consideration to such factors as the balance in retained earnings and the company's cash position. Four dates are usually involved in the distribution of a dividend:
a Date of declaration.
b Date of record.
c Ex-dividend date.
d Date of payment.

14 Dividends are sometimes paid in a form other than cash, such as securities of other corporations or merchandise. A *liquidating dividend* usually takes place when a corporation goes out of business and distributes assets in final liquidation. A *stock dividend* is a distribution to stockholders of additional shares of the corporation's own stock.

15 A *stock dividend* causes no change in assets or in the total amount of the stockholders' equity. The only effect of a stock dividend is the transfer of a portion of the retained earnings into the Capital Stock and the Paid-in Capital from Stock Dividends accounts. A stock dividend increases the number of common shares outstanding and decreases the book value per share. Each stockholder owns a larger number of shares after the stock dividend, but his or her total equity in the corporation remains unchanged.

16 What, then, are the reasons for distributing stock dividends? The reasons usually are:
a To conserve cash. During profitable years when business is expanding, a stock dividend may be distributed in lieu of a cash dividend so that all available cash can be used in the business.
b To reduce the price per share of stock. When the price of a share of stock is high, a large stock dividend will reduce the price per share to a more convenient trading range.
c To avoid income tax on stockholders. Stock dividends are not considered as taxable income to the recipients.

17 A "small" stock dividend may range from 1% of the outstanding stock to a maximum of 20 to 25%. Stock dividends of this size

are recorded by a debit to Retained Earnings equal to the total *market value* of the additional shares being distributed, a credit to Stock Dividend to Be Distributed equal to the par or stated value of the additional shares, and a credit to Paid-in Capital from Stock Dividends equal to the excess of market value over par (or stated) value of the "dividend" shares. When the shares are distributed, Stock Dividend to Be Distributed is debited and Capital Stock is credited.

18 Stock dividends in excess of, say, 20 to 25% are not considered small and are subject to different accounting treatment. They should be recorded by transferring only the *par or stated value* of the dividend shares from Retained Earnings to the Capital Stock account.

19 A *stock split* is effected by reducing the par or stated value of the capital stock and issuing a larger number of shares to each stockholder. In a 5 for 1 split, for example, the par value may be reduced from $10 to $2, and a shareholder owning 100 shares before the split would own 500 shares after the split.

20 Assume that a company discovers that a material error was made in the measurement of the net income of a prior year. How should this error be corrected? Since the net income of the prior year has been closed into Retained Earnings, the error is corrected by adjusting the balance of the Retained Earnings account. Such adjustments are called *prior period adjustments*. A prior period adjustment has no effect upon the net income of the current period and does not appear in the income statement; it is shown in the statement of retained earnings.

21 The *statement of retained earnings* is a vehicle for reconciling the beginning balance in retained earnings with the ending balance. The usual format of the statement is to combine any prior period adjustments with the beginning balance as originally reported. The restated beginning balance is then increased by the net income for the current year and reduced by the amount of dividends declared in arriving at the ending balance.

22 Some companies employ a *combined statement of income and retained earnings* which shows operating results as well as a reconciliation of the beginning and ending balances

in retained earnings. This form of reporting is sometimes criticized because it "buries" the important net income figure within the body of the "combined" statement.

23 Retained earnings of a corporation are either unrestricted and available for dividends or restricted (earmarked) for some specific purpose, such as to absorb possible losses or to show that retained earnings are not available for dividends because the funds generated by profitable operations are needed to finance an expansion of plant facilities.

24 Most companies disclose restrictions upon the availability of retained earnings for dividends in a note to their financial statements. A few companies, however, formally record the restriction in their accounting records by *appropriating* a portion of the balance of the Retained Earnings account. An appropriation of retained earnings is recorded by a debit to Retained Earnings and a credit to an appropriations account. The appropriation does not consist of cash or any other asset; it is simply a separate account reported within the stockholders' equity in the balance sheet. When the appropriation is no longer needed, it is returned to retained earnings by a debit to the appropriation account and a credit to Retained Earnings.

25 If a corporation acquires its own stock from stockholders, the reacquired stock is referred to as *treasury stock*. Treasury stock may be held indefinitely or may be reissued; it is not entitled to receive dividends or to vote.

26 Treasury stock is generally recorded at cost and is deducted from the total of the paid-in capital and retained earnings in the balance sheet. *Treasury stock is not an asset*. If the treasury stock is reissued, the Treasury Stock account is credited for the cost of the shares sold, and Paid-in Capital from Treasury Stock Transactions is debited or credited for the difference between the cost and the resale price.

27 The purchase of treasury stock is similar to a dividend in that a distribution of cash is made to stockholders. If a corporation is to keep its paid-in capital intact, it must not pay out to its stockholders any more than it earns. Thus retained earnings equal to the cost of treasury stock purchased is restricted and is not available for cash dividends.

TEST YOURSELF ON CORPORATIONS

True or False

For each of the following statements, circle the T or the F to indicate whether the statement is true or false.

T F 1 The net income figure generally is considered to be a better indicator of future operating results than is the subtotal, Income before Extraordinary Items.

T F 2 The income statement of a corporation should always include the subtotal Income from Continuing Operations.

T F 3 Fully diluted earnings per share usually is a larger figure than primary earnings per share.

T F 4 Most corporations whose stock is publicly owned report the results of the current year's operations in comparison with the results of the previous year.

T F 5 When retained earnings are appropriated to cover a contingency, cash is set aside as a reserve to pay for the contingency if it occurs.

T F 6 When an appropriation of retained earnings is no longer required, the appropriation (reserve) account is closed by a debit and an extraordinary gain account is credited.

T F 7 Any cash paid by a corporation to a stockholder is properly referred to as a dividend.

T F 8 An event which is unusual and occurs only once every three or four years should be classified as an extraordinary item.

T F 9 The reason for showing Income before Extraordinary Items or Income from Continuing Operations in an income statement is that these subtotals are considered useful in forecasting future earnings.

T F 10 Stockholders must approve a dividend action taken by the board of directors.

T F 11 A policy of paying regular quarterly dividends tends to give a higher investment quality to common stock.

T F 12 Income tax effects should be ignored in computing the income or loss from a discontinued segment of the business.

T F 13 The investor who purchases shares of the X Co. on the ex-dividend date will not receive the next dividend paid by X Co.

T F 14 A 3 for 1 split places stockholders of a company in essentially the same position as a 200% stock dividend.

T F 15 A corporation's stockholders' equity accounts will be the same whether it declares a 100% stock dividend or splits its stock 2 for 1.

T F 16 It may be argued that a stock dividend is not really a dividend since the corporation distributes no assets to its stockholders as a result of such action; however, stockholders welcome stock dividends and some corporations continue to distribute them from time to time.

T F 17 Prior period adjustments are reported in the statement of retained earnings rather than in the income statement.

T F 18 The reissuance of treasury stock at a price in excess of the cost of these shares is a source of paid-in capital.

T F 19 A corporation cannot acquire its own stock in the open market unless it has retained earnings at least equal to the purchase price.

Completion Statements

Fill in the necessary words or amounts to complete the following statements:

1 Large unexpected losses from inability to collect accounts receivable or from the shrinkage in the value of inventories should be taken into account in computing _____ before _____ _____ .

2 Companies with convertible preferred stock outstanding generally report both _____ earnings per share based upon the _____ _____ number of common shares outstanding, and _____ _____ earnings per share, based upon the potential number of outstanding common shares.

3 The correction of an error in the measurement of the net income of a prior year is called a _____ _____ _____ and is reported in the _____ _____ _____ as an adjustment to the balance of _____ _____ at the _____ of the current period.

4 Dividends in arrears on preferred stock are not reported as a liability in the balance sheet but should be disclosed by a _____ accompanying the financial statements.

5 On January 1, the Avery Corporation had 100,000 shares of capital stock with a par value of $10, paid-in capital in excess of par of $300,000, and retained earnings of $700,000. During the year the company split its stock 2 for 1 (reducing the par value to $5 per share) and subsequently declared a 2% stock dividend (its first) when the market value of the stock was $40. It earned $200,000 during the year and paid no cash dividends. (a) At the end of the year the balance in the Capital Stock account will be $_____; (b) the balance in Paid-in Capital in Excess of Par will be $_____; and (c) the balance in Retained Earnings will be $_____.

6 Given below is a list of accounts which appear in a balance sheet for a corporation. The stock dividend, which has not yet been distributed, is the first in the company's history.

Appropriation for purchase of treasury stock	$ 20,000
Accumulated earnings—unappropriated	780,000
Paid-in capital in excess of par	317,400
Paid-in capital from stock dividends . .	103,400
Stock dividend to be distributed (10%)	94,000
Treasury stock, 1,000 shares at cost . .	20,000(debit)
Capital stock, $10 par value	950,000
Paid-in capital from treasury stock transactions	14,000
Cash dividends payable	18,800
Appropriation for bond sinking fund .	100,000

Complete the following: (a) Total of accumulated (retained) earnings, including appropriations, is $_____; (b) the latest cash dividend per share amounted to $_____; (c) treasury stock was acquired (before, after) _____ the declaration of the 10% stock dividend; (d) total stockholders' equity is $_____; (e) the market price of stock at the time the 10% stock dividend was declared was $_____ per share.

7 The book value of a share of capital stock is $10 per share. For each of the independent events listed below, use a check mark to indicate whether the transaction or event will increase, decrease, or have no effect on the book value per share of stock.

	Transaction or Event	Increase	Decrease	No Effect
a	Declaration of cash dividend			
b	Distribution of a 20% stock dividend			
c	A 4 for 1 stock split			
d	Net income is reported for latest year			
e	Additional stock is sold at $8 per share			
f	Treasury stock is acquired at $12 per share			
g	Additional stock is sold at $14 per share			

Multiple Choice

Choose the best answer for each of the following questions and enter the identifying letter in the space provided.

_____ **1** Which of the following is *least* important in determining the fair market value of a share of stock?
a Earnings and dividends per share.
b Book value per share.
c The available supply of the shares and the demand to purchase the shares.
d The par or stated value per share.

_____ **2** Which of the following qualifies as an extraordinary item?

a Gain on sale of unprofitable consumer goods division.

b A large, unexpected write-off of an account receivable.

c A write-off and abandonment of goods in process inventory because of a new government regulation prohibiting the use of one of the ingredients.

d Additional depreciation recorded because of reduction in useful life of assets.

_____ 3 The financial statements of Fields Corporation reported earnings of $4,000,000 from continuing operations, a $700,000 loss from a segment of the business discontinued during the year, a $300,000 decrease in retained earnings as a result of a prior period adjustment, and a $500,000 extraordinary loss. The amount appearing in the income statement as Income before Extraordinary Items was:

a $4,000,000

b $3,300,000

c $3,000,000

d Some other amount.

_____ 4 The book value per share of Company B stock on January 1, Year 4, was $31.50 per share. During Year 4, the stock was split 3 for 1, and shortly afterwards a 5% stock dividend was distributed. At the end of the year, a $1 cash dividend was declared and earnings per share of $3.10 were announced. The book value per share of stock as of December 31, Year 4, amounted to:

a $10.50

b $10.70

c $12.10

d $13.10

_____ 5 The James Corporation had 100,000 shares of common stock and 5,000 shares of preferred stock outstanding at the beginning of Year 1. On April 1, 10,000 shares of common stock were sold for cash and on November 3, the common stock was split 2 for 1. The weighted-average number of shares outstanding for Year 1 in computing primary earnings per share is:

a 255,000

b 220,000

c 205,000

d 215,000

_____ 6 The distribution of a 20% stock dividend on common stock:

a Reduces the book value per share of common stock outstanding.

b Does not change the number of shares of common stock outstanding.

c Decreases total stockholders' equity.

d Increases the net assets of the corporation.

_____ 7 When a corporation declares a cash dividend on common stock, which of the following should be excluded in determining the *total amount* of the dividend?

a Shares issued in exchange for preferred stock.

b Shares held by officers and directors.

c Shares held by other corporations.

d Shares reacquired and held in treasury.

_____ 8 Revenue and expenses relating to a segment of business discontinued during the year are:

a Netted and reported as an extraordinary item.

b Included in total revenue and expenses as reported in the income statement.

c Netted and reported as a separate item following income from continuing operations.

d Netted and reported as a prior period adjustment.

_____ 9 In recording a large stock dividend, say 50 or 100%, the amount of retained earnings transferred to paid-in capital is generally measured by:

a The market value of the stock on the date of declaration.

b The book value of the stock on the date of declaration.

c The par (or stated) value of the additional shares issued.

d The amount authorized by the board of directors to be transferred from the Retained Earnings account.

_____ 10 Treasury stock is best described as:

a Unissued stock.

b Reacquired stock which was previously outstanding.

c An asset acquired by making a cash disbursement.

d Retirement of a portion of outstanding stock which increases total stockholders' equity.

Exercises

1 The Axel Company had issued 105,000 shares of capital stock, of which 5,000 shares were held in the treasury throughout the year. During the year, the company reported income from continuing operations of 5% of sales, and a loss from a segment of the business discontinued during the year of $300,000 (net of the income tax benefit). Sales from continuing operations were $4,200,000, gross profit rate on sales amounted to 30%, and income taxes were 40% of income before taxes. In the space below prepare the income statement for Axel Company, including the earnings per share figures.

AXEL COMPANY
Income Statement
for the Current Year

Sales	$4,200,000
Cost of goods sold	
Gross profit on sales (30%)	$
Operating expenses	
Operating income (before taxes)	$
Income taxes (40% of operating income) . .	
Income from continuing operations	$
Loss from discontinued operations, net of	
income tax benefit	(300,000)
Net loss	$
Per share of capital stock:	
Income from continuing operations . . .	$
Loss from discontinued operations	
Net loss	$

2 The income statement of Windjammer Company shows income from continuing operations of $490,000 and income from a segment of the business discontinued near year-end of $182,000 (net of income taxes). The company had 100,000 shares of common stock and 10,000 shares of $6 preferred stock outstanding throughout the year. Compute the following earnings per share figures for Windjammer company:

Earnings from continuing operations:

$ _____

Net earnings:

$ _____

3 At the beginning of Year 1, Bender Mfg. Company had 250,000 shares of $5 par value common stock outstanding. In the space provided below, prepare journal entries to record the following selected transactions during Year 1:

Mar. 1 Declared a cash dividend of 80 cents per share, payable on Mar. 21.

Mar. 21 Paid cash dividend declared on Mar. 1.

Aug. 10 Declared 5% stock dividend. The market price of the stock on this date was $40 per share.

Sept. 2 Issued 12,500 shares pursuant to 5% stock dividend declared on Aug. 10.

Dec. 21 Declared and issued a 100% stock dividend. The market price of the stock on this date was $60 per share.

Dec. 30 Acquired 1,000 shares of its own common stock on the open market at $30 per share.

	General Journal		
Year 1			
Mar. 1	Retained Earnings		
	Declared cash dividend of $0.80 per share on 250,000 shares.		
Mar. 21			
Aug. 10			
Sept. 2			
Dec. 21			
Dec. 30			

18

CORPORATIONS: BONDS PAYABLE, LEASES, AND OTHER LIABILITIES

HIGHLIGHTS OF THE CHAPTER

1 Bonds payable are a popular form of long-term financing. Bonds payable may be secured by specific property or may be unsecured. An unsecured bond is referred to as a *debenture bond*. Most bonds have a single maturity date (for example, 20 or 25 years from date of issue); some bond issues provide for varying maturity dates and are known as *serial bonds*.

2 Most bonds are *callable* at the option of the issuing corporation at stipulated dates and prices. Some bonds are *convertible* into common stock at the option of the bondholder. If the corporation is successful and the price of its common stock appreciates substantially, the owner of convertible bonds can share in the company's success by converting the bonds into common stock.

3 Most bonds today are *registered*, in contrast to *coupon* bonds which were popular some years ago. When bonds are registered, the issuing corporation maintains a record of the individual bondholders and mails them the periodic interest checks. When bonds have coupons attached, the bondholder receives the interest payment by depositing the appropriate interest coupon in a bank; the corporation maintains no record identifying the bondholders.

4 Bonds of large, well-established companies are readily transferable because they are generally traded on one or more securities exchanges. The quotations for bonds are usually given in terms of a percentage of the par value. Thus, a $1,000 bond sold at $101\frac{7}{8}$ would bring $1,018.75, before deducting commissions or taking accrued interest into account.

5 A major advantage of raising capital by issuing bonds rather than stock is that bond interest payments are deductible in determining taxable income, while dividend payments are not. Also, if a company can earn a return higher than the fixed cost of bonds, net income and earnings per share will increase. If stock were issued, the additional shares would tend to offset the increase in earnings per share.

6 Bonds generally pay interest every six months. When bonds are issued between interest dates, the buyer is charged for the accrued interest from the last interest payment date to date of sale, and the issuing corporation credits Bond Interest Payable. This account is then debited (along with Interest Expense) at the next interest payment date.

7 The *present value* of a future cash payment is the amount that a knowledgeable investor would pay *today* for the right to receive that future payment. The present value will always be less than the future amount, because money on hand today can be invested to become equivalent to a larger amount in the future. This principle is sometimes called the *time value of money*.

8 The rate of interest which will cause a given present value to grow to a given future amount is called the *effective interest rate*. At any given time, the effective interest rate required by investors is the *going market*

rate of interest. The price at which bonds will sell is the present value to investors of the future principal and interest payments. The *higher* the going market rate of interest (effective interest rate), the *less* investors will pay for bonds with a given contract rate of interest.

9 If the contractual rate of interest that the bonds pay is lower than the "going market rate," the *bonds will sell at a discount*. If the bonds pay a rate in excess of the going market rate, the *bonds will sell at a premium*. The bond discount is deducted from the par value of the bonds and the premium is added to the par value in reporting bonds payable in the balance sheet.

10 The *carrying value* (or book value) of a bond issue is its face value plus any premium or minus any discount. At the date of issuance, the carrying value is equal to the amount for which the bonds were sold. Over the life of the bonds, however, the carrying value will gradually move toward the maturity value of the bonds as the discount or premium is *amortized*.

11 When bonds are sold at a discount, the corporation must repay more than it borrowed. Total interest expense over the life of the bond issue is equal to the regular cash interest payments *plus the amount of the discount*. To measure annual interest expense, the discount should be *amortized into interest expense over the life of the bonds*.

12 A discount is amortized by an entry debiting Interest Expense and crediting the contra-liability account Discount on Bonds Payable. The effects of this entry are (a) to *increase* the amount of interest expense recognized in the current period and (b) to *increase* the carrying value of the liability for bonds payable (by decreasing the balance of the contra-liability account) toward its maturity value.

13 Amortization of a discount increases interest expense but involves no additional cash payment in the current period. The additional interest expense corresponds to an increase in the long-term liability for bonds payable.

14 When bonds are sold at a premium, the corporation must repay *less* than the amount borrowed. Total interest expense over the life of the bond issue is equal to the regular cash interest payments *minus the amount of the premium*. To measure annual interest expense, the premium must be *amortized as*

a reduction in interest expense over the life of the bonds.

15 A premium is amortized by an entry crediting Interest Expense and debiting the liability account Premium on Bonds Payable. The effects of this entry are (a) to *reduce* the amount of interest expense recognized in the current period and (b) to *reduce* the carrying value of the liability for bonds payable toward its maturity value.

16 Amortization of the premium reduces interest expense but it does not reduce the amount of the cash interest payment for the current period. The reduction in interest expense is accompanied by a reduction in the long-term liability for bonds payable.

17 Bond discount or premium may be amortized by two methods:

a *Straight-line method* This method amortizes an equal portion of the discount or premium each period over the life of the bonds. Mechanically, straight-life amortization is similar to straight-line depreciation.

b *Effective interest method* In this method, the carrying value of the bonds at the beginning of each period is multiplied by the effective interest rate for the bond issue. The amount of discount or premium amortized is the *difference* between the interest expense computed in this manner and the contractual (cash) interest expense for the period. Since the carrying value of the liability for bonds payable moves closer to maturity value every period, this method results in a *slightly different interest expense every period*. However, the interest expense will always be a *constant percentage* of the carrying value of the liability for bonds payable.

18 The FASB requires the use of the effective interest method of amortization whenever it would produce results *materially different* from those obtained by the straight-line method. An *amortization table* can be prepared to show the effective interest expense and amount of discount or premium amortization for each period in the life of the bond issue. The periodic journal entries may then be made directly from this table.

19 A *bond sinking fund* may be accumulated in order to have sufficient cash when the bonds mature to pay off the liability. The fund is accumulated through periodic deposits with a trustee who invests the cash in the company's bonds or in other income-yielding

securities. The fund represents an asset (reported as an investment) of the corporation.

20 If bonds are retired before maturity at a price above their carrying value, a loss results; if bonds are retired at a price below their carrying value, a gain is realized. Gains and losses on the early retirement of bonds should be shown in the income statement as *extraordinary items*. No gain or loss is recognized by the issuing corporation upon the conversion of bonds into common stock; the carrying value of the bonds converted is assigned to the common stock issued.

21 Companies making *long-term investments* in bonds are required by the FASB to amortize the difference between the cost of the investment and its maturity value over the life of the bonds. This amortization should follow the effective interest method, which results in a constant rate of return over the life of the investment. Investors do not use separate accounts to record the face value of the investment and any related discount or premium. Thus, amortization of the difference between cost and maturity value results in a direct adjustment of the Investment account.

22 A *lease* is a contract in which the *lessor* gives the *lessee* the right to use an asset in return for periodic rental payments. Lease contracts may be *operating leases*, in which the lessor retains the risks and returns of ownership, or *capital leases*, in which the objectives are to provide financing to the lessee for the eventual purchase of the property. Lessees should make full disclosure of the terms of all noncancelable leases in their financial statements.

23 In an operating lease, the periodic rentals are recorded as revenue by the lessor and as rental expense by the lessee. No liability is recognized by the lessee other than for any accrued monthly rentals.

24 A capital lease, which is essentially equivalent to a sale and purchase, should be recorded as a sale by the lessor and as a purchase by the lessee. The asset and related liability should be recorded by the lessee at the *present value* of the future lease payments. The lessee should depreciate the asset over its estimated useful life rather than over the life of the lease.

25 Mortgages payable generally call for monthly payments, including interest and repayment of principal. The portion of unpaid principal maturing within one year should be classified as a current liability in the balance sheet.

26 A pension plan is a contract between a company and its employees under which the company agrees to pay retirement benefits to eligible employees. In a *funded* pension plan, the employer makes regular payments to an insurance company or other agency (debit Pension Expense and credit Cash). When employees retire, their retirement benefits are paid by the insurance company.

27 An *estimated liability* is one *known to exist* but for which the dollar amount is uncertain. An example is the liability of a manufacturer to honor any warranty on products sold. To achieve the objective of matching revenue with related expenses, the liability for future warranty repairs on products sold during the current year is estimated and recorded at the balance sheet date. The estimate generally is based upon the company's past experience.

28 A *loss contingency* is a situation involving uncertainty as to whether or not a loss has been incurred. The uncertainty will be resolved by a future event. An example of a loss contingency is a lawsuit pending against a company. Until the lawsuit is resolved, uncertainty exists as to whether or not a liability exists. Many loss contingencies may also be called *contingency liabilities*. However, the term *loss contingency* encompasses the possible impairment of assets as well as the possible existence of liabilities.

29 Loss contingencies are recorded in the accounting records only when (a) it is probable that a loss has been incurred and (b) the amount of loss can be reasonably estimated. Loss contingencies which do not meet both of these criteria should still be disclosed in notes to the financial statements.

APPENDIX: APPLICATIONS OF PRESENT VALUE

30 As stated in paragraph **7.** the *present value* of a future amount is the amount that a knowledgeable investor would pay *today* for the right to receive the future amount. The present value is always less than the future amount, because money on hand today can be invested to become equivalent to a larger amount in the future. The difference between

a future amount and its present value may be regarded as interest revenue (or expense) included in the future amount.

31 The present value of a future amount depends upon (a) the estimated *amount* of the future cash receipt (or payment), (b) the *length of time* until the future amount will be received (or paid); and (c) the *rate of return* required by the investor. The required rate of return is called the *discount rate* and depends upon the amount of *risk* associated with the investment opportunity and upon the return available from alternative investment opportunities.

32 Computing the present value of a future cash flow is called *discounting* the future amount. The easiest method of discounting future amounts is by the use of *present value tables*. Your textbook includes present value tables which show (a) the present value of a single, lump sum amount to be received at a future date and (b) the present value of a series of equal-sized periodic cash flows, called an *annuity*.

33 We will now demonstrate the use of present value tables by finding the present value of $800 to be received annually for 10 years, discounted at an annual rate of 12%. Since we are dealing with a series of 10 equal-sized payments, we will use the annuity table on page 708 in the textbook. This table shows us that the present value of $1 received annually for 10 years, discounted at 12%, is *5.650*, meaning $5.65. Therefore, the present value of the $800 annuity is $800 × 5.650, or *$4,520.*

34 The concept of present value has many applications in accounting, including:

a *Valuation of long-term notes receivable and payable* When a long-term note does not bear a realistic stated rate of interest, a portion of the face amount of the note should be regarded as representing an interest charge. The principal amount of the note can be found by discounting the maturity value of the note and any future interest payments at a realistic interest rate.

b *Estimating the value of goodwill* Goodwill represents the present value of expected future earnings in excess of a normal return on net identifiable assets.

c *Evaluating bond prices* The market price of a bond is the present value to investors of the future principal and interest payments.

d *Valuation of capital leases* When an asset is "sold" under a capital lease agreement, the present value of the future lease payments is recorded as a receivable by the lessor and as a liability by the lessee.

TEST YOURSELF ON BONDS PAYABLE AND LEASES

True or False

For each of the following statements, circle the T or the F to indicate whether the statement is true or false.

T F 1 Total interest expense on a bond sold for less than its face value will be the cash paid as interest less the amortization of the discount.

T F 2 Unissued bonds may be reported as an asset in the balance sheet since they represent a potential source of cash.

T F 3 When the going rate of interest on the open market is 12%, a 9% bond will sell at a discount.

T F 4 A debenture bond may be convertible, callable, and registered as to ownership.

T F 5 The time value of money concept means that the present value of a future payment is always less than the future amount.

T F 6 The lower the effective rate of interest required by investors, the lower the price at which a given bond should sell.

T F 7 In the effective interest method of amortization, bond interest expense is found by applying the effective interest rate to the carrying value of the liability at the beginning of the current period.

T F 8 When bond premium is amortized by the effective interest method, interest expense will decrease slightly from one period to the next.

T F 9 The effective interest method of amortizing bond discount or premium causes interest expense to be a uniform amount over the life of the bond issue.

T F 10 Mortgages payable usually call for equal monthly payments, consisting of interest on the unpaid balance for one month and a partial repayment on the principal.

T F 11 In accruing interest expense at the end of the period, the premium or discount on bonds payable should be amortized to the balance sheet date.

T F 12 If a company issues bonds payable at a discount, the rate of interest stated on the bond is greater than the effective rate.

T F 13 An investor who buys a bond at a premium is willing to earn a lesser rate of interest than the rate stated on the bond.

T F 14 Amortization of a discount on bonds payable increases interest expense and increases the carrying value of the liability.

T F 15 Amortization of a premium on an investment in bonds reduces interest revenue and reduces the carrying value of the investment.

T F 16 Material gains and losses on the early retirement of bonds payable are reported in the income statement as extraordinary items.

T F 17 Leases which contain provisions indicating that they are in effect equivalent to a sale and purchase of assets are called operating leases.

T F 18 When lease payments are regarded as rent expense, no liability for the present value of future lease payments appears in the lessee's balance sheet.

T F 19 When the lessee records an asset and a liability equal in amount to the present value of the future lease payments, part of each lease payment is regarded as interest expense.

T F 20 A funded pension plan does not require the recognition of pension expense in the accounting records of the employer company.

T F 21 A loss contingency is an appropriation of retained earnings to provide for unexpected losses in future periods.

Completion Statements

Fill in the necessary words or amounts to complete the following statements:

1 Bonds payable reacquired by the issuing company through purchase on the open market at a price (less, greater) _____ than carrying value will cause the recording of a gain, whereas bonds reacquired at a price (less, greater) _____ than carrying value will cause the recording of a loss.

2 In the accounts of the issuing company, the carrying value of bonds equals the face value plus any _____ or minus any _____ .

3 Most corporate bonds are issued in denominations of $ _____ and pay interest _____ a year.

4 For each 9%, 30-year bond issued, the X Company received $925. The market quotation as shown in the newspaper for these bonds would be _____ .

5 The _____ _____ of a future payment is always (more, less) _____ than the future amount because money on hand today can be invested to become a _____ amount in the future.

6 In using the effective interest method to amortize a discount or premium, interest expense is found by _____ the _____ _____ of the bonds by the _____ _____ _____ . The amount of discount or premium amortized is the difference between interest expense determined in this manner and the interest based upon the _____ rate of interest.

7 As the discount on bonds payable is amortized, the amount of the net bond liability (increases, decreases) _____ ; as the premium on bonds payable is amortized, the amount of the net bond liability (increases, decreases) _____ .

8 The lessee accounts for the monthly payments on an operating lease by debiting _____ _____ . The type of lease is often called _____ _____ _____ financing because the lessee records no _____ _____ for future lease payments.

9 In accounting for a capital lease used to finance the sale of merchandise, the lessor debits _____ _____ _____ and credits _____ for the _____ _____ of the future lease payments. When lease payments are received, the lessor recognizes part of each payment as _____ _____ and the remainder as a reduction in _____ _____ _____ .

Multiple Choice

Choose the best answer for each of the following questions and enter the identifying letter in the space provided.

_____ 1 The discount on bonds payable is best described as:

a An element of interest expense on borrowed funds that will be paid by issuing corporation at maturity.

b The payment of periodic interest at less than the rate called for in the bond contract.

c An amount below par which the bondholder may be called upon to make good.

d An asset representing interest that has been paid in advance.

_____ 2 The account Premium on Bonds Payable is best classified in the balance sheet as:

a An addition to bonds payable.

b An appropriation of retained earnings.

c A deduction from bonds payable.

d An asset.

_____ 3 Bonds containing a provision for exchange into other securities of the issuing company are called:

a Callable bonds.

b Redeemable bonds.

c Convertible bonds.

d Debenture bonds.

_____ 4 Riverton Corporation has authorized an issue of 14%, 10-year bonds. At the issue date the market rate of interest for this type of bonds is 13.7%. On these facts it might be expected that:

a The company will find it difficult to sell the bonds.

b The bonds will be sold at a premium.

c The bonds will be sold at a discount.

d The bond contract will be rewritten.

_____ 5 The effective interest method of amortization results in:

a A constant amount of interest expense from one period to the next.

b An increasing amount of interest expense each period.

c A decreasing amount of interest expense each period.

d Either an increasing or a decreasing amount of interest expense each period, depending upon whether the bonds were issued at a discount or a premium.

_____ 6 Assume that a capital lease is erroneously treated as an operating lease in the accounting records of the lessee. One effect of this error will be:

a An overstatement of assets and liabilities.

b An overstatement of rent expense and understatement of interest expense and depreciation expense.

c An understatement of rent expense and an overstatement of liabilities.

d None of the above.

_____ 7 Loss contingencies relating to pending litigation usually are:

a Disclosed in notes to the financial statements.

b Shown as current liabilities in the balance sheet.

c Shown as extraordinary items in the income statement.

d Not disclosed or recorded until the litigation has been settled.

Exercises

1 On July 1, Year 1, Caldwell Company issued $600,000 of 16%, 10-year bonds with interest payable on March 1 and September 1. The company received cash of $637,800, including the accrued interest from March 1, Year 1. Bond discount or premium is amortized at each interest payment date and at year-end using the *straight-line* method. Place the correct answer to each of the following questions in the space provided. (Use the space provided for computations.)

a What was the amount of accrued interest on July 1, Year 1? $ _____ .

b What was the amount of bond discount or premium (state which) to be amortized over the period that the bonds will be outstanding, 116 months? $ _____ .

c What was the amount of cash paid to bondholders on September 1, Year 1?

$ _____ .

d What amount of accrued interest payable should appear on the balance sheet on December 31, Year 1? $ _____ .

e What was the amount of the unamortized discount or premium on December 31, Year 1? $ _____ .

f What was the total interest expense for Year 1 relating to this bond issue? $ _____ .

Computations

2 From the data in Exercise 1, prepare journal entries required on each of the following dates.
a July 1, Year 1 (issuance of bonds).
b September 1, Year 1 (payment of interest and amortization for two months).
c December 31, Year 1 (accrual of interest and amortization from Sept. 1 to Dec. 31).

		General Journal		
a	July 1			
b	Sept. 1			
c	Dec. 31			

3 Shown below is a portion of the amortization table prepared after the issuance of *$800,000* face value, 10-year bonds, with interest payable on June 30 and December 31. The bonds were issued on January 1, Year 1. Bond discount or premium is amortized by the *effective interest* method.

Six-Month Interest Period	Semiannual Interest Payment	Effective Semiannual Interest	Carrying Value of Bonds, End of Period
			$757,624
1	$52,000	$53,034	758,658
2	52,000	53,106	759,764
3	52,000	53,183	760,947
4	52,000	53,266	762,213
5	52,000	53,355	763,568

a What is the amount of the bond discount or premium (state which) to be amortized over the life of the bonds? $_____ .

b What is the amount of interest paid to bondholders *annually*? $ _____ .

c What is the annual *contractual* rate of interest stated on the bonds? _____ %

d What is the *semiannual effective* rate of interest? _____ %

e What is the total amount of interest expense to be recognized during *Year 2*? $_____

f In the space below, show how the bonds would appear in the balance sheet of the issuing company at the end of Year 2.

Bonds payable . . . . $

_____ $_____ .

Computations

19

CORPORATIONS: INVESTMENTS IN CORPORATE SECURITIES

HIGHLIGHTS OF THE CHAPTER

1 Many companies invest cash not needed for current operations in high-grade *marketable securities*, such as government bonds and the bonds and stocks of large corporations. Investments in marketable securities are preferable to holding idle cash because of the interest or dividend revenue which they produce. Marketable securities may be purchased or sold at quoted market prices through organized securities exchanges, such as the *New York Stock Exchange*.

2 The market price of stocks is quoted in dollars per share. Bond prices are quoted as a *percentage* of the bond's maturity value (or face value), which usually is $1,000. Thus, a bond quoted at 102 has a market value of $1,020.

3 Investments in marketable securities originally are recorded in the accounting records at cost. Commissions paid to a broker for purchase of securities are included in cost of the investment. When investors buy bonds between interest-payment dates, they pay the current market price of the bond plus the interest accrued since the last interest date. This payment for interest is not part of the cost of the bond, but is debited to a separate account and collected as part of the next semiannual interest payment from the issuing corporation. Interest accrues from day to day on bonds, but dividends do not accrue on stock. Usually cash dividends are not recognized as earned until the date of receipt.

4 Additional shares of stock received in stock splits or stock dividends reduce the cost basis per share *but are not income to the stockholder*. Only a *memorandum* entry is necessary to record the additional number of shares received and the new cost basis per share.

5 When marketable securities are sold, any difference between the sales price and the cost of the securities should be recognized as a gain or a loss. Since bonds sell at the quoted market price *plus accrued interest*, the seller will receive any interest which has accrued since the last interest payment date. When an investment in bonds is sold, the seller should credit *Interest Revenue* for any portion of the proceeds which represents accrued interest.

6 Gains and losses on the sale of marketable securities, as well as interest and dividends earned, are all nonoperating income. These items should be shown separately on the income statement after the determination of income from operations.

7 In the balance sheet, most companies classify their investments in marketable equity securities as current assets. If a company has a definite intention to hold certain securities on a long-term basis, however, it may elect to classify these securities as a noncurrent asset under a caption such as Long-Term Investments. When securities owned are *not readily marketable* or are held for the *purpose of exercising control* over the issuing company, they must be classified as long-term investments.

8 A short-term investment in marketable *debt* securities (bonds) generally is carried in the

accounting records at cost until the bonds are sold. If bonds are held as a long-term investment, the carrying value of the investment is adjusted each year for amortization of the discount or premium.

9 Investments in marketable *equity* securities (stocks) are valued in the balance sheet at the *lower of aggregate cost or market value at the balance sheet date.* In applying this lower-of-cost-or-market rule, the total cost of the entire portfolio of marketable equity securities is compared with its cost, and the lower of these two amounts is used as the balance sheet valuation.

10 The carrying value of the portfolio is reduced to a market value below cost by an entry debiting *Unrealized Loss on Marketable Securities* and crediting *Valuation Allowance for Marketable Securities.* The loss from decline in market value is termed *unrealized* to distinguish it from a loss which is realized by an actual sale of the securities. The valuation allowance is a *contra-asset* account; it appears in the balance sheet as a *deduction from Marketable Securities*, thus reducing the carrying value of the portfolio to its market value.

11 The balance of the valuation allowance is adjusted at the end of every accounting period. If the valuation allowance must be increased because of further declines in market value, the adjusting entry will recognize an additional unrealized loss. If market prices have increased since the last balance sheet date, the adjusting entry will reduce or eliminate the valuation allowance and recognize an *unrealized gain.*

12 The amount of unrealized gain which can be recognized is limited to that which results from eliminating the credit balance of the valuation allowance. In brief, when marketable equity securities have been written down to a market value below cost, they can be written back up to original cost if the market prices recover. However, the rules of the FASB *do not* permit recognition of any market rises *above* original cost.

13 Lower-of-cost-or-market adjustments affect the carrying value of the portfolio as a whole but do not change the carrying values of specific investments within that portfolio. These adjustments, therefore, have *no effect* upon the gain or loss recognized when an investment is sold. When specific securities are sold, the gain or loss realized from the sale is determined by comparing the *cost* of the securities (without regard to lower-of-cost-or-market adjustment) to their selling price.

14 The lower-of-cost-or-market adjustments described above are *not acceptable* for determining income subject to income taxes. The only gains and losses recognized for income tax purposes are realized gains and losses resulting from sale of an investment.

15 The unrealized gains and losses resulting from application of the lower-of-cost-or-market rule are presented differently in the financial statements, depending upon whether the securities are classified as a current asset or a long-term investment. When the securities are considered a current asset, any unrealized gains or losses are shown in the income statement. Unrealized gains and losses on long-term investments *do not appear in the income statement*; they are closed directly into an account called Unrealized Loss on Long-Term Investments, which appears in the balance sheet as a *reduction in stockholders' equity.*

16 Many accountants are convinced that investments in securities should be valued in the balance sheet at *current market price.* This value is the most significant to the banker or other user of the balance sheet in judging financial strength and debt-paying ability. Moreover, the market value is readily obtainable and can be objectively verified. Remember, valuation of marketable equity securities at current market prices is *not* in accordance with current accounting practice.

17 Long-term investment in common stock made for the purpose of exercising control over the issuing company (called the *investee*) should be accounted for by the equity method. Ownership of 20% or more of the investee's outstanding common stock generally is considered an investment for purposes of control.

18 The accounting procedures for applying the equity method are as follows:

a The investment originally is recorded at cost.

b The investor subsequently records its proportionate share of the investee's net income by debiting the investment account and crediting Investment Income. If the investee reports a net loss, the investor debits Investment Loss and credits the investment account.

c   The investor views its share of cash dividends paid by the investee as a conversion of the investment into cash. Thus, the investor debits Cash and credits the investment account when dividends are received from the investee.

No lower-of-cost-or-market adjustments are made to investments accounted for by the equity method.

19   When one corporation controls another corporation through ownership of a *majority* of its voting stock, the controlling corporation is called the *parent* company and the controlled corporation is called the *subsidiary* company. Financial statements prepared for the *affiliated* companies (the parent company and its subsidiaries) are called *consolidated financial statements*.

20   We usually think of a large organization such as IBM, General Electric, or Exxon as a single company. Actually, such organizations are really *groups* of affiliated companies. It is logical to think of an affiliated group such as IBM as a single economic entity, because all the companies in the affiliated group are under the control of one parent company.

21   Consolidated financial statements show the combined financial position and combined operating results of all the individual companies in the affiliated group *as if they were one company*. In a *consolidated balance sheet*, the assets and liabilities of the affiliated companies are combined and reported as though only a single entity existed. Similarly, in a *consolidated income statement* the revenue and expenses of the affiliated companies are combined.

22   The amounts shown in consolidated financial statements *do not come from a ledger*; they are determined on a working paper by combining the amounts of like items in the financial statements of the affiliated companies. In the combining process, certain adjustments must be made to eliminate the effects of *intercompany transactions*.

23   Intercompany transactions are transactions among affiliated companies which do not give rise to assets, liabilities, revenue, or expenses when the affiliated companies are viewed as parts of a single consolidated entity. Intercompany eliminations fall into three categories:

a   Elimination of intercompany stock ownership.

b   Elimination of intercompany debt.

c   Elimination of intercompany revenue and expenses.

24   When a parent company invests in a subsidiary, the parent records the investment in an asset account entitled *Investment in Subsidiary*. However, in a consolidated balance sheet, we want to show the individual assets and liabilities of the subsidiary company. It would not be logical to show the assets and liabilities of the subsidiary *and also* to show the parent company's investment in those assets and liabilities. Therefore, the Investment in Subsidiary account is *eliminated* (offset) against the stockholders' equity of the subsidiary company.

25   After the parent's Investment in Subsidiary and the subsidiary's stockholders' equity have been eliminated (offset against one another), the *stockholders' equity of the parent company* is the stockholders' equity on the consolidated balance sheet. Also, the individual assets and liabilities of the subsidiary are presented *in place of* the Investment in Subsidiary account.

26   If the parent company acquires *less than 100%* of the stock issued by the subsidiary, the entry on the consolidated working papers to eliminate the Investment in Subsidiary account will not offset all of the stockholders' equity of the subsidiary. The remaining equity of the subsidiary is called a *minority interest* and is shown in the equity section of the consolidated balance sheet.

27   Often the parent company acquires the subsidiary's stock at a price above book value, indicating that either (1) certain assets are undervalued in the subsidiary's accounting records, or (2) the subsidiary possesses *unrecorded goodwill*. In the consolidated balance sheet, the subsidiary's assets should be valued at the value indicated by the parent company's purchase price, and any unrecorded goodwill purchased by the parent company should *appear as an asset* and be amortized over its useful life.

28   A consolidated income statement is prepared by combining on a working paper the revenue and expense accounts of the affiliated companies. Revenue and expenses arising from *intercompany transactions* are eliminated because they reflect transfers of assets from one affiliated company to another and do not change the net assets of the consolidated entity. Examples of intercompany revenue and expense transactions include the

payment of rent or interest by one affiliated company to another.

29 If control of a subsidiary is acquired through issuance of stock and the stockholders of the subsidiary become stockholders of the parent, the consolidated statements for the two companies may be prepared on a *pooling-of-interests* basis. Consolidated statements on a *pooling* basis will differ from those on the *purchase* basis in the following respects:

a Regardless of the market value of the stock issued by the parent company, the assets of the subsidiary will appear in the consolidated balance sheet at their book values and no goodwill is recorded.

b Since no goodwill appears in the consolidated balance sheet, consolidated net income is not reduced by amortization expense relating to this asset.

c Earnings of a subsidiary for the entire year in which control was acquired are included in the consolidated income statement, even if control was achieved on the last day of the fiscal year.

30 Consolidation of a particular subsidiary may not be appropriate if the subsidiary is in a different line of business than the other companies in the affiliated group. *Unconsolidated subsidiaries* appear in the financial statements as long-term investments, accounted for by the equity method.

31 Consolidated financial statements primarily are of interest to managers, creditors, and stockholders in the parent company, because the long-run well-being of the parent company depends upon the success of the entire group of companies it controls. Consolidated financial statements are not significant to the minority stockholders or creditors of a subsidiary company.

32 We have now discussed marketable securities, investments accounted for by the equity method, and consolidated financial statements. The accounting treatment of an investment in stock depends primarily upon the *degree of control* which the investor is able to exercise over the issuing corporation. These relationships are summarized as follows:

a *Controlling interest* (ownership of 50% or more of the voting stock)—consolidate, unless the activities of a subsidiary are significantly different from those of the parent. Unconsolidated subsidiaries are accounted for by the equity method.

b *Influential but not controlling interest* (between 20 and 50% of the voting stock)—show as a long-term investment, accounted for by the equity method.

c *Noninfluential interest* (less than 20% of the voting stock)—show as a marketable security.

TEST YOURSELF ON INVESTMENTS IN CORPORATE SECURITIES

True or False

For each of the following statements, circle the T or the F to indicate whether the statement is true or false.

T F   1 The quoted market price of marketable securities is established every morning by an agency of the federal government.

T F   2 A company which has owned marketable securities for more than one year must classify the investment as a noncurrent asset.

T F   3 When an investment in bonds is sold between interest dates, the seller forfeits the interest which has accrued since the last interest payment date.

T F   4 Investments in marketable equity securities are valued at the lower of aggregate cost or market value, while investments in marketable debt securities generally are valued at cost.

T F   5 Jay Corporation purchased marketable equity securities at a cost of $1 million, but at the next balance sheet date the market value of the securities had dropped to $950,000. If Jay Corporation reduces the carrying value of the securities to market, it may deduct a $50,000 unrealized loss on its income tax return.

T F   6 A company with a long-term investment in bonds should amortize the discount or premium as a step toward computing interest earned.

T F   7 An unrealized loss relating to an investment in marketable equity securities is deducted in the income statement if the investment is classified as a current asset, but does not reduce net income if the investment is classified as long-term.

T F   8 An investor using the equity method

recognizes investment income whenever cash dividends are received.

T F 9 Under the rules of the FASB, the amount of unrealized gain which an investor can recognize on an investment in marketable equity securities is limited to the amount of unrealized losses recognized in prior periods.

T F 10 Many accountants believe that investments in marketable securities should be shown in the balance sheet at current market value and that changes in market value should be recognized as gains and losses. However, this approach is not in accordance with current practice.

T F 11 A consolidated balance sheet reports the financial condition for a group of separate legal entities.

T F 12 Stockholders of the parent company elect the board of directors of the subsidiary company.

T F 13 Most published financial statements issued by large corporations are prepared on a consolidated basis.

T F 14 Consolidated financial statements are prepared from the general ledger of the consolidated entity.

T F 15 If consolidated retained earnings are $100,000 and the retained earnings of a 100%-owned subsidiary amount to $10,000, the retained earnings of the parent must be $90,000.

T F 16 Minority interest should be reported as an asset in the consolidated balance sheet.

T F 17 Minority interest is *increased* when the subsidiary company reports net income or when the parent company reduces the percentage of stock held in the subsidiary.

T F 18 The eliminations required on the working papers for the consolidated balance sheet to eliminate intercompany receivables and payables are not recorded in the ledger of either the parent or the subsidiary company.

T F 19 If the parent company owns 90% of stock of the subsidiary and the subsidiary owes the parent $10,000 on open account, only $9,000 of intercompany receivables and payables would be eliminated in preparing a consolidated balance sheet.

T F 20 When a business combination is accounted for as a *pooling of inter-*

ests, the consolidated income statement will include the earnings of the subsidiary for the entire year, even if the combination occurred near year-end.

T F 21 As a general rule, consolidation is appropriate whenever the parent company owns 20% or more of the voting stock of a subsidiary.

T F 22 If the business activities of a 100%-owned subsidiary are significantly different from those of the parent company, consolidation may be inappropriate.

T F 23 Investments in unconsolidated subsidiaries are not included in consolidated financial statements.

T F 24 Consolidated financial statements are of interest primarily to the creditors and minority stockholders of the individual subsidiaries.

Completion Statements

Fill in the necessary words or amounts to complete the following statements:

1 When a company purchases bonds between interest dates, the excess of its payment over the price of the bond and the commission will be debited to an account entitled

_____ _____ _____ .

2 Lee Jones paid $84 a share for 100 shares of common stock. Later he received an additional 5 shares as a stock dividend. His cost basis per share is now $_____ , computed by _____ $ _____ by_____ _____ .

3 In managing an investment portfolio, an investor seeks to maximize _____ while minimizing _____ . Purchasing securities of companies in different industries is called _____ and is one means of reducing _____ .

4 The loss which results from reducing the carrying value of a portfolio of marketable equity securities to a market value below _____ is called an_____ loss, because the securities have not been _____ .

5 A company using the equity method recognizes as investment income its proportionate

share of the investee's _____ _____ .
The investor regards _____ received
from the investee as a conversion of the
investment into _____ .

6 Zee Company owns a majority of the voting
shares of Bee Company; Zee Company is
said to own a _____ interest in Bee
Company, and the two companies may be
viewed as a single economic_____ .

7 (a) The Investment in Subsidiary account
appears in the ledger of the parent company
but does not appear in the _____
balance sheet; (b) minority interest (is, is not)
_____ found in the ledger of the parent
company or the ledger of the subsidiary
company.

8 If the consolidated balance sheet for the
parent and a 90%-owned subsidiary shows
minority interest at $80,000 and the subsid-
iary has $500,000 of paid-in capital, the
subsidiary's retained earnings balance is
$ _____ .

9 On November 1, Year 1, P Company acquired
100% of the stock of S Company. During
Year 1, P Company earned $2 million (omit-
ting any income from S Company), and S
Company earned $25,000 per month. If the
business combination is accounted for as a
purchase, consolidated net income for Year
1 will be $ _____ ; if it is viewed as a
pooling of interests, consolidated net income
will be $ _____ .

Multiple Choice

Choose the best answer for each of the following
questions and enter the identifying letter in the
space provided.

____ 1 Dart Company bought $10,000 (ma-
turity value) of 8% bonds at a price of 92. The
brokerage commission was $30, and accrued
interest amounted to $200. Dart Company
should debit investment in Bonds:
a $9,200
b $9,230
c $9,430
d Some other amount.

____ 2 Which of the following investments
should *not* be classified as a current asset?
a U.S. government bonds which will not mature
for several years.
b Preferred stock issued by a public utility company.
c Common stock that has paid no dividends for
several years.
d Common stock held for the purpose of exercising control over the issuing company.

____ 3 Under current accounting practice:
a The same valuation concepts are applied to
marketable debt securities and marketable
equity securities.
b The same income is recognized from an investment in common stock regardless of
whether the shares are held for temporary
investment or for purposes of controlling
the issuing company.
c All marketable equity securities owned for
more than one year should be classified as
noncurrent assets.
d The treatment accorded to fluctuations in
the market value of securities owned depends
upon whether the market value is above or
below cost.

____ 4 The only securities owned by Gear
Company are 1,000 shares of Delta Corporation
common stock, which were purchased in Year 2
at a price of $45 per share plus a total broker's
commission of $300. At December 31 of Year 2
the market price of Delta Corporation stock was
$40, and at December 31 of Year 3 the price
was $55. The carrying value of the investment in
Gear Company's balance sheet at December 31
of each year is:
a $45,300 at December 31 of both years.
b $40,000 at December 31 of Year 2 and
$45,300 at December 31 of Year 3.
c $40,000 at December 31 of Year 2 and
$55,000 at December 31 of Year 3.
d None of the above.

____ 5 Which of the following does *not*
appear in a consolidated balance sheet?
a Capital stock of parent company.
b Capital stock of subsidiary.
c Investment in unconsolidated companies.
d Minority interest.

____ 6 Total assets of the parent company
are $300,000, total assets of the subsidiary are

$200,000, and consolidated assets amount to only $420,000 on the date of acquisition. The most likely explanation of this is:

a The parent company owes $80,000 to the subsidiary.

b The subsidiary owes the parent $80,000.

c The minority interest amounts to $80,000.

d The parent company has an $80,000 investment in the subsidiary.

_____ 7 The parent company paid *more than book value* for its 100% interest in the subsidiary. The most likely reason for this is:

a The subsidiary assets are overvalued.

b The parent company assets are understated.

c The subsidiary has sustained large net losses.

d The subsidiary company has unrecorded goodwill.

_____ 8 Which of the following offers a good reason for preparing consolidated statements?

a The legal boundaries between affiliated companies are clearly presented.

b Only one set of accounting records need be kept for the affiliated companies, thus reducing operating expense.

c A financial picture of the resources and operations of an economic entity is helpful to stockholders and management of the parent company.

d Minority stockholders can ascertain the soundness of their investment.

_____ 9 Minority interest, as it appears in a consolidated balance sheet, refers to:

a Owners of less than 50% of the parent company stock.

b Parent's interest in subsidiary companies.

c Interest expense on subsidiary's bonds payable.

d Equity in the subsidiary's net assets held by stockholders other than the parent company.

_____ 10 Dividends payable on December 31, 19__, are as follows: parent company, $120,000; 100%-owned subsidiary, $30,000. The amount of dividends payable in the consolidated balance sheet is:

a $150,000

b $120,000

c $ 90,000

d $ 30,000

Exercises

1 On September 1, Year 5, National Company bought $100,000 par value of World Airlines 12% bonds at a price of 87¾ and accrued interest, plus a brokerage commission of $500. Interest dates of the bonds were August 1 and February 1. On April 1, Year 6, the National Company sold the bonds at a price of 91 plus accrued interest and less a commission of $500.

Complete the journal entries for the several transactions relating to the bonds in the space on the following page.

		General Journal		
Year 5				
Sept. 1		Accrued Bond Interest Receivable		
		Purchased $100,000 par value of World Airlines 12% bonds		
		at 87¾ and accrued interest, plus commission of $1,000.		
Dec. 31				
		To accrue bond interest earned to Dec. 31 ($100,000 × $\frac{4}{12}$).		
Year 6				
Feb. 1				
		Received semiannual bond interest on World Airlines bonds ($100,000		
		× 12% × ½).		
Apr. 1				
		To accrue interest to date of sale of investment in World Airlines		
		bonds ($100,000 × 12% × $\frac{2}{12}$).		
Apr. 1				
		To record sale of $100,000 par value of World Airlines 12% bonds		
		at 91 plus accrued interest of $2,000 and minus commission of		
		$500.		

2 Milestone Corporation acquired a portfolio of marketable equity securities in Year 1. The portfolio is regarded as a current asset, and securities are frequently purchased and sold from the portfolio. The cost and market value of the portfolio is shown below for the first three years:

	Cost	Market Value Dec. 31
Year 1	$325,000	$301,000
Year 2	270,000	255,000
Year 3	310,000	330,000

On January 2, Year 4, the company sold from the portfolio securities which had cost $45,000. The sales proceeds amounted to $52,000. Prepare the adjusting entry at the end of each of the three years to value the portfolio at the lower of cost or market. Also prepare the entry on January 2, Year 4, to record the sale of securities.

	General Journal		
Year 1			
Dec. 31			

3 On April 30, Year 4, Par Company purchased 100% of the stock of Sub Company for $520,000 cash. Par Company paid a purchase price in excess of book value because Sub Company possesses unrecorded goodwill. The condensed balance sheets immediately after the purchase are shown below:

	Par Co.	Sub Co.
Cash	$ 120,000	$ 70,000
Investment in Sub Co.	520,000	
Other assets	450,000	600,000
Totals	$1,090,000	$670,000
Liabilities	$ 400,000	$240,000
Capital stock	300,000	150,000
Retained earnings	390,000	280,000
Totals	$1,090,000	$670,000

In the space provided, prepare a consolidated balance sheet immediately after Par Company acquired control of Sub Company.

PAR CO. AND SUBSIDIARY
Consolidated Balance Sheet
April 30, Year 4

Assets

Cash . . . . $

Total assets . . . . $

Liabilities & Stockholders' Equity

Liabilities . . . . $

Total liabilities & stockholders' equity . . . $

20
INCOME TAXES AND BUSINESS DECISIONS

HIGHLIGHTS OF THE CHAPTER

1 As the role of government in our society increases, so does the level of taxes. Taxes, which were almost insignificant in the early part of this century, now represent a major expense of doing business.

2 Because taxes have become such a significant expenditure, careful *tax planning* is essential to operating a business efficiently. Tax planning refers to determining in advance the income tax effect of every proposed business action, and so the burden of taxes may be considered in the business decision.

3 In terms of revenue produced (to government), the four most important taxes are *income taxes*, *sales taxes*, *property taxes*, and *excise taxes*. Income taxes probably exceed all others and are most important in business decisions.

4 There are four classes of taxpayers: *individuals*, *corporations*, *estates*, and *trusts*. A *partnership* does not pay any income tax, but it must file an *information* return. Partners must include their share of the partnership net income in their *personal* income tax returns, regardless of the amount they withdraw from the business.

5 The earnings of corporations are subject to *double taxation*. Corporate earnings are subject to corporate income tax when earned by the corporation and then are subject to personal income tax when distributed as dividends to stockholders.

6 Almost all individual tax returns are prepared on the *cash basis* of measuring income. In-

dividuals may use the accrual basis if they choose, but the cash basis is simpler, requires less record keeping, and permits tax savings by allowing the taxpayer to shift the timing of revenue and expenses from one year to another.

7 Taxes may be *proportional* (constant percentage of the base), *progressive* (increasing percentage of the base as the base increases), or *regressive* (decreasing percentage of the base as the base increases). Income tax rates on individuals are *highly progressive*, ranging in recent years from 11 to 50% of taxable income.

8 Because of the progressive nature of income taxes, an individual whose income fluctuates from year to year would have to pay more taxes than an individual who earned the same total amount at a more even annual rate. Therefore, individuals whose income fluctuates widely are permitted to average out their income and pay income taxes as if the income had been earned at an even rate over the last five years.

9 Income taxes are increased each year *as a result of inflation* even though the schedule of tax rates remains unchanged. Inflation moves people into higher tax brackets even though their higher salaries represent no increase in purchasing power. This problem may end in 1985 when *indexing* is scheduled to begin. Indexing refers to adjusting the tax brackets each year to reflect changes in the Consumer Price Index.

10 In analyzing the tax effect of a transaction, the *marginal* tax rate, not the average tax rate, should be used.

11 The income tax formula for individuals is as follows: Total income minus exclusions equals gross income. Gross income minus deductions equals adjusted gross income. Adjusted gross income minus excess itemized deductions minus personal exemptions equals taxable income. The tax on the taxable income minus any tax credits equals the tax payable to the government.

12 Gross income of individuals includes *all items of income not specifically excluded by law*. Among the items *excluded* are:
 a Interest on state and municipal bonds.
 b Gifts and inheritances received.
 c Life insurance proceeds resulting from death of insured.
 d Workmen's compensation and sick pay.
 e Social security benefits, military bonuses, and pensions to veterans.
 f Compensation for personal damages.
 g Certain income earned outside the United States.
 h First $100 of dividends from domestic corporations ($200 on a joint return).

13 Deductions *to arrive at* adjusted gross income are:
 a Business expenses.
 b Employees' expenses.
 c Expenses attributable to rents and royalties.
 d Losses from the sale of property used in a trade or business.
 e Net capital losses up to $3,000 in any one year.
 f Sixty percent of the excess of net long-term capital gains over net short-term capital losses.
 g Net operating loss carry-overs from preceding years.
 h Contributions to retirement plans (IRAs and Keoghs).
 i The "two-earner married couple" deduction, which is 10% of the income of the lower earning spouse, with the deduction limited to $3,000.

14 Deductions from adjusted gross income are limited to excess itemized deductions and personal exemptions. *Excess itemized deductions* consist of such items as charitable contributions, interest paid on home mortgage and other borrowings, and taxes paid to state, cities, or counties. The term *excess* means that these items are deductible only to the extent that they exceed the zero bracket amount (presently $3,400 for married taxpayers filing a joint return and $2,300 for single taxpayers).

15 The *zero bracket amount* is a specified amount of income which is subject to a tax rate of 0%. The zero bracket amount is built into the tax tables to assure that a given amount of the income earned by every taxpayer is not subject to income taxes. In effect, the zero bracket amount represents an "automatic" deduction from adjusted gross income in determining the amount of income actually subject to income tax. As stated in paragraph 14, taxable income can be reduced further if the taxpayer can itemize deductions in *excess* of the zero bracket amount.

16 *Personal exemptions* (presently $1,000 each) may be deducted for the taxpayer, spouse, and each dependent. A taxpayer and spouse may each claim an additional exemption if he or she is blind, and another exemption if he or she has reached the age of 65.

17 The preceding steps lead us to the taxable income of the individual, the amount to which the appropriate tax rates are applied.

18 *Gains and losses from the sale or exchange of capital assets* are granted special treatment for income tax purposes. A gain or loss on the sale or exchange of capital assets held more than one year is a *long-term* gain or loss; the sale or exchange of capital assets held for less than one year results in a *short-term* gain or loss.

19 The amount of capital gain or loss included in the tax return for individuals is determined as follows:
 a Long-term gains and losses are combined to produce a *net long-term gain or loss*. Short-term gains and losses are similarly combined into a *net short-term gain or loss*.
 b If there is a net long-term gain and a net short-term gain, only 40% of the net long-term gain is included in taxable income, but 100% of the net short-term gain is included. Similar rates are applied when the net gain (of either type) exceeds the net loss (of either type).
 c If there is a net short-term loss and a net long-term loss, the short-term loss is combined with 50% of the long-term loss, and up to $3,000 of this total may be deducted to arrive at adjusted gross income. If the total exceeds $3,000, the excess may be carried to future tax years.

20 Many people believe that investors benefit

from losing money because of "tax losses." This is simply not true. Except for the allowable $3,000 deduction for capital losses, capital losses are deductible only against capital gains. Thus, an investor who loses $50,000 and has no capital gains may take only a $3,000 tax deduction in the current year. Even if this investor is in the maximum 50% tax bracket, a $3,000 deduction saves only $1,500 in taxes. Although the excess may be carried forward to future years, the investor will *never* come out ahead for having lost money.

21 The ratio of capital investment to gross national product in the United States has fallen below that of many other countries. Capital investment is, of course, vital to high employment, high productivity, and a high standard of living. To encourage investment, some countries have *no* tax on capital gains. In the United States, gains are taxed heavily while large capital losses are deductible only against capital gains. This policy may be inconsistent with the national policy of encouraging private investment.

22 *Tax credits* differ from deductions. A deduction, such as a charitable contribution, reduces the *income subject to tax*, but a tax credit is subtracted *directly from the tax owed*. Major types of tax credits include the investment tax credit, new jobs credit, credit for the elderly, and foreign tax credit.

23 The investment credit exists as an incentive to investment. When a business buys certain types of long-lived productive assets, it can take a credit of from 4 to 10% of the cost of the property as a deduction from its income taxes.

24 Individuals who compute their income on the calendar-year basis must file an income tax return by April 15 of each year. Corporations must file a return 2½ months after the end of their fiscal year.

25 Quarterly payments of estimated tax are required for self-employed persons and for others having income not subject to withholding. An example of such income is rent received from tenants.

26 A *corporation* is a separate taxable entity. Income tax expense therefore appears on the income statement of a corporation and income taxes payable appear as a current liability on the balance sheet.

27 Tax rates for corporations are in a graduated five-step structure. The rates in effect at the time of publication are:

	Tax Rate, %
First $25,000 of taxable income	15
Second $25,000 of taxable income	18
Third $25,000 of taxable income	30
Fourth $25,000 of taxable income	40
All taxable income over $100,000	46

A short-cut method of computing the tax for a corporation with taxable income above $100,000 is to multiply the *entire amount* of taxable income by 46% and then subtract $20,250 from the resulting figure.

28 Corporations cannot deduct a net capital loss. However, a corporation can offset the net capital loss of one year against any capital gains in the three preceding years or in the following five years. The concepts of excess itemized deductions and personal exemptions are not applicable to corporations.

29 Corporations are not entitled to the dividend exclusion of $100 allowed to individuals; corporations are, however, allowed to deduct 85% of the dividends they receive from other domestic corporations. Corporations are subject to a maximum tax rate of 28% on net long-term capital gains.

30 *Accounting income* often differs from *taxable income* because each is computed with different purposes in mind. Furthermore, taxable income is computed by reference to specific laws, and laws generally do not govern the computation of accounting income.

31 A taxpayer usually can elect to use either the *cash* or the *accrual* basis of determining taxable income. When merchandise is a significant factor in a business, the accrual method is required. If the cash basis is used, depreciation must be computed in the same way as under the accrual basis, and income *constructively* received must be included in income even though cash has not been physically received.

32 The three major sources of differences between *accounting income* and *taxable income* are:
a *Special tax treatment* of revenue and expenses. (For example, municipal bond interest and 85% of intercompany dividends are excluded from taxable income, whereas

political contributions and amortization of goodwill are not deductible.)

b *Differences in timing* of revenue and expenses. (For example, income received in advance is taxed in the year of receipt, while certain expenses are not deductible for tax purposes until they are actually paid.)

c *Alternative accounting methods* for tax purposes and financial reporting (for such items as inventories, depreciation, and installment sales). Business executives will generally select an accounting method for tax purposes that will minimize their current tax liabilities.

33 Significant differences between accounting income and taxable income may be caused by differences in timing of revenue and expenses or by using alternative accounting methods. *Interperiod income tax allocation* should be used to avoid the distortion of net income computed for financial reporting purposes. The objective of interperiod tax allocation is to *accrue income taxes in relation to accounting income* whenever differences between accounting and taxable income are caused by *differences in timing* of revenues and expenses (including those differences resulting from the use of alternative accounting methods).

34 Income tax considerations may be of great importance in making certain business decisions. Some of these decisions are:

a Choice of the form of business organization.

b Choice of accounting methods for inventories, depreciation of plant and equipment, long-term construction contracts, etc.

c Timing and manner in which property is sold.

d Allocation of values to assets when a business is acquired or sold.

e Types of securities to be issued in raising capital to finance a business.

35 *Tax shelters* are investments which produce a loss for tax purposes in the near term but hopefully will prove profitable in the long run. For example, investments in real estate may show a short-term loss because of deductions for interest, property taxes, and depreciation but may prove profitable in the long run because of rising market values. Many tax shelters lose money, however, and the tax savings *never offset the full amount of the loss.*

TEST YOURSELF ON INCOME TAXES

True or False

For each of the following statements, circle the T or the F to indicate whether the statement is true or false.

T F 1 Planning a business transaction in advance to minimize the amount of tax that will become due is termed *tax avoidance* and is usually illegal.

T F 2 Individuals with large incomes pay a lower percentage of their incomes as income taxes than do individuals with low incomes.

T F 3 Individuals, corporations, and partnerships must all pay taxes on business income.

T F 4 Interest on municipal bonds, life insurance proceeds, social security benefits, and the first $100 of dividends from domestic corporations are examples of items which may be excluded from gross income for tax purposes by an unmarried taxpayer.

T F 5 The highest tax rate applied to a corporation is higher than the highest tax rate applied to individuals.

T F 6 Income averaging is designed to benefit individuals whose income fluctuates widely from year to year.

T F 7 A taxpayer with a net long-term capital gain of $8,000 and a net short-term capital loss of $14,000 may deduct $6,000 as a net short-term capital loss.

T F 8 A taxpayer with a net long-term capital loss of $1,800, and no net short-term gain or loss, has a $900 deduction to arrive at adjusted gross income.

T F 9 The federal income tax is designed to serve a number of purposes other than obtaining revenue for the government.

T F 10 Any action by a high-bracket taxpayer which reduces taxable income tends to reduce income taxes; therefore, any investment which results in a loss will be advantageous to such a taxpayer.

T F 11 From the viewpoint of tax planning, a corporation will usually find it advantageous to finance expansion through the issuance of preferred stock rather than bonds payable.

T F   12 Full-time students earning $2,500 per year can qualify as dependents for their parents.

T F   13 Corporations are not entitled to a $100 dividend exclusion but may deduct 85% of dividends received from other domestic corporations.

T F   14 If a taxpayer used the accrual basis in preparing a tax return, income for tax purposes would always be the same as income for accounting purposes.

T F   15 The cash basis of determining taxable income is more commonly used by individuals than the accrual basis.

T F   16 Any business, whether incorporated or not, can elect to use a different method of depreciation on its income tax return from that used in its financial statements.

T F   17 The objective of interperiod income tax allocation is to accrue income taxes in relation to accounting income whenever differences between accounting and taxable income are caused by differences in the timing of revenue or expenses.

T F   18 The cash basis is often more beneficial to the taxpayer than the accrual basis because it often permits postponing the recognition of taxable income by controlling the timing of expenses and collections.

Completion Statements

Fill in the necessary words to complete the following statements:

1 If income tax rates remain constant during a period of inflation, most people will pay a _____ _____ of their earnings as income taxes merely as a result of inflation.

2 The four classes of taxpayers are _____, _____, _____, and _____.

3 The four types of taxes which raise the most revenue for government are _____ taxes, _____ taxes, _____ taxes, and _____ taxes.

4 A partnership does not pay any tax but must file an _____ return.

5 Interest credited by a bank to a savings account is taxable to the depositor even though not withdrawn, because it is _____ _____ _____.

6 The major categories of itemized deductions on the tax returns of individuals are _____, _____, _____, _____, _____ _____ (in excess of 3% of adjusted gross income), _____ _____ and expenses related to the _____ of _____.

7 A procedure designed to accrue income tax expense in relation to pretax accounting income is called _____ _____ _____ _____. This procedure is used when differences in accounting income and _____ income are caused by differences in the _____ of revenue or expenses.

Multiple Choice

Choose the best answer for each of the following questions and enter the identifying letter in the space provided.

_____ 1 The expression *tax planning* is usually taken to mean:
a The analysis of the tax consequences of alternative business decisions and the means of minimizing the tax burden on the taxable entity.
b Preparing the various tax returns and making sure that cash is available to make the payments.
c The classification of various types of taxes in the accounts and the presentation in financial statements.
d Preparation and filing of a declaration of estimated tax.

_____ 2 The income tax rules affecting corporations:
a Treat all corporations alike regardless of size.
b Deliberately favor small corporations.
c Deliberately favor large corporations.
d Specify a wider range of tax rates than do the tax rules affecting individuals.

_____ **3** The investment tax credit is:

a Deductible from adjusted gross income to the extent it exceeds the zero bracket amount.

b Computed as a percentage of dividend income and deducted from adjusted gross income.

c Computed as a percentage of the cost of depreciable business property acquired during the year and deducted from the tax owed.

d Used in place of the zero bracket amount.

_____ **4** John has ordinary income of $18,600, a long-term capital gain of $1,600, and a short-term capital loss of $5,600. Based on these facts, John should report adjusted gross income for federal income tax purposes of:

a $15,600

b $14,600

c $13,000

d Some other amount

_____ **5** Susan has short-term capital gains of $2,000 and short-term capital losses of $3,000. She also has long-term gains of $6,000 and long-term losses of $1,000. The net amount of capital gains that she would include in taxable income is:

a $4,500

b $1,600

c $2,000

d Some other amount

_____ **6** The taxable income for an individual is determined as follows:

a Gross income less personal exemptions.

b Adjusted gross income less exclusions.

c Total income less exclusions less adjusted gross income.

d Adjusted gross income less excess itemized deductions less personal exemptions.

_____ **7** John and Judy Lee have an adjusted gross income of $25,000 on their joint tax return. They have paid property tax of $500, state income tax of $400, and interest of $2,200. The zero bracket amount is $3,400, and each personal exemption is $1,000. The Lees have two small children. The taxable income the Lees should report is:

a $14,500

b $17,600

c $21,000

d Some other amount

_____ **8** In determining whether the corporate or noncorporate form of business organization is preferable from an income tax standpoint for a small enterprise, which of the following factors would *favor incorporation?*

a The major stockholder is the active manager of the business.

b The major stockholder is single and withdraws most of the earnings of the business to meet personal living expenses.

c The sole stockholder has substantial income from holdings of municipal bonds.

d The owner-manager has substantial income from dividends on blue-chip stocks and prefers that earnings of the business be used to finance its expansion.

_____ **9** The cash basis of accounting:

a Cannot be used in filing income tax returns.

b Is widely used by manufacturing corporations.

c Should be used whenever possible since it enables the taxpayer to postpone the payment of income tax.

d Is permissible but usually results in a larger amount of tax than does the accrual method.

_____ **10** Which of the following would *not* be a source of difference between accounting income and taxable income?

a Straight-line amortization of a patent over its useful life.

b Depreciation computed by different methods in tax return and accounting records.

c Inventory valuation by different methods in tax return and accounting records.

d Straight-line amortization of goodwill over 40 years.

Exercises

1 The income statement of Miller Corporation shows income before taxes of $100,000, which includes, among other items, the following:

Dividends from other corporations	$ 20,000
Net long-term capital loss	8,000
Amortization of goodwill	5,000
Interest received on municipal bonds	4,500

Compute the income that would be taxable to the Miller Corporation.

Income before taxes		$100,000
Add:	$	
Subtotal		
Less:	$	
Taxable income		$

2 Robert and Betty Hill have six dependent children. In preparing their income tax return you obtain the following information:

Gross income:

Salaries (before deductions)

Robert Hill 22,000

Betty Hill 22,000

Dividends from domestic corporations

(assume joint ownership) 580

Proceeds on life insurance policy upon

death of father 5,000

Interest on City of Medford bonds 2,100

Interest on savings account 1,320

Gain on stock held over one year 8,200

Loss on stock held two months . . . . (4,200)

Inheritance from father's estate 12,500

Christmas gift from family friend 50

Personal expenses:

Living expenses: food, clothes, etc. 5,800

Sales taxes 400

State income taxes paid. 2,300

Contribution to church and other

allowable organizations. 800

Property taxes on residence 1,650

Federal excise taxes 150

Interest on mortgage and personal loan 6,520

Medical expenses 1,800

Subscription to investment advisory

service 200

Federal income tax withheld by

employer 4,840

Social security taxes withheld by

employer 3,080

Instructions Assuming that the zero bracket amount is $3,400 and each personal exemption is $1,000, compute the taxable income that Robert and Betty Hill should report on a joint return.

ROBERT AND BETTY HILL
Computation of Taxable Income for 19___

Gross income: $

$

Deduction to arrive at
adjusted gross income:

Adjusted gross income . . . . . $

Deductions from adjusted
gross income:
Itemized deductions: $

$

Less: Zero bracket
amount . . . .

Excess itemized deductions . . . . $

Personal exemptions
(___ × $1,000) . . . .

Taxable income . . . . $

21

STATEMENT OF CHANGES IN FINANCIAL POSITION: CASH FLOWS

HIGHLIGHTS OF THE CHAPTER

1 We have seen how the income statement measures the profitability of a business. But profitability alone does not assure success; a business must also maintain adequate liquid resources to pay its maturing obligations and to take advantage of new investment opportunities. The *statement of changes in financial position* helps measure the quantity and quality of resources employed by a business. This financial statement shows the *sources and uses of working capital* and helps answer such questions as: What became of the proceeds of a bond issue? Is the company becoming more or less solvent?

2 The statement of changes in financial position is often called a *funds statement*. The word *funds* is used to mean *all working capital*, not just cash.

3 A statement of changes in financial position measures changes in working capital. If working capital continued to decrease long enough, a business would become insolvent; excessive working capital means resources are not efficiently employed. In the short run, increases and decreases in working capital may be *independent of profitability*.

4 Sources of (increases in) working capital may come from (a) operations (revenue minus expenses that require funds), (b) sale of noncurrent assets, (c) borrowing through long-term debt, and (d) issuing additional shares of capital stock.

5 Funds provided by operations are revenue minus expenses that require funds. This is the same thing as net income *plus* expenses that *do not* require funds. Examples of expenses that do not require funds are depreciation, amortization, and depletion. These items required funds when the *asset was acquired*, not when the expense is being recognized.

6 Extraordinary and nonoperating gains and losses (if material) should be *eliminated* from net income in computing the funds generated by operations. This is because the funds generated by the disposition (or destruction) of the asset causing the extraordinary or nonoperating gain or loss will *already be included* in the statement of changes in financial position as a source of funds resulting from the disposition of a noncurrent asset.

7 Uses of working capital are (a) declaration of a cash dividend, (b) repayment of long-term debt, (c) purchase of noncurrent assets, and (d) repurchase of outstanding capital stock.

8 Transactions involving only working capital accounts (current assets and current liabilities), such as short-term borrowing or the collection of an account receivable, *do not change* the amount of working capital.

9 Transactions involving a working capital account and a nonworking capital account *must* either increase or decrease working capital. For example, the purchase of a building for cash is a *use* of working capital, and long-term borrowing is a *source* of working capital.

10 Transactions involving only nonworking capital accounts, such as the issuance of long-term debt in exchange for a building, do not change the *amount* of working capi-

tal. This is because such an *exchange transaction* consists of both a *source* of working capital (sale of bonds) and a *use* of working capital (purchase of building). Since the source and the use of funds are equal, there is no change in the amount of working capital. Instead of ignoring these transactions, a clearer picture will result if we include them in the statement of changes in financial position as *both* a source and a use of working capital.

11 Most transactions involving only nonworking capital accounts are exchange transactions. Two exceptions are stock dividends and stock splits. Stock dividends and stock splits do not involve an exchange and do not affect the financial position of the business. Thus, they are not shown in a statement of changes in financial position.

12 It is not necessary to have a list of all transactions occurring during a period to prepare a statement of changes in financial position. In practice, the statement is usually prepared on a working paper from analysis of changes in *noncurrent accounts* as presented in *comparative balance sheets*.

13 Working papers for analysis of the changes in noncurrent accounts are prepared by listing the amount of working capital and the balances of the noncurrent accounts at the beginning of the period in the left-hand column, and the balances at the end of the period in the right-hand column. In the middle columns, the total change which has occurred in each account during the period is entered as a debit or a credit, and the resulting effect on working capital is listed below as a source or use of working capital. Each change in a noncurrent account generally results in a change in working capital.

14 After all the changes in noncurrent accounts have been recorded as changes in working capital, a total *increase or decrease* in working capital for the period is computed by *subtracting the uses of working capital from the sources of working capital*. This total increase (or decrease) in working capital should be the difference between the beginning and ending amounts of working capital listed in the working papers. (Carefully study the working papers for the Allison Corporation shown in your text.)

15 A formal statement of changes in financial position is prepared from the working papers once the total change in working capital has been confirmed. The statement of changes in financial position should be followed by a schedule showing the *changes in the composition of working capital*. This schedule shows the change occurring during the year in each current asset and current liability account.

16 A statement of changes in financial position shows the inflow and outflow of liquid resources (working capital) during a period. However, a company may have adequate working capital and still not be able to pay its debts if the working capital is primarily tied up in inventory and receivables. Management may therefore prepare a *cash flow statement* which shows the cash position of a business.

17 A cash flow statement shows (in summary form) all cash payments, all cash receipts, and the increase or decrease in cash during the period.

18 Much of a company's cash flow is generated by operations. We may prepare a report of cash flow from operations from an income statement by converting from the accrual to the cash basis of accounting.

19 Net sales can be converted to cash receipts from customers by *adding any decrease* (or subtracting any increase) *in accounts receivable*. The cost of goods sold can be converted to cash payments for merchandise by *adding any increase* (subtracting any decrease) in inventory to find the total merchandise purchases, and *adding any decrease* (subtracting any increase) in accounts payable.

20 Expenses can be converted to the cash basis by two steps. From the listed expenses, (a) subtract any increase (or add any decrease) in accrued liabilities and (b) add any increase (subtract any decrease) in short-term prepayments.

21 Some expenses, such as depreciation and amortization of bond discount, correspond to changes in the carrying value of a noncurrent asset or liability. Such expenses do not involve cash outflows in the current period.

22 When an income statement is restated on the cash basis, the net income figure will be converted to *cash flow from operations*. In the short run, cash flow may be independent of profitability.

TEST YOURSELF ON FUNDS FLOW ANALYSIS

True or False

For each of the following statements, circle the T or the F to indicate whether the statement is true or false.

T F 1 The primary purpose of a statement of changes in financial position is to measure short-run profitability.

T F 2 The statement of changes in financial position is sometimes referred to as a funds statement.

T F 3 A statement of changes in financial position shows the sources and uses of working capital during an accounting period.

T F 4 In accounting terminology, the word *funds* is used to refer only to cash.

T F 5 Short-term borrowing may be a source of cash, but it is not a source of working capital.

T F 6 Selling a noncurrent asset is a source of working capital, even if the asset is sold at a loss.

T F 7 If the income statement shows a net loss for the period, there cannot have been any funds provided by operations.

T F 8 A company which is profitable cannot have decreasing working capital.

T F 9 A company with decreasing working capital cannot be profitable.

T F 10 If a long-term liability is incurred for the purchase price of a noncurrent asset, there will be no change in the amount of working capital, but the event will appear in the statement of changes in financial position as both a source and a use of working capital.

T F 11 A transaction that affects only current assets and current liabilities cannot cause a change in working capital.

T F 12 The payment of a cash dividend, not the declaration of the dividend, is a use of working capital.

T F 13 Transactions which affect a current asset or current liability account and a noncurrent account will cause a change in working capital.

T F 14 Depreciation expense is not a use of funds in the current period and should be added back to net income to determine working capital provided by operations.

T F 15 Extraordinary gains or losses are sources or uses of working capital and should be included in the working capital provided by operations figure.

T F 16 A cash flow statement shows only receipts and payments of cash and does not show other changes in working capital.

T F 17 Net sales may be converted to cash received from customers by adding any decrease (subtracting any increase) in receivables from customers.

T F 18 The delivered cost of net purchases may be converted to cash paid for merchandise by adding any increase (subtracting any decrease) in accounts payable to suppliers.

T F 19 Short-term prepayments increased during the year by more than the increase in accrued liabilities. This means that more cash was paid for expenses than is shown in the accrual basis income statement.

Completion Statement

Fill in the necessary words to complete the following statements:

1 The statement of changes in _____ _____ shows _____ and _____ of _____ _____ .

2 A statement prepared by management to analyze the sources and uses of cash is called a ____ _____ statement.

3 The _____ of a cash dividend is a _____ of working capital. The sale of a noncurrent asset at a loss is a _____ of working capital. Repurchase of outstanding capital stock, at a price below the original issue price, is a _____ of working capital.

4 Depreciation expense should be _____ to _____ _____ to determine working capital _____ ____ _____ , because depreciation expense does not decrease working capital.

5 It is possible to prepare a statement of changes in financial position by analyzing the changes in _____ accounts.

6 A transaction which changes only

_____ accounts is neither a source nor a use of working capital.

7 The cash flow from operations may be determined by converting an income statement from the _____ basis to the _____ basis of accounting.

8 To convert net sales to cash receipts from customers, you should add any _____ in receivables from customers. Expenses may be converted to the cash basis by adding any _____ in short-term prepayments and subtracting any _____ in accrued liabilities.

Multiple Choice

Choose the best answer to the following questions and enter the identifying letter in the space provided.

_____ **1** Which of the following is *not* a use of working capital?
a Repayment of long-term debt.
b Acquisition of treasury stock.
c Cash dividend declared but not paid.
d Payment of an account payable.

_____ **2** Net income may be adjusted to show the working capital provided by operations by:
a Adding expenses not requiring working capital, adding nonoperating gains, and subtracting nonoperating losses.
b Adding expenses not requiring working capital, subtracting nonoperating gains, and adding nonoperating losses.
c Subtracting depreciation and amortization expenses.
d Adding any decreases in receivables and subtracting any increases in accounts payable and notes payable.

_____ **3** Purchases amounted to $10,000; inventories increased by $4,000; accounts payable decreased by $1,500. The cash paid to creditors was:
a $ 8,500
b $10,000
c $11,500
d $15,500

_____ **4** The purpose of a statement of cash flow is to:
a Compute cash earnings per share.
b Explain increases or decreases in the cash balance from one date to another.

c Explain the reasons for changes in working capital.
d Restate net income on a cash basis.

_____ **5** Which of the following events would appear on a statement of changes in financial position?
a Issuing long-term bonds in exchange for land.
b Purchasing inventory on credit.
c Repayment of a short-term loan.
d None of the above.

_____ **6** Bondholders in Bluebell Corporation converted $2 million of long-term convertible bonds payable into 80,000 shares of common stock. In Bluebell Corporation's statement of changes in financial position, this transaction should be shown as:
a Neither a source nor a use of funds, because working capital was not affected.
b Only a $2 million source of funds from the issuance of common stock.
c Only a $2 million use of funds for the retirement of long-term debt.
d Both a $2 million source and a $2 million use of funds.

_____ **7** The composition of working capital at the beginning and end of a period:
a Appears in the working paper for the statement of changes in financial position.
b Appears in comparative balance sheets and therefore should not be included in the statement of changes in financial position.
c Appears in a schedule accompanying the statement of changes in financial position.
d Has little or no significance for users of financial statements.

Exercises

1 Indicate the immediate effect upon working capital of each transaction listed below. Use the following code:
S = A source of working capital
U = A use of working capital
SU = Both a source *and* a use of working capital
N = Neither a source nor a use of working capital

____ Paid semiannual interest on bonds payable.

____ Recognized depreciation expense.

____ Made monthly payment on operating lease.

____ Paid six months' rent in advance.

____ Declared cash dividend for payment in the next accounting period.

____ Declared a stock dividend for distribution in the next accounting period.

____ Outstanding convertible preferred stock is converted into common stock.

____ Sold treasury stock at a price below cost.

____ Sold marketable securities (a current asset) at a price below carrying value.

____ Issued common stock in exchange for the net assets of another corporation.

2 From the following information, prepare a statement of changes in financial position (without showing the composition of working capital) for Year 2 for Patriotic Fireworks Corporation:

a Net income for Year 2 was $112,000.

b Depreciation expense for Year 2 was $25,000.

c During Year 2, land which had cost $40,000 was sold for $60,000, net of the tax on the gain.

d A six-month bank loan of $50,000 made in Year 1 was repaid in Year 2.

e Additional equipment was acquired during Year 2 at a cost of $84,000.

f An earthquake caused $30,000 of damage to plant assets.

g A cash dividend of $50,000 was declared at the end of Year 2 to be paid in January of Year 3.

PATRIOTIC FIREWORKS CORPORATION
Statement of Changes in Financial Position
For Year Ended December 31, Year 2

Sources of working capital:
   Operations:
      Income before nonoperating gain and loss $
      Add:

                                     $

     Total sources of working capital. . . . $
Uses of working capital:
                        $

     Total uses of working capital . . . . .
Increase in working capital . . . . $

3 The net income for the Baker Corporation in Year 1 amounted to $100,000 and included the following items:

Interest revenue.	$ 2,000
Depreciation expense	40,000
Accrued salaries and wages	4,000
Amortization of patents	5,000
Gain on sale of plant assets (net of taxes) . . .	20,000
Amortization of premium on bonds payable .	2,500
Income tax expense	80,500

In the space provided below, compute the working capital provided by regular operations:

Net income	$100,000
Add:	
Subtotal	$
Less:	
	$
Working capital provided by operations	$

4 The financial statements of Stacy Corporation provide the following information:

	Year 5	Year 4
Accounts receivable	$ 29,000	$25,000
Inventory	35,000	28,000
Prepaid expenses	500	1,500
Accounts payable (for merchandise) . .	17,000	14,000
Accrued liabilities	2,000	750
Net sales	320,000	
Cost of goods sold	200,000	
Operating expenses (including deprecia-		
tion of $8,000)	90,000	
Net income	30,000	

Using the given data, compute for Year 5:

a Cash collected from customers.

b Cash paid for merchandise.

c Cash paid for operating expenses.

d Cash provided by operations.

22

ANALYSIS AND INTERPRETATION OF FINANCIAL STATEMENTS

HIGHLIGHTS OF THE CHAPTER

1 *Financial statements* represent a report on managerial performance. In order to interpret the information contained in financial statements, the user should understand the workings of the accounting system. Financial statements are of interest to many groups, each with a different set of needs.

2 The published financial statements of corporations have been audited by CPA firms and reviewed in detail by governmental agencies such as the Securities and Exchange Commission. Consequently, users of these financial statements may have confidence that the information in the statements is reasonably reliable and is presented in accordance with generally accepted accounting principles.

3 Some sources of financial data available to users other than management include:

a Annual reports of corporation.

b Data filed with the Securities and Exchange Commission.

c Investment advisory services and stock brokerage firms.

d Organizations such as Moody's Investors Service, Standard & Poor's Corporation, and Dun & Bradstreet, Inc.

4 A given figure contained in financial statements is seldom significant to the reader; the *relationship* of figures, or the *change* over time, is generally much more useful.

5 Critics of business often blame "excessive" corporate profits for rising prices and other economic problems. In evaluating the reasonableness of corporate profits, we must relate the dollar amount of net income to the volume of sales and the value of the economic resources necessary to produce that profit. Also, we must consider the need for profits as a means of financing expansion, creating jobs, and increasing the supply of goods and services.

6 It is also important to remember that during periods of inflation, financial statements based upon historical cost tend to overstate the profitability of a business by failing to recognize the current value of the resources consumed in the production of revenue. The SEC requires large corporations to disclose the replacement cost of their inventories, cost of goods sold, plant assets, and depreciation expense. This information should be used to help answer such questions as: Are the company's earnings sufficient to keep "physical capital" intact *given the rising cost of replacing inventories and plant assets*?

7 Three techniques commonly used in the analysis of financial statements are:

a Dollar and percentage changes.

b Component percentages.

c Ratios.

8 *Dollar and percentage changes* are taken from *comparative* financial statements and give valuable clues to growth and other important trends affecting the business. The percentage of relationship between any figure appearing in financial statements and the total which includes this figure (total assets on a balance sheet, and net sales on an income statement) is known as a *component percentage*. It can be used to measure the importance (or possible imbalance) of the item in question. A *ratio* measures the rela-

tionship of one financial item to another and calls attention to a significant relationship which may suggest further investigation.

9 In interpreting the significance of percentage changes, component percentages, and ratios, some *standards of comparison* should be used. Two widely used *standards* are:

a The past performance of the company.

b The performance of other companies in the same industry or the performance of the industry as a whole.

10 Comparison of data over time gives some idea of the company's performance compared with its past record and may be helpful in forecasting future performance.

11 Comparison of a company's performance with that of other companies similarly situated or with the aggregate results for an industry offers valuable clues relating to a company's ability to compete and perhaps to surpass the industry's performance.

12 The key objectives of financial analysis are to determine a company's *future earnings performance* and the *soundness of its financial position*. To evaluate earnings performance and financial soundness, we are interested not only in the *amount* of earnings and assets, but also in the *quality of earnings*, the *quality of assets*, and the *amount of debt*.

13 The quality of earnings depends upon the *source* and *stability* of those earnings. The quality of earnings helps us to evaluate how likely it is that earnings will continue to grow or whether future earnings are likely to fluctuate widely. An analysis of the accounting principles and methods used by a company is helpful in evaluating the quality of earnings reported by the company.

14 A company may become insolvent even though it is profitable. The health and even the survival of a company may therefore be dependent not only on earnings, but also on the *quality of assets* and the *amount of liabilities* outstanding. A firm with inadequate cash position, slow-moving inventories, past-due receivables, and large amounts of short-term liabilities may be facing serious financial difficulties.

15 The concept of return on investment (called *ROI*) is a measure of management's efficiency in using the resources under its control. The ROI concept is used in many situations, such as evaluating the performance of a branch, product line, total business, or par-

ticular investment. ROI is computed several different ways, depending upon the circumstances; two common measures of ROI are *return on assets* and *return on stockholders' equity*. A summary of these and other ratios is contained at the end of the chapter in your textbook.

16 *Stockholders and potential investors* in the common stock of a company are primarily interested in the following:

a Earnings per share.

b Price-earnings ratio.

c Dividends paid and the yield based on the market value of the stock.

d Book value per share.

e Revenue and expense analysis (the increase or decrease in specific revenue and expense items).

f The rate of return on assets used in the business.

g The rate of return on common stockholders' equity.

h Equity ratio (the proportion of total assets financed by stockholders).

17 Financing a business with fixed-return securities (bonds and notes payable and preferred stock) is known as using *leverage* or *trading on the equity*. If the rate earned on total assets is *greater* than the rate paid on the fixed-return securities (the cost of borrowing), the common stockholders will gain from the use of leverage. Common stockholders will gain because the capital provided by the fixed-return securities is being invested to earn more than the amount which must be paid to the providers of that capital. The excess of the earnings generated by that capital over the fixed return paid out belongs to the common stockholders.

18 If the return earned on total assets is *less* than the cost of borrowing, the common stockholder will *lose* by trading on the equity.

19 The *debt ratio* (total liabilities ÷ total assets) measured the degree to which a company is trading on the equity. A high debt ratio means that a high percentage of the total assets is financed by creditors and that the company is making extensive use of leverage.

20 The *equity ratio* (stockholders' equity ÷ total assets) shows the percentage of total assets financed by stockholders. The equity ratio plus the debt ratio must always equal 1, so a low equity ratio means a high debt ratio. A

low equity ratio may be profitable to common stockholders in periods of prosperity (when return on assets is greater than cost of borrowing) but can lead to serious trouble in a period of low earnings if return on assets falls *below* the cost of borrowing.

21 *Long-term creditors* are primarily interested in the following measurements:

a The rate of return on investment, known as the *yield* on investment in bonds.

b The firm's ability to meet periodic interest requirements.

c The firm's ability to repay the principal of the debt at maturity.

22 The *yield* on bonds is the *effective interest rate* (after amortization of any discount or premium) that an investor will earn by buying the bonds at their current market price and holding them to maturity. The yield varies *inversely* with changes in the market price of a bond. The safety of an investment in bonds depends on the ability of a firm to meet the interest and principal payments. An indication of the ability to pay interest is the *number of times* that the interest requirement was earned. This is computed by dividing the income from operations by the annual interest expense. The safety of principal is, to some extent, measured by the *debt ratio*. The lower the debt ratio, the safer the position of creditors.

23 *Preferred stockholders* are primarily interested in the yield on their investment and the number of times that preferred dividends were earned. The *yield* is computed by dividing the annual dividend received on a share of preferred stock by the market value of a share of stock. The *times preferred dividends were earned* is computed by dividing net income by the annual dividends paid on the preferred stock.

24 *Short-term creditors* are primarily concerned with the relationship of *liquid assets* to current liabilities and the *turnover* of accounts receivable and inventories. These are usually analyzed by computing the following:

a Working capital, the excess of current assets over current liabilities.

b Current ratio, current assets divided by current liabilities.

c Quick ratio, quick assets (cash, marketable securities, and receivables) divided by current liabilities.

d Inventory turnover, cost of goods sold for the year divided by the average inventory during the year.

e Turnover of accounts receivable, credit sales for the year divided by the average receivables for the year.

25 Short-term creditors consider the quality of working capital as well as the dollar amount. Factors affecting the quality of working capital include (a) the nature of the assets comprising the working capital and (b) the length of time required to convert these assets into cash. Turnover ratios give an indication of how rapidly inventory and receivables can be converted into cash.

26 The inventory turnover and accounts receivable turnover may be expressed in *days* by dividing 365 (days in a year) by the number of times the average inventory or receivables have turned over in one year. The result is the number of days necessary to turn inventory into receivables · and receivables into cash.

27 Adding the days required to turn over inventory to the days required to turn over receivables gives the days necessary to convert inventory into cash. This is the *operating cycle* for a merchandising business (for firms that manufacture their inventory, this would be only part of the operating cycle). An operating cycle which lengthens from one period to the next may indicate that the firm is having trouble selling its inventory or collecting its accounts receivable.

TEST YOURSELF ON ANALYSIS OF FINANCIAL STATEMENTS

True or False

For each of the following statements, circle the T or the F to indicate whether the statement is true or false.

T F 1 The dollar amount of a change during a period in a certain item appearing in financial statements is probably less significant than the change measured as a percentage.

T F 2 Percentage changes are usually computed by using the latest figure as a base.

T F 3 It is possible that a decrease in gross profit rate may be more than offset by a decrease in expenses, thus resulting in an increase in net income.

T F 4 In a common size income statement each item is expressed as a percentage of net sales.

T F 5 Industry standards tend to place the performance of a company in a more meaningful perspective.

T F 6 Two earnings per share figures frequently appear in an income statement: earnings per share before taxes and earnings per share after taxes.

T F 7 Dividing the market price of a share of common stock by the dividends per share gives the price-earnings ratio.

T F 8 If some expenses are fixed (do not fluctuate in proportion to change in sales volume), net income should increase by a greater percentage than the increase in sales volume.

T F 9 Dividing net sales by average inventory gives the inventory turnover rate, which is a measure of how quickly inventory is selling.

T F 10 If the rate of return on assets is substantially higher than the cost of borrowing, the common stockholder should want the company to have a high equity ratio.

T F 11 If a company gets into financial difficulty, both the debt ratio and the equity ratio might decline at the same time.

T F 12 The common stockholder will lose from trading on the equity when the cost of borrowing exceeds the return on assets.

T F 13 The number of times preferred dividend requirements were earned is computed by dividing income *before* taxes by the amount of the annual dividend requirement of the preferred stock.

T F 14 A high current ratio may indicate that capital is not productively used and that inventories and receivables may be excessive.

T F 15 It is possible to improve many balance sheet ratios by completing certain transactions just before the close of the fiscal period.

T F 16 Certain account balances at the end of the accounting period may not be representative for the entire year, and as a result the ratios (or turnover figures) may be misleading.

Completion Statements

Fill in the necessary words or amounts to complete the following statements:

1 The three most widely used analytical techniques are _____ and _____ change, _____ _____ , and _____ .

2 The four groups that supply capital to a corporation are _____ _____ , _____ _____ , _____ _____ , and _____ _____ .

3 The market price of common stock divided by earnings per share is known as the _____ _____ _____ _____ .

4 The debt ratio may be found by deducting the _____ _____ from 100%.

5 The current ratio is 3 to 1; working capital amounts to $100,000, and the quick ratio is 1.5 to 1. Compute the following: (a) current assets, $ _____ ; (b) current liabilities, $ _____ ; (c) total investment in inventories and short-term prepayments, $ _____ .

6 The number of times interest is earned is primarily important to _____ _____ , and may be found by dividing _____ _____ _____ by the annual _____ _____ .

7 When the _____ _____ _____ is less than the cost of borrowing, common stockholders should prefer a _____ debt ratio.

8 Cost of goods sold during a year divided by the average cost of _____ gives the _____ _____ for the year.

9 The _____ turnover plus the _____ _____ turnover, expressed in days, measures the length of the _____ _____ of a merchandising business.

Multiple Choice

Choose the best answer for each of the following questions and enter the identifying letter in the space provided.

_____ **1** An income statement showing only component percentages is known as a:
a Common dollar statement.
b Condensed income statement.
c Common size income statement.
d Comparative income statement.

_____ **2** Which of the following *is not* a valuable standard of comparison in analyzing financial statements of a company engaged in the manufacture of mobile homes?
a Past performance of the company.
b Performance of another company engaged in the manufacture of mobile homes.
c Performance of all companies engaged in manufacture of mobile homes.
d Performance of companies engaged in construction of apartment buildings.

_____ **3** Common stockholders would be *least concerned* with which of the following?
a Earnings per share of stock.
b Revenue and expense analysis.
c Book value per share.
d Number of times interest earned.

_____ **4** A company has a current ratio of 2 to 1 at the end of Year 1. Which one of the following transactions will *increase* this ratio?
a Sale of bonds payable at a discount.
b Declaration of a 50% stock dividend.
c Collection of a large account receivable.
d Borrowed cash from bank, issuing a six-month note.

_____ **5** Bondholders would be *most* interested in which of the following?
a Quick ratio.
b Inventory turnover.

c Times interest earned.
d Operating cycle.

_____ **6** If we added the average number of days required to turn the inventory over and the average age of receivables (in number of days), we would have an estimate of:
a The company's fiscal period.
b The sales volume of the business.
c The company's operating cycle.
d Nothing meaningful.

_____ **7** In projecting the future profitability of a merchandising company, investors will be least concerned with changes in:
a The gross profit rate.
b The rate earned on total assets.
c The quick ratio.
d Sales volume.

_____ **8** If sales increase by 10% from Year 1 to Year 2 and cost of goods sold increases only 6%, the gross profit on sales will increase by:
a 4%
b 10%
c 6%
d Some other percentage.

Exercises

1 There are 10 transactions or events listed next. Opposite each item is listed a particular ratio used in financial analysis. Indicate the effect of each transaction or event on the ratio listed opposite it. Use the following symbols: Increase = *I*; Decrease = *D*; No Effect = *NE*. (Assume that the current ratio and the quick ratio are higher than 1 to 1.)

	Transaction or Event	Ratio	Effect
a	Purchased inventory on open account.	Quick ratio	
b	A larger physical volume of goods was sold at reduced prices.	Gross profit percentage	
c	Declared a cash dividend of $1 per share.	Current ratio	
d	An uncollectible account receivable was written off against the allowance account.	Current ratio	
e	Issued additional shares of common stock and used proceeds to retire long-term debt.	Rate earned on total assets (before interest and income taxes)	
f	Distributed a 20% stock dividend on common stock.	Earnings per share of common stock	
g	Operating income increased 25%; interest expense increased 10%.	Times interest charges earned	
h	During period of rising prices, company changed from fifo to lifo method of inventory pricing.	Inventory turnover	
i	Paid previously declared cash dividend.	Debt ratio	
j	Issued shares of common stock in exchange for plant assets.	Equity ratio	

2 From the following comparative balance sheet for the Gulfstream Company, compute the dollar and percentage changes from Year 1 to Year 2:

GULFSTREAM COMPANY
Comparative Balance Sheet
Year 1 and Year 2

Assets	Year 2	Year 1	Increase (or Decrease) Amount	Increase (or Decrease) Percentage
Current assets	$150,000	$120,000	$	
Investments	160,000	80,000		
Plant and equipment (net)	360,000	300,000		
Intangibles	80,000	100,000		
Total assets	$750,000	$600,000	$	

Liabilities & Stockholders' Equity

	Year 2	Year 1	Amount	Percentage
Current liabilities	$ 76,000	$ 80,000	$	
Long-term debt	116,000	100,000		
Capital stock, $5 par	250,000	200,000		
Retained earnings	308,000	220,000		
Total liabilities & stockholders' equity	$750,000	$600,000	$	

3 The balance sheets of the Olympia Corporation at the beginning and end of Year 1 and the income statement for Year 1 are presented below:

OLYMPIA CORPORATION
Comparative Balance Sheet

Assets	Dec. 31, Year 1	Jan. 1, Year 1
Cash	$ 60,000	$ 45,000
Marketable securities	30,000	40,000
Accounts receivable (net)	50,000	70,000
Inventory	140,000	130,000
Plant and equipment (net of accumulated depreciation)	420,000	330,000
Total assets	$700,000	$615,000

Liabilities & Stockholders' Equity

Accounts payable	$ 95,000	$ 30,000
Accrued liabilities	10,000	15,000
7% bonds payable	80,000	100,000
Capital stock, $5 par	300,000	300,000
Retained earnings*	215,000	170,000
Total liabilities & stockholders' equity	$700,000	$615,000

*Dividends paid amounted to $0.65 per share.

OLYMPIA CORPORATION
Income Statement
For Year Ended December 31, Year 1

Net sales (all on credit)		$800,000
Cost of goods sold:		
Inventory, Jan. 1, Year 1	$130,000	
Purchases	500,000	
Goods available for sale	$630,000	
Inventory, Dec. 31, Year 1	140,000	490,000
Gross profit on sales		$310,000
Operating expenses (includes depreciation of $25,000)		160,000
Income from operations		$150,000
Other expense: Bond interest expense		7,000
Income before income taxes		$143,000
Income taxes		59,000
Net income		$ 84,000
Earnings per share		$ 1.40

On the basis of the information in the Olympia Corporation financial statements, fill in the blanks below with the appropriate amounts (do not compute the ratios):

a The *current ratio* at the end of Year 1 would be computed by dividing $_____ by $_____ .

b The *acid test* (or *quick ratio*) at the end of Year 1 would be computed by dividing $_____ by $_____ .

c The *average turnover of receivables* during the year would be computed by dividing $_____ by $_____ .

d The *average turnover of inventories* during the year would be computed by dividing $_____ by $_____ .

e The number of times bond interest charges were earned during Year 1 (before income taxes) would be determined by dividing $_____ by $_____ .

f The *rate earned on average investment in assets* would be determined by dividing $_____ by $_____ .

g The *equity ratio* at the end of Year 1 would be determined by dividing $_____ by $_____ .

h The *rate of return on the average stockholders' equity* would be determined by dividing $_____ by $_____ .

i The *earnings per share* of capital stock would be determined by dividing $_____ by _____ shares outstanding.

j If the capital stock had a market value at the end of the year of $42 per share, the *price-earnings ratio* would be determined by dividing $_____ by $_____ .

k The *yield* on the stock, assuming a market value of $42, is computed by dividing $_____ by $_____ .

l The book value per share of capital stock at the end of Year 1 would be computed by dividing $_____ by _____ shares outstanding.

m The *gross profit percentage* would be computed by dividing $_____ by $_____ .

23

RESPONSIBILITY ACCOUNTING: DEPARTMENTS AND BRANCHES

HIGHLIGHTS OF THE CHAPTER

1 Past chapters have emphasized financial accounting. Financial accounting information is developed in conformity with generally accepted accounting principles and is used in financial statements. In this chapter, we shift our emphasis more toward the field of managerial accounting. Relative to financial accounting, managerial accounting has the following characteristics:

a The information is used by managers and generally is not distributed to outsiders.

b The information is specifically designed to assist managers in planning and controlling business activities.

c There are no formal standards for presentation; thus, the information may be tailored to suit the decision at hand.

2 There is a considerable overlap between the fields of financial and managerial accounting. Much of the accounting information used in financial statements is also relevant to many managerial decisions. Cost accounting, for example, involves the determination of the unit cost of manufacturing a product or performing a manufacturing process. Cost accounting is an integral part of both financial and managerial accounting.

3 One function of managerial accounting is to provide detailed information about the operations of each department within the business. A department is a segment of a business which handles a certain type of merchandise or performs a certain function. For example, a retail store may have several departments with a manager in charge of each one. Information regarding the revenue and expenses of each department is needed in order to evaluate the profitability of the department and the effectiveness of the department manager.

4 There are two basic types of departments: (a) *cost centers*, which incur costs but do not directly generate revenue, and (b) *profit centers*, which incur costs and also generate revenue.

5 The information system designed to measure the performance of a particular segment of a business for which a given manager is responsible is often called a *responsibility accounting system*.

6 A responsibility accounting system enables managers to be judged by the expenses incurred (or revenues earned) which are *directly under their control*. For example, a report designed to measure the effectiveness of a production manager should not include advertising expense, since it is not under the control of the production manager.

7 All items of expense are the responsibility of some individual and should be charged to that individual at the *point where the cost originates*.

8 Responsibility accounting systems should exist at all levels of a large business; we shall emphasize two of the most important types of accountability units—departments and branches.

9 There are two basic approaches to developing departmental information: (a) establishing *separate departmental accounts* for each item of revenue and expense and (b) main-

143

taining *one general ledger account* for each item of revenue and expense and *allocating* the totals among the departments at the end of the period.

10   *Departmental gross profit* is an important factor in evaluating the profitability of a department. Departmental gross profit may quickly be determined if accounts are maintained for each department's sales, purchases, and inventories.

11   Operating expenses should also be allocated to departments to determine departmental net income. How expenses are allocated depends on whether they are *direct* or *indirect*.

12   *Direct expenses* are those that benefit only one department and should be assigned to that department.

13   *Indirect expenses* benefit the business as a whole and should be allocated among the departments in a manner to charge each department with the approximate cost of the benefits it received.

14   A departmental expense allocation sheet, such as the one for the Day Corporation illustrated in your text, is often used to allocate both direct and indirect expenses to departments. Study the Day Corporation example, paying special attention to the *basis of allocation* of the various expenses.

15   Departmental income statements commonly are prepared in either of two ways. The first approach is to allocate both the direct and indirect expenses to each department, thus measuring each department's net income. A second approach is to allocate *only the direct expenses* to the departments, thus measuring each department's *contribution to the indirect expenses of the business*. Many accountants argue that the second approach provides a better basis for evaluating the performance of departmental managers, because indirect expenses often are beyond the departmental manager's control.

16   Just because a department shows a net loss in a departmental income statement does not mean that the overall income of the business would increase if the department were closed. This is because some of the indirect expenses allocated to the unprofitable department (such as depreciation) would *not be eliminated* by closing the department. These expenses would then have to be allocated against other departments.

17   The decision of whether or not closing a particular department would increase the profitability of the business requires a careful analysis of the department's revenue and expenses. The key question is whether closing the department would eliminate expenses in excess of the department's revenue. There also are other considerations, such as the effect that closing one department might have upon the sales of other departments.

18   A *branch store* is a profit center and may be evaluated by a responsibility accounting system similar to that used to evaluate departments. Branch accounting systems may be *centralized* at the *home office* or *decentralized* at the *branch*.

19   Three features of a centralized branch accounting system are (a) the branch is provided with a *working fund* (similar to a petty cash fund) for small expenses, (b) all business documents originating at the branch are sent to the home office, and (c) separate records are maintained for each branch by the home office.

20   With a decentralized system, the branch keeps records *as if it were a separate business* and forwards its completed financial statements to the home office.

21   When a centralized system is in use, branch revenues are deposited in a home office bank account, and branch expenses are paid by the home office (except for small expenses paid from the working fund). With a decentralized system, the branch maintains its own bank account and pays its own bills.

22   Frequently the home office will invest cash or assets in the branch. In a decentralized system, the home office will carry its investment in the branch in an asset account named after the branch. The branch will record the investments by the home office as debits to the appropriate asset accounts and a credit to an equity account entitled Home Office.

23   At the end of a period, the branch will close the revenue and expense accounts into the Income Summary account and close the Income Summary account into the Home Office account.

24   When the home office receives financial statements from all the branches, these statements are combined through working papers to prepare financial statements for the business as a whole.

TEST YOURSELF ON RESPONSIBILITY ACCOUNTING

True or False

For each of the following statements, circle the T or the F to indicate whether the statement is true or false.

T F   1 Managerial accounting information is developed in conformity with the same generally accepted accounting principles as apply to financial accounting.

T F   2 Information about the unit cost of manufacturing inventories is used in managerial accounting, but not in financial accounting.

T F   3 An information system designed to measure the performance of a segment of a business for which a given manager is responsible is called a responsibility accounting system.

T F   4 As managers move higher in the organization, fewer expenses will be charged against them by a responsibility accounting system.

T F   5 A cost center is a unit of business which incurs cost but does not directly generate revenue.

T F   6 Unless separate revenue and expense accounts are maintained by each department, information about departmental revenue, gross profit, and net income cannot be determined.

T F   7 The salary of a drill press operator would be a direct expense to the production department.

T F   8 The salary of a night security guard in a department store is a direct expense of each sales department.

T F   9 If a department consistently shows a net loss on a departmental income statement, the business as a whole would always show a greater profit if that department were discontinued.

T F 10 A department's contribution to the indirect expenses of the business is equal to the department's revenue less its direct expenses.

T F 11 Closing a department is more likely to eliminate the indirect expenses charged to that department than the direct expenses of the department.

T F 12 A department which shows a net loss in a departmental income statement might still make a positive contribu-

tion to the indirect expenses of the business.

T F 13 The decision of closing a department should be based only upon the revenue and expenses of that department. Management should not consider the possible effect upon the revenue of other departments.

T F 14 A branch uses a working fund provided by the home office only when a decentralized accounting system is in use.

T F 15 If a multibranch business uses a centralized accounting system, bills for expenses incurred by the branches are usually paid by the home office.

T F 16 When a decentralized system is used, a branch would record the acquisition of office equipment paid for by the home office by debiting the Office Equipment account and crediting the Home Office account.

T F 17 In a decentralized system, the home office will maintain asset accounts to show the investment in each branch.

T F 18 A home office using a decentralized system will record the net income of each branch by debiting the asset account for the specific branch and crediting a revenue account.

T F 19 The Home Office account appears only on the books of the branch and should be viewed as an asset account.

T F 20 A branch is an example of a profit center.

Completion Statements

Fill in the necessary words to complete the following statements:

1 A responsibility accounting system helps judge the effectiveness of particular managers on the basis of expenses that are directly

_____ ____ _____ .

2 A ____ _____ is a unit of a business which incurs expenses but does not directly generate revenue; a _____ _____ generates revenue and incurs costs.

3 The elimination of an unprofitable department will reduce total _____ by more than it will reduce total _____ .

4 The two basic ways to collect departmental information are to maintain _____ _____ accounts for each item of revenue and expense, or maintain one _____ _____ account for each item of revenue and expense, and allocate each account _____ among the various departments at the end of the period.

5 Expenses which can be traced straight to specific departments are called _____ expenses, whereas expenses incurred for the benefit of the business as a whole are called _____ expenses.

6 Deducting direct departmental costs and expenses from departmental revenue indicates the department's _____ of the business.

7 If the North Branch remits cash to the home office and if a decentralized system is in use, the North Branch will debit a proprietorship account entitled _____ _____ and credit Cash; the home office will debit the Cash account and credit an _____ account entitled _____ _____ .

Multiple Choice

Choose the best answer for each of the following questions and enter the identifying letter in the space provided.

_____ 1 Which of the following would not be a direct expense of the Western division of the Nationwide Corporation?
a Salaries to employees of the Western division.
b Plant security at the Western division's factory.
c A portion of the cost of fighting an antipollution lawsuit against Nationwide Corporation.
d The salary of the Western division's manager.

_____ 2 Which of the following expenses could not be eliminated if a department store discontinued the shoe department which occupies the entire basement?
a The salary of the shoe salespersons.
b Depreciation on the building charged to the shoe department.
c Shoe advertising.
d None of the above.

_____ 3 If several departments share the same building, which is the best basis for allocating heating expense?
a Cubic feet of space occupied by each department.
b Number of employees in each department.
c Dollar sales of each department.
d The ratio used to allocate indirect advertising expense.

_____ 4 If a department store buys a health insurance policy covering all employees, the best basis for allocating this expense among the departments would be:
a Departmental gross profit.
b Cubic feet of space occupied by each department.
c Number of employees in each department.
d Dollar sales of each department.

_____ 5 An entry debiting Cash and crediting Home Office on the books of a branch would:
a Result from a cash sale by the branch.
b Mean the branch had deposited cash in the bank account of the home office.
c Occur only if the branch were unprofitable.
d Indicate that the home office deposited cash in the bank account of the branch.

_____ 6 If a department store sought to determine the contribution of each sales department to the indirect expenses of the business, the depreciation on the building:
a Should be charged to the departments as a direct expense.
b Should be allocated among the departments as an indirect expense.
c Should not be charged to the departments at all.
d Should be recorded by each department in departmental accounts.

Exercises

1 Using the information below, complete the Departmental Expense Allocation Sheet for the Stylesetter Corporation:
a All sales personnel receive the same salary and work exclusively for one department or the other. The Women's Department has five salespeople, the Men's Department has three. All salespeople receive equal salaries.
b The Women's Department had $45,000 of direct advertising, while the Men's Department had $15,000. Indirect advertising is allocated in the same ratio as direct advertising.

c Floor space is the basis used to allocate building expenses: the Women's Department occupies 3,000 square feet; the Men's Department occupies 2,000 square feet.

d Each department has a separate buyer; the expenses incurred by the Men's Department buyer amounted to $50,000.

e Direct administrative expenses amounted to $40,000 for each department. Indirect administrative expenses are allocated on the basis of net sales. Net sales amounted to $900,000 in the Women's Department and $600,000 in the Men's Department.

STYLESETTER CORPORATION
Departmental Expense Allocation Sheet
Current Year

	Total Expenses	Women's Dept. Direct	Women's Dept. Indirect	Men's Dept. Direct	Men's Dept. Indirect
Sales force salaries	$240,000	$	$	$	$
Advertising expense	90,000				
Building expense	75,000				
Buying expense	115,000				
Administrative expense	130,000				
Totals—direct and indirect	$650,000	$	$	$	$
Totals for each department:					
Women's Department	$				
Men's Department					
Total—direct and indirect	$650,000				

2 On the schedule provided, fill in the general journal entries (omitting explanations) that would be required on the books of both the branch and the home office to record the following events.

Events	Branch Books			Home Office Books		
Example: Home office opens East Branch and transfers $10,000 cash and $1,500 store supplies to branch	Cash	10,000		East Branch	11,500	
	Store Supplies	1,500		Cash		10,000
	Home Office		11,500	Store Supplies		1,500
1 Merchandise purchased by branch from outside supplier for $16,000						
2 $10,000 in sales on account made by branch						
3 Rent expense of $1,200 paid by branch						
4 Wages expense of $4,000 at branch is paid by home office in cash to avoid cash shortage at branch						
5 Cash sales of $8,000 made by branch						
6 Branch collects $7,000 of branch accounts receivable						
7 Branch remits $5,000 cash to home office						
8 Branch closes Income Summary with $3,200 debit balance at end of period; home office also records net income (loss) of branch						

24

ACCOUNTING FOR
MANUFACTURING OPERATIONS

HIGHLIGHTS OF THE CHAPTER

1 A manufacturing business differs from a merchandising company because the manufacturing company *makes* its inventory. Thus, *Cost of Finished Goods Manufactured* replaces Purchases in determining the cost of goods sold.

2 Costs incurred to manufacture inventories are called *manufacturing costs*. Manufacturing costs are classified into three groups: (a) raw materials used, (b) direct labor costs, and (c) factory overhead costs.

3 The cost of *raw materials used* is computed by subtracting the amount of raw materials on hand at the end of the period (ending inventory of raw materials) from the total of the beginning inventory of raw materials, plus any purchases of raw materials during the period. (Note how computing raw materials used resembles computing the cost of goods sold in a merchandising business.)

4 *Direct labor* costs consist of wages paid to factory employees who work *directly* on the product. Direct labor costs would include wages paid to assemblers and machine operators but not to supervisors or timekeepers.

5 *Factory overhead* includes *all* costs incurred in the factory other than the costs of raw materials and direct labor. Major factory overhead costs include (a) indirect labor (such as supervisors and timekeepers), (b) occupancy costs (such as heat, taxes, and depreciation on building), and (c) machinery and equipment costs (such as repairs and depreciation on machinery).

6 When several products are being produced, it is difficult to allocate factory overhead costs accurately among the products. Therefore, factory overhead costs are often called *indirect costs*, while direct labor and raw materials are called *direct costs*.

7 A manufacturing company has three inventories: raw materials, goods in process, and finished goods, all of which are classified as current assets on the balance sheet.

8 Manufacturing costs are *product costs*, not period costs. Product costs are the costs of creating an asset (inventory) and are not viewed as operating expenses applicable to a particular time period. Product costs associated with ending inventories of goods in process and finished goods represent the cost of those inventories and are shown on the balance sheet as an asset. The only product costs deducted from revenue are those associated with goods *sold* during the period.

9 Costs deducted from revenue in the period they occur are called *period costs*. Period costs *do not* relate to the production of goods and *are not* manufacturing costs. Examples of period costs are selling expenses and administrative expenses.

10 The cost of manufacturing inventories is computed in a supplementary schedule which often accompanies the income statement of a manufacturing company. A *Schedule of Cost of Finished Goods Manufactured* begins with the cost of goods in process at the beginning of the period. To this amount the total manufacturing costs incurred during the period are added to give the total

cost of goods in process during the period. This total is then allocated between the goods finished during the period and those which are still in process at the end of the period. The cost allocated to goods finished during the period is termed *Cost of Finished Goods Manufactured* and is used in the cost of goods sold section of the income statement.

11 The format and content of a schedule of cost of finished goods manufactured is illustrated below:

Goods in process, beginning of period		$ XXX
Add manufacturing costs:		
Raw materials used	$ XXX	
Direct labor	XXX	
Factory overhead	XXX	
Total manufacturing costs		XXX
Total cost of goods in process		
during the period		$ XXX
Less: Goods in process, end of period		(XXX)
Cost of finished goods manufactured.		$ XXX

12 The cost of the goods in process inventory is an *estimate* including (a) an estimate of the raw materials in the partially completed units, (b) an estimate of the direct labor incurred on goods still in process, and (c) an appropriate portion of the factory overhead. The ending goods in process inventory is carried forward to become the beginning goods in process inventory for the next period.

13 Since factory overhead is not directly associated with specific units of output, some method must be developed to assign an appropriate amount of factory overhead to the ending inventory of goods in process. A common method is to express total factory overhead for the period as a *percentage* of total direct labor costs. The resulting percentage is called an *overhead application rate*. The amount of factory overhead assigned to the ending inventory of goods in process is then determined by applying the overhead application rate to the amount of direct labor cost assigned to those units.

14 In the process of closing their accounts, manufacturing companies use a *Manufacturing Summary* account to bring together all of the costs relating to the manufacture of finished goods. All of the manufacturing cost accounts and the beginning inventories of raw materials and of goods in process are closed by crediting these accounts for their respective balances and debiting Manufactur-

ing Summary. The ending inventories of raw materials and of goods in process are recorded by debiting the two inventory accounts and crediting Manufacturing Summary. After these two closing entries have been made, the Manufacturing Summary has a debit balance representing the cost of finished goods manufactured, which is then closed into the Income Summary account.

15 Notice that the determination of the cost of finished goods manufactured in the Manufacturing Summary account involves the same inventory accounts and manufacturing cost accounts that are used in preparing a Schedule of Cost of Finished Goods Manufactured.

16 Working papers for a manufacturing company include two "Manufacturing" columns, from which the formal Schedule of Cost of Finished Goods Manufactured can be prepared. The items extended into the Manufacturing columns on the work sheet parallel the debit and credit entries to the Manufacturing Summary account discussed in paragraph 15.

17 The procedures discussed in this chapter relate to the *periodic inventory* method used by many small manufacturing firms. A limitation of the periodic inventory method is that a physical inventory must be taken to determine the cost of goods manufactured and the cost of inventories on hand. More timely information is available when *perpetual inventory* records are maintained. For this reason, most large manufacturing firms maintain perpetual inventory records and make frequent comparisons between forecast and actual operating results. Cost accounting systems based upon the perpetual inventory method are discussed in the next chapter.

TEST YOURSELF ON ACCOUNTING FOR MANUFACTURING OPERATIONS

True or False

For each of the following statements, circle the T or the F to indicate whether the statement is true or false.

T F 1 Cost of finished goods manufactured appears in the income statement of a manufacturing business as part of cost of goods available for sale.

T F 2 An inventory of finished goods is an

asset, but inventories of raw materials and goods in process are not considered assets until production is completed.

T F 3 The cost of finished goods manufactured includes the total cost of all goods completed during the current period, even if much of the work on these goods was performed in an earlier period.

T F 4 All raw materials purchased in a period are part of total manufacturing costs.

T F 5 Factory overhead includes all manufacturing costs except direct labor and raw materials.

T F 6 The wages paid to supervisors are an example of direct labor.

T F 7 Product costs are all deducted from revenue in the period in which they are incurred.

T F 8 Product costs associated with goods in process and unsold inventories of finished goods appear on the balance sheet as current assets until the goods are sold.

T F 9 All costs and expenses incurred by a manufacturing company are considered product costs rather than period costs.

T F 10 If the levels of finished goods and goods in process inventories are increasing, the amount of product costs deducted from revenue during the period will be less than the amount of product costs incurred.

T F 11 A manufacturing company usually has three separate inventories: raw materials, manufacturing supplies, and finished goods.

T F 12 The cost of finished goods manufactured is equal to the beginning inventory of goods in process plus total manufacturing costs less the ending inventory of goods in process.

T F 13 A company which does not manufacture any of its inventory generally has no product costs other than the cost of purchases and transportation-in.

T F 14 For convenience, factory supplies on hand are often included in the raw materials inventory.

T F 15 The goods in process inventory is computed in a manner very similar to determining the cost of goods sold for a merchandising company.

T F 16 The balance of the Manufacturing Summary account is total manufacturing costs.

T F 17 All manufacturing costs appear as debits to the Manufacturing Summary account; ending inventories of raw materials and goods in process appear as credits.

T F 18 The Manufacturing Summary account is closed by an entry which debits Manufacturing Summary and credits the Income Summary.

T F 19 The Manufacturing Summary account, the Manufacturing columns of the work sheet, and a schedule of cost of finished goods manufactured all contain the same information.

T F 20 Using an overhead application rate to allocate factory overhead to goods in process and finished goods inventories causes all factory overhead costs to be assigned to ending inventories.

Completion Statements

Fill in the necessary words or amounts to complete the following statements:

1 In the income statement of a manufacturing firm, the _____ __ _____ _____ _____ replaces the item labeled _____ in the income statement of a merchandising business.

2 The major classifications of manufacturing costs are ____ _____ _____ , ____ _____ , and _____ _____ .

3 Manufacturing costs are considered to be _____ costs because they are deducted from revenue in the period in which the related goods are sold, rather than being treated as operating _____ of the current period.

4 The (debit, credit) _____ balance of the Manufacturing Summary account represents the ____ __ _____ _____ _____ _____ and is closed into the _____ _____ account.

5 In classifying manufacturing costs, the wages paid to a production scheduling engineer should be considered _____ _____ , and wages paid to a drill press operator should be included in _____ _____ .

6 Given below is certain information for a manufacturing concern:

Cost of raw materials used.	$ 80,000
Direct labor	200,000
Total manufacturing cost incurred	400,000
Total cost of goods in process during the year.	450,000
Goods in process inventory, end of year	20,000
Decrease in finished goods inventory during the year	7,500

From the information given above, evaluate the following:

a Goods in process inventory, beginning of year: $ _____.

b Factory overhead for the year: $_____

c Cost of finished goods manufactured: $ _____

d Cost of goods sold: $ _____

7 In the ledgers, the cost of finished goods manufactured is determined in the _____ _____ _____ account. This account is _____ with the balances of Direct Labor, Factory Overhead, Purchases of Raw Materials, and the _____ inventories of raw materials and finished goods in process.

8 The cost of finished goods manufactured is transferred to the Income Summary account by an entry which _____ the Income Summary and _____ the _____ _____ account.

Multiple Choice

Choose the best answer for each of the following questions and enter the identifying letter in the space provided.

_____ 1 The cost of finished goods manufactured is computed by:
a Adding ending inventory of goods in process, raw materials used, direct labor, and factory overhead; subtracting beginning inventory of goods in process.
b Adding beginning inventory of goods in process, raw materials purchased, direct labor, and factory overhead; subtracting ending inventory of goods in process.

c Adding beginning inventory of goods in process, raw materials used, direct labor, and factory overhead; subtracting ending inventory of goods in process.
d Adding beginning inventory of finished goods, raw materials used, direct labor, and factory overhead; subtracting ending inventory of finished goods.

_____ 2 Which of the following would not be part of the factory overhead of an automobile manufacturer?
a The cost of maintaining equipment.
b The cost of sheet steel for auto bodies.
c The salaries of assembly-line supervisors.
d The salaries of plant security guards.

_____ 3 Which of the following is not likely to be treated as a product cost?
a Depreciation on the factory.
b Portion of the cost of running the quality control department.
c Salaries paid to factory workers.
d Interest paid bonds payable.

_____ 4 Company B had total factory overhead of $80,000 and total direct labor of $60,000. Using the factory overhead rate, how much factory overhead would be allocated to goods in process at the end of the period, which are estimated to contain $12,000 of direct labor?
a $45,000
b $16,000
c $11,250
d $ 9,000

_____ 5 Total cost of goods in process during the period was $180,000. Finished units required $10 in raw materials and $10 in direct labor. The factory overhead rate is 200%. The ending inventory of goods in process consists of 200 units 50% complete as to materials and labor. The cost of finished goods manufactured during the period is:
a $177,000
b $176,000
c $174,000
d $172,000

_____ 6 A product cost is deducted from revenue when:
a The finished goods are sold.
b The expenditure is incurred.
c The production process takes place.
d The production process is completed.

Exercises

1 Pleasurecraft Corporation manufactures sail boats. To manufacture one boat requires $1,000 of raw materials and $2,000 of direct labor. During the current year, the company's manufacturing costs were:

Raw materials used . . . . $ 84,500
Direct labor 160,000
Factory overhead 200,000

At the end of the current year, 20 boats are still in process. Each boat is 70% complete as to materials and 20% complete as to direct labor. Compute the factory overhead rate, and determine the ending inventory of goods in process.

a Factory overhead rate =

b Raw materials used (   ) $
    Direct labor (   )
    Factory overhead (   )
    Ending inventory, goods in process $

2 Using the items listed below and the information from exercise 1, prepare a statement of cost of goods manufactured and an income statement for Pleasurecraft Corporation for the current year. Disregard income taxes.

Goods in process (beginning of year) . . . . . . $ 27,500
Finished goods (beginning of year) 60,500
Finished goods (end of year) 55,000
Sales 700,000
Selling expenses 90,000
General and administrative expenses 130,000

Statement of Cost of Goods Manufactured

Income Statement

25
COST ACCOUNTING SYSTEMS

HIGHLIGHTS OF THE CHAPTER

1 Cost accounting systems have developed principally in manufacturing companies where they are used for two purposes: (a) to determine the unit costs of production and (b) to control the cost of operations.

2 The *control of costs* requires first of all that management know the cost of making a product or performing a business function, so that this cost can be compared with budgets, past performance, or other yardsticks.

3 The first essential of a cost accounting system is the maintenance of three *perpetual* inventory accounts: (a) a raw materials inventory, (b) a work in process inventory, and (c) a finished goods inventory.

4 Two basic types of cost accounting systems are (a) a *job order cost system* and (b) a *process cost system*.

5 A job order cost system is appropriate when each job or batch of product is different and can be identified all the way through the manufacturing process. For example, job cost systems are used in the fields of construction, aerospace, and motion pictures. A *job cost sheet* shows the cost of raw materials, direct labor, and factory overhead on each job, such as a group of airplanes of a given type. The average unit cost per airplane can also be computed.

6 The perpetual inventory account for raw materials is debited for the cost of materials purchased and credited with the cost of materials requisitioned for specific jobs. Subsidiary ledger accounts are kept for each type of materials. These subsidiary ledger accounts agree in total with the controlling account for raw materials.

7 At the end of the month the total of the materials requisitions is the basis of an entry debiting Goods in Process Inventory and Factory Overhead with an offsetting credit to Materials Inventory.

8 Factory labor cost is classified into two types: direct labor and indirect labor. The wages of employees working on a specific job are a direct labor cost recorded by charging a job cost sheet. Wages of employees not directly associated with a particular job constitute *indirect labor*, which is charged to Factory Overhead. *Time tickets* for each employee showing the hours spent on each job enable us to compute the labor cost of each job and also provide data for compiling the payroll.

9 *Factory overhead* includes all costs incurred in manufacturing other than direct labor and direct materials. Examples are indirect labor, factory supplies, power and light, and depreciation of plant assets.

10 Factory overhead is an indirect cost and cannot be traced directly to specific jobs or units. Therefore, an overhead application rate is used to assign a reasonable portion of factory overhead to each job. The overhead application rate is based upon some measure

which can be traced directly to specific units, such as direct labor costs.

11 Factory overhead includes both *fixed costs* and *variable costs*. Fixed costs are constant from month to month regardless of changes in the level of factory output, as, for example, property taxes or the factory superintendent's salary. Variable costs change in direct proportion to output as, for example, electric power to operate a machine.

12 *Fixed overhead cost per unit* depends on how many units are produced each month. In high-volume months, unit costs will be low; in low-volume months, unit costs will be high. If normal production were 1,000 units per month, but in July, because of a vacation shutdown, only 200 units were produced, the cost per unit would be so high as to be meaningless. To avoid such monthly fluctuations, management uses a predetermined overhead application rate for an entire year.

13 To compute a predetermined *overhead application rate*, we estimate the total dollar amount of factory overhead a year in advance and divide this amount by the estimated direct labor cost for the coming year. The resulting figure is the factory overhead rate per direct labor dollar.

14 As each job is completed, the overhead applicable to the job is determined by multiplying the predetermined overhead rate times the direct labor cost incurred on the job. Thus, the total cost of the job (direct labor, raw materials, and factory overhead) can be computed as soon as a job is finished.

15 The total amount of overhead applied to jobs during the period will be debited to Goods in Process Inventory and credited to Factory Overhead.

16 Applied overhead will not exactly equal actual overhead because the predetermined rate was based on estimates. The difference between overhead actually incurred during the year and overhead charged to Goods in Process Inventory is usually closed to the Cost of Goods Sold account.

17 The perpetual inventory account for Goods in Process is charged with the cost of raw materials used, direct labor, and estimated overhead applicable to all jobs. Supporting this controlling account are individual job cost sheets for all jobs in process.

18 When a job is completed, the total cost as shown by the job cost sheet is the basis for an entry debiting Finished Goods Inventory and crediting Goods in Process Inventory. A subsidiary ledger for Finished Goods Inventory consists of a card showing the cost of each type of finished product.

19 When sales are made, two entries are necessary: (a) debit Cash (or Accounts Receivable) and credit Sales for the *sales price* and (b) debit Cost of Goods Sold and credit Finished Goods Inventory for the *cost* of the goods sold.

20 *Process cost systems* are used in businesses manufacturing a homogeneous product through a series of operations, for example, cement, chemicals, and petroleum. Costs are accumulated for each process (or departmental cost center) rather than for batches of product as previously described for a job cost system.

21 The costs incurred each period in each department are accumulated in separate goods in process accounts. The units produced in each department are also tabulated, and an *average cost* per unit for each process is determined. The cost of a finished unit consists of the sum of the unit costs of performing each process in the unit's manufacture.

22 Some units of product usually will be only partially processed at the end of the period. These partially processed units are expressed in *equivalent full units* in order to compute unit costs. For example, an ending inventory of 200 units which are 60% complete would represent 120 equivalent full units (200 $\times$ 60%).

23 To determine the units of output by a department for the month, we must combine the equivalent full units of work performed to (a) complete the units which were already in process at the beginning of the month, (b) start and complete new units during the month, and (c) partially complete the units still in process at month-end. The result is the equivalent production in terms of finished units for the month, and this is divided into the costs for the month to get a unit production cost.

24 The computation of the average unit production cost is computed monthly for each processing department in a departmental *cost report*. The purposes of the cost report are (a) to determine the equivalent full units

of work performed by the department, (b) to summarize the units and costs charged to the department during the month, (c) to compute the average unit cost of production, and (d) to allocate the costs charged to the department between completed units and the ending inventory of goods in process.

25 Unit costs are used to value the units transferred during the month from one department to another, and from the Goods in Process of the final production department into the Finished Goods Inventory.

TEST YOURSELF ON COST ACCOUNTING

True or False

For each of the following statements, circle the T or F to indicate whether the statement is true or false.

T F 1 A well-designed cost accounting system will work equally well with the periodic inventory system or the perpetual inventory system.

T F 2 The concepts of cost accounting are applicable to banks, hospitals, and government agencies, as well as to manufacturing businesses.

T F 3 A job order cost system is one that accumulates the costs applicable to each department or process during a given accounting period.

T F 4 Effective control of costs in a manufacturing plant is possible only when a cost accounting system exists to measure the cost of making a product or performing a process.

T F 5 If a company manufactures only one product and the accounts contain no arithmetical errors, the precise cost of manufacturing a unit of product in a given accounting period can be computed.

T F 6 The use of a predetermined overhead rate requires that estimates be made of the factory overhead cost for a future accounting period.

T F 7 In a job cost system, the three inventory accounts used are the Raw Materials Inventory, Goods in Process Inventory, and Finished Goods Inventory.

T F 8 The Raw Materials Inventory account is supported by a subsidiary ledger consisting of job cost sheets.

T F 9 The allocation of factory overhead to units of output is accomplished by relating factory overhead to some other cost factor such as direct labor cost or direct hours which can be directly identified with units or lots of output.

T F 10 The fixed cost per unit increases when the volume of production decreases.

T F 11 The use of predetermined overhead rates in a job cost system eliminates the need for recording actual overhead costs incurred during the period.

T F 12 The use of predetermined overhead rates in a job cost system makes it possible to know the total cost of a given job as soon as that job is finished.

T F 13 A process cost system is appropriate when production consists of standard products such as paint, cement, or dairy products.

T F 14 It is necessary to determine the equivalent full units of production by a department before it is possible to compute the departmental unit production cost.

T F 15 The number of equivalent full units of production may be either larger or smaller than the number of units completed during the period.

T F 16 Completing 1,000 units which were each 40% complete at the beginning of the period represents 400 equivalent full units of work.

T F 17 Unit costs are ordinarily determined by dividing the total costs of the period by the number of units worked on during the period.

T F 18 The unit cost computed in a department of a company using a process cost system includes both variable and fixed costs and is used as the basis for the entry transferring the cost of goods to the next department or to the Finished Goods Inventory.

T F 19 When finished goods are sold, the transaction is recorded by a debit to Cost of Goods Sold and a credit to Sales.

Completion Statements

Fill in the necessary words or amounts to complete the following statements;

1 A process cost system stresses the accu-

mulation of costs by _____ or
_____ , whereas a job cost system
stresses the accumulation of costs by
_____ or _____.

2 Two important managerial objectives of cost
accounting are (a) to determine _____
costs and (b) to _____ the _____ of
business operations.

3 In a job order cost system the Raw Materials
Inventory controlling account is supported
by _____ _____ accounts,
the debits to which are posted from suppliers _____ and the credits from materials _____ .

4 In job order cost accounting, if the direct
labor cost for the next period is estimated to
be $60,000 and _____ _____ is
estimated to be $90,000, a specific job com-
pleted with a direct labor cost of $3,000
would be charged with _____ _____
of $ _____ .

5 In a job cost system, the _____ _____
_____ constitute a subsidiary ledger for
the Goods in Process Inventory account.

6 If factory overhead is to be applied on the
basis of direct labor costs, a predetermined
_____ _____ _____ is com-
puted by dividing _____ factory overhead costs for the period by the _____
_____ _____ costs.

7 If the Factory Overhead account has a debit
balance at the end of the year, overhead has
been (overapplied, underapplied) _____
_____ , and the goods in process inventory, finished goods inventory, and _____
___ _____ _____ are all (overstated,
understated) _____ .

8 In a process cost system, the monthly unit
cost for a processing department is determined by dividing the manufacturing costs
charged to the department by the _____
_____ _____ _____ produced during the
month.

9 In a process cost system, a departmental cost
report shows (a) the _____ _____
_____ produced, (b) the _____ and _____

charged to the department, (c) the computation of the _____ costs of production, and
(d) the allocation of total costs between
_____ units and the ending inventory of _____ _____ _____ .

Multiple Choice

Choose the best answer for each of the following
questions and enter the identifying letter in the
space provided.

_____ 1 A condition favorable for the use of a
job order cost system exists when:
a A single product is manufactured.
b Each product or batch of product can be
identified in each step of the manufacturing
process.
c Factory overhead is substantially greater than
the cost of direct labor.
d Prime costs exceed conversion costs.

_____ 2 Factory overhead includes:
a All manufacturing costs other than raw materials and direct labor.
b All prime costs and conversion costs.
c All period costs other than product costs and
indirect labor.
d Indirect labor and general and administrative
expenses other than those included in finished
goods inventory.

_____ 3 A predetermined factory overhead rate
is determined by:
a Dividing actual factory overhead for the current year by actual direct labor hours.
b Multiplying average unit costs by estimated
output.
c Dividing estimated factory overhead for the
coming year by actual prime costs.
d Dividing budgeted factory overhead by the
estimated direct labor cost or other overhead
application base.

_____ 4 In a job order cost system, the subsidiary ledger for the Goods in Process Inventory
controlling account consists of:
a Job cost sheets.
b Material requisitions.
c Prime costs.
d None of these.

_____ 5 The most commonly used basis for
charging factory overhead to jobs is:
a Payroll summary sheets.
b Prime costs.
c Indirect labor and factory supplies.
d Direct labor cost or direct labor hours.

_____ **6** A process cost system is feasible if the company:

a Engages in mass production of a homogeneous product.

b Is subject to substantial seasonal variation in output.

c Produces a wide variety of products.

d Has a decentralized management structure.

_____ **7** The journal entry to record the normal transfer of goods out of the Goods in Process Inventory account is:

a Debit Cost of Goods Sold; credit Goods in Process Inventory.

b Debit Goods in Process Inventory; credit Finished Goods Inventory.

c Debit Finished Goods Inventory; credit Goods in Process Inventory.

d None of these.

Exercises

1 The Magic Forest Company builds custom vacation cabins on site to the customer's order and uses a job order system. The predetermined overhead rate for the current year is 60% of direct labor cost.

At the end of the current year the direct labor cost amounts in total to $320,000 and the actual overhead to $208,000.

A cabin built for Avery Jones required $40,000 of raw materials and $15,000 of direct labor. It was completed in April of the current year.

a What was the total cost of the Jones cabin as shown on the Magic Forest Company's accounts at date of completion?

Direct materials . . . . $
Direct labor . . . .
Overhead. . . . . _____
    Total cost . . . . $

b Was overhead overapplied or underapplied for the current year as a whole? Explain.

_____

_____

_____

_____

c What disposition should be made of the difference between actual overhead and applied overhead at the end of the year?

_____

_____

2 Winchester Company uses a process cost system. At the beginning of March the Raw Materials account showed a balance of $14,000. During March, purchases of materials totaled $119,000. At the end of March the documents showing materials issued in response to requisitions were summarized as follows:

Materials requisitioned by Cutting
    Department $102,900
Materials requisitioned by Assembly
    Department 19,100

a Draft a summary entry to record the purchase of materials and supplies during March.

_____

_____

_____

_____

b Draft a summary entry to record the issuance of materials and supplies during March.

_____

_____

_____

_____

_____

c What was the balance of the Raw Materials Inventory account at the end of March? In what financial statement or schedule would it appear?

_____

_____

_____

BUDGETING AND STANDARD COSTS: TOOLS FOR PLANNING AND CONTROL

HIGHLIGHTS OF THE CHAPTER

1 Two of management's most basic responsibilities are planning and controlling the operations of the business. *Planning* means setting financial and operating goals for the business. *Control* means seeing that everything goes according to plan and that proper corrective action is taken when actual results fall short of plans. *Budgeting* and *standard costs* are two accounting tools designed to assist managers in planning and controlling business operations.

2 A budget is a comprehensive *financial plan* for future operations. The benefits to a business of a thorough budgeting process include:

a Enhanced managerial perspective. Budgeting makes managers more aware of the economic environment of the business.

b Advance warning of problems. Budgets often provide advance warning of such problems as cash shortages or rising costs.

c Coordination of activities. Preparation of a budget provides an opportunity to coordinate the activities of all the departments within the business.

d Performance evaluation. Budgets provide a financial yardstick against which each department's performance may be measured.

3 Budgeted amounts should be set at *realistic and achievable levels*. This is accomplished by having managers at all levels of the business participate in the budgeting process.

4 Planning all the activities of a business usually requires the preparation of several types of budgets. Together, these various budgets are called the *master budget*, which is the overall financial and operating plan for the upcoming year. The master budget usually includes:

a Operating budgets, such as forecasts of sales, production, and operating expenses.

b Responsibility budgets, operating budgets relating to the aspects of a business that are the responsibility of a particular manager.

c Capital budgets, long-run forecasts of major expenditures.

d Cash budgets, short-run forecasts of cash flows.

e Budgeted financial statements, forecasts of the financial statements for the upcoming budget period.

5 A master budget is prepared as follows:

a Prepare a sales forecast for the budget period.

b Prepare budgets for production, manufacturing costs, operating expenses, and capital expenditures.

c Prepare a budgeted income statement.

d Prepare a cash budget.

e Prepare a budgeted balance sheet.

6 Dividing a master budget into responsibility segments ensures that managers know what is expected of them and how their actual individual performances compare with planned performances.

7 A *flexible budget* is a *series of budgets* for *different levels of activity*. Use of a flexible budget prevents the budget from being made obsolete by a change in the level of business activity.

8 We have seen how cost accounting systems are used to determine the actual unit cost of

producing a product. A cost accounting system becomes even more useful when it includes budgeted amounts to serve as standards for comparison with actual costs. The budgeted amounts used in a cost accounting system are called *standard costs*. Standard costs may be used in both job-order and process cost accounting systems.

9 Standard costs are the per unit costs that *should* be incurred in producing a product *under normal conditions*. Comparison of actual costs to the budgeted standard costs alerts managers to those areas in which the actual costs appear excessive. Standard costs should periodically be reviewed and revised so that they remain *attainable* under current conditions.

10 The differences between standard costs and actual costs are called *cost variances*. Under standard cost procedure, costs charged to Goods in Process, Finished Goods, and Cost of Goods Sold are standard costs, *not actual costs*. Any differences in standard costs and actual costs are recorded in *variance accounts*.

11 The variance in actual material costs and the standard cost for materials is divided into two types of variances:

a The *material price variance* is the variance in the price actually paid for materials and the standard price.

b The *material quantity variance* is the variance in the quantity of materials actually used and the quantity which should have been used at that level of production.

12 Direct labor variance also takes two forms:

a The *direct labor rate variance* is the variance in the wage rate paid for direct labor.

b The *direct labor usage variance* is the variance in the amount of labor actually used from the estimated labor required at a given level of production.

13 Factory overhead variance is allocated between:

a *Controllable factory overhead variance*, the difference between the actual factory overhead incurred and the budgeted overhead for the actual level of production attained; and

b *Volume variance*, the difference between the budgeted overhead at the level of production attained and the standard unit cost of factory overhead applied to the level of production attained.

14 A volume variance results when the actual level of output differs from the normal output because the amount of fixed factory overhead included in the standard unit cost is based on the normal level of output. The volume variance will be favorable when actual volume exceeds normal volume and will be unfavorable when actual volume is less than normal volume.

15 An unfavorable volume variance is often called an *idle capacity loss*, because it represents the fixed factory overhead applicable to productive capacity which is not being used.

16 When a *standard cost system* is used, the amounts transferred from the Materials Inventory, Direct Labor, and Factory Overhead accounts to the Goods in Process account are the *standard costs* of goods in process during the period. Thus, a debit balance remaining in a cost account means an *unfavorable variance* (actual costs exceeded standard costs), and a credit balance indicates a *favorable variance* (standard costs exceeded actual costs). The remaining balances in the cost accounts are transferred to the proper variance accounts.

17 At the end of the year the variance accounts are generally closed into the Cost of Goods Sold account. Thus, unfavorable variances increase the cost of goods sold, and favorable variances decrease the cost of goods sold.

18 As a result of this procedure, all *unfavorable cost variances* are deducted from revenue in the period the excessive costs were incurred, instead of part of them being carried forward as assets (inventories of goods in process and finished goods) until the goods are sold. *Favorable cost variances* would cause a larger gross profit on sales in the period of efficient production, rather than in the period that the goods are sold.

19 However, if cost variances are very large, indicating that the standard costs were unrealistic, the cost variances should be prorated among Goods in Process, Finished Goods, and Cost of Goods Sold in order to restate these accounts in terms of actual cost.

20 Standard costs are an effective tool for management control but currently are not used in the preparation of published financial statements.

TEST YOURSELF ON STANDARD COSTS AND BUDGETING

True or False

For each of the following statements, circle the T or the F to indicate whether the statement is true or false.

T F   1 A budget is a fund from which all expenditures must be made.

T F   2 Every budget is a forecast of future events.

T F   3 A master budget states the absolute maximum level of expenditures and cannot be exceeded.

T F   4 A responsibility budget is a financial plan for a segment of a business that is the responsibility of a specific manager.

T F   5 Capital budgets are usually long-term, whereas cash budgets are usually short-term.

T F   6 Budgets are tools useful in planning but have little to do with controlling a business enterprise.

T F   7 Forecasts of sales, units to be manufactured, and operating expenses are all necessary to prepare a master budget.

T F   8 The payment of a bank loan reduces assets and liabilities by the same amount and would therefore not appear in a cash budget.

T F   9 A flexible budget is a series of budgets showing forecast results at many different levels of business activity.

T F   10 Standard costs are budgeted costs.

T F   11 A standard cost system eliminates the need to keep track of actual manufacturing costs.

T F   12 Standard costs are not fixed standards, but must often be revised because of changes in wage rates, material prices, and production methods.

T F   13 A volume variance exists when the standard unit cost fails to allocate the proper amount of fixed overhead to production, due to a difference in normal and actual volume of output.

T F   14 When more hours of direct labor are necessary to complete a process than the standard allows, a labor rate variance exists.

T F   15 There may be a net favorable material variance even though more material was needed to complete a process than was estimated.

T F   16 The direct labor usage variance has nothing to do with overtime wage rates being paid to employees.

T F   17 Unfavorable variances will result in credit balances in the cost accounts, which are then transferred to the variance accounts.

T F   18 If inventories are valued at standard cost, production cost variances will affect net income in the period of production rather than the period in which output is sold.

T F   19 If a small net favorable variance exists, inventories are restated at actual cost to prevent the premature recognition of revenue.

T F   20 Standard costs are often used in preparing the financial statements of manufacturing businesses.

Completion Statements

Fill in the necessary words or amounts to complete the following statements:

1 A budget is often viewed as a comprehensive

_____ _____ .

2 Identify the following budgets:

a A _____ _____ is a segment of the master budget relating to the aspect of a business that is the responsibility of one manager.

b A _____ _____ is a long-range budget that incorporates plans for major plant and equipment expenditures.

c A _____ _____ is the overall financial and operating plan for the next fiscal period.

d A _____ _____ is a budget which shows budgeted results at many different levels of business activity.

3 The use of a budget serves the control function in two ways: (a) by disclosing areas that require _____ _____ and (b) by serving as a yardstick for _____

_____ .

4 Standard costs are the costs that _____ _____ incurred under relatively ideal conditions. When actual costs exceed standard

costs, an _____ cost _____ is said to exist.

5 If there is an unfavorable total material variance of $900 but a favorable material price variance of $200, there must have been an _____ material _____ _____ of $_____ .

6 If less labor is used than estimated to complete a job, but employees have to be paid at overtime rates which exceeded estimates, there is a _____ labor _____ _____ and an _____ labor _____ _____ .

7 If variable factory overhead exceeds the amount budgeted for the actual production, and actual production exceeds forecast production, there will be an _____ _____ factory overhead variance and a _____ _____ _____ .

8 Because less labor was used than had been estimated to complete the first of several manufacturing processes, actual direct labor costs were $1,200 and standard direct labor costs were $1,400. An entry to cost the inventory of goods in process would _____ Goods in Process for $_____ , _____ an account called _____ _____ _____ for $_____ , and _____ Direct Labor for $_____ .

Multiple Choice

Choose the best answer for each of the following questions and enter the identifying letter in the space provided.

_____ 1 Which of the following is *not* a benefit derived from budgeting?
a Management is made more aware of the economic environment of the business.
b The budget may provide advance warning of future financial problems.
c The budget fund provides assurance that cash will be available to meet budgeted expenditures.
d The budget provides a yardstick for evaluating departmental performance.

_____ 2 Which of the following steps in the preparation of a master budget would logically be performed first?

a Prepare a production schedule.
b Prepare a sales forecast.
c Prepare a cash budget.
d Prepare a budget of manufacturing costs.

_____ 3 Manmoth Company sells all the units it can produce at a price of $6 per unit. Average unit cost is $5 per unit at the 70% level of production, and $4 per unit at the 90% level. If the company's cost of goods sold is $350,000 at the 70% production level, the projected gross profit on sales at the 90% level would then be:
a $180,000
b $140,000
c $360,000
d $450,000

_____ 4 At the end of the year the journal entry to close a variance account with a small favorable variance might:
a Debit the variance account and credit Goods in Process.
b Credit the variance account and debit Goods in Process.
c Debit the variance account and credit Cost of Goods Sold.
d Debit Cost of Goods Sold and credit the variance account.

_____ 5 If the actual amount of raw materials used in a process exceeded the standard amount of materials, there was:
a An unfavorable materials price variance.
b A favorable materials price variance.
c An unfavorable materials quantity variance.
d A favorable materials quantity variance.

_____ 6 If fewer units are produced than had been estimated when standard unit cost was computed, there will always be:
a A favorable material quantity variance.
b An unfavorable volume variance.
c A favorable labor usage variance.
d An unfavorable controllable factory overhead variance.

_____ 7 The most important advantage of a standard cost system is that standard costs:
a Highlight trouble spots and facilitate prompt corrective action.
b Make financial statements more comparable because different companies cost their inventories in the same manner.
c Can be determined with great precision so that inventories are valued with complete accuracy.
d Always cause a lower net income resulting in lower income taxes.

Exercises

1 Use the following information to prepare a cash budget for Eagle Corporation for the month of December 19___.

a In November, 30-day credit sales were $120,000; 90% of this amount is estimated to be collectible in December.

b December sales are estimated to be $200,000; cash sales are usually 25% of total sales.

c Total fixed expenses are $30,000 per month, including $6,000 depreciation. Variable expenses are 62% of sales. All expenses requiring funds are paid in cash when incurred.

d A $12,000 note payable must be paid on December 31.

e On November 30, the cash balance is $18,000.

EAGLE CORPORATION
Cash Budget
For the month of December 19___

Cash balance at beginning of month . . . . $		
Receipts:	$	
	_____	
Total cash available		
Disbursements:		
	$	
	_____	
Total cash disbursements		
		_____
Cash balance at end of month . . . . $		

2 During the current month, the Whidbey Company transferred $30,000 of raw materials, $40,000 of direct labor, and $90,000 of factory overhead to goods in process. Whidbey Company uses a standard cost system, and the month-end variances are as follows:

Material price variance (unfavorable)	$3,000
Material quantity variance (favorable)	500
Labor rate variance (unfavorable).	2,000
Labor usage variance (unfavorable).	2,500
Controllable factory overhead (favorable)	1,500
Volume variance (favorable)	1,200

The ending balance of Goods in Process exceeds the beginning balance by $2,000. Total standard unit cost is $10 per unit. Compute the following:

a Actual raw material cost incurred during the month: $_____ .

b Actual direct labor cost incurred: $_____ .

c Actual factory overhead during the month: $_____ .

d The number of units completed during the month: _____ .

27

COST-VOLUME-PROFIT ANALYSIS

HIGHLIGHTS OF THE CHAPTER

1 *Cost-volume-profit analysis* is a *predictive* tool used by management to plan and control the activities of a business. With this tool, management can forecast future costs, revenues, and profits at *various levels* of business activity.

2 Some questions answered by cost-volume-profit analysis are: What level of sales must be reached for the business to break even? What will happen to net income if we reduce unit sales price by $1 and increase unit sales by 10%? These questions may be answered by *forecasting the revenues and expenses* associated with various levels of business activity.

3 The first step in cost-volume-profit analysis is to know *how costs behave* in response to changes in the level of activity.

4 Levels of business activity must be measured by some type of *volume index*. A volume index may be stated in terms of *inputs* (such as tons of raw materials used), or in terms of *outputs* (such as units produced or dollar sales revenue). *Miles driven* is the output of service rendered by an automobile, and would be an appropriate volume index for analyzing the cost of operating the automobile.

5 *Variable costs* are those costs that increase and decrease in *direct proportion* to changes in volume. An example of a variable cost associated with driving an automobile would be the cost of gasoline used.

6 *Fixed costs* (nonvariable costs) *do not change* with changes in volume. Your annual registration fee is a fixed cost of operating an automobile.

7 *Semivariable (or mixed) costs* are those costs that increase and decrease *directly with volume*, and by *less than a proportionate amount*. Semivariable costs include some minimum level, which is a *fixed* portion of the cost. Beyond that minimum level, the cost varies in proportion to volume. Repair costs constitute a semivariable cost of operating an automobile.

8 By combining all variable, semivariable, and fixed costs, we may formulate *cost-volume relationships*, such as, "It costs $900 per year plus 20 cents per mile to operate an automobile." The $900 represents all fixed costs and fixed portion of the mixed costs; the 20 cents per mile represents all variable costs and variable portion of mixed costs.

9 *Average unit cost* is the total cost divided by the units of output. Within certain limits, average unit cost tends to go down as volume goes up because the fixed costs are being spread over more units.

10 The *relevant range* is the range of volume (or production) levels over which the assumptions made about cost-volume relationships remain valid.

11 Cost-volume relationships may be expressed graphically with dollar cost as the vertical axis and volume as the horizontal axis.

12 *Cost-volume-profit analysis* includes the forecast revenue at the various levels of volume. By graphing both costs and revenues at all levels of volume on the same graph, a *cost-*

volume-profit graph may be developed. This type of graph illustrates the amount of expected profit or loss at any level of volume.

13 The zero profit point on a cost-volume-profit graph is called the *break-even* point.

14 A key relationship in cost-volume-profit analysis is the *contribution margin*. The contribution margin is the amount of revenue left over after variable costs have been paid. Contribution margin may be expressed in total dollars (sales revenue − total variable costs), or on a per unit basis (unit sales price − variable costs per unit).

15 When the contribution margin is expressed as a *percentage of sales*, it is called the *contribution rate*. The contribution rate may be computed as follows: contribution margin per unit divided by unit sales price.

16 The contribution margin may be used to compute the sales volume required to break even or to earn any desired level of operating income. The required sales volume *in units* may be computed as follows:

$$\frac{\text{Fixed costs} + \text{operating income}}{\text{Contribution margin per unit}}$$

To find the required sales volume *stated in dollars*, the formula is modified as shown below:

$$\frac{\text{Fixed costs} + \text{operating income}}{\text{Contribution rate}}$$

17 The dollar amount by which actual sales volume is expected to exceed the break-even point is called the *margin of safety*. The margin of safety provides a quick means of estimating the operating income at any sales volume above the break-even point. The estimated operating income may be computed as follows:

Margin of safety × contribution rate

18 The contribution rate also may be used to estimate the *change* in operating income which is likely to result from any expected change in sales volume. The change in operating income can be determined as:

Change in sales volume × contribution rate

19 Cost-volume-profit relationships are widely used during the budgeting process. In addition, these relationships can provide information which is useful in a wide variety of planning decisions, such as the formulation of marketing strategies.

20 The higher the contribution rate, the lower the dollar sales volume needed to cover fixed expenses and to provide a given amount of operating income. At any given sales volume, *selling products with high contribution rates is more profitable than selling products with lower contribution rates*. Thus, sales with high contribution rates are said to be *high quality* sales.

21 Sometimes one resource, such as direct labor, is limited in supply. If so, profitability will be maximized by producing the product with the highest contribution margin *per unit of input* of this scarce resource. The contribution margin per hour of direct labor is computed as follows:

Contribution margin per hour of direct labor	=	contribution margin per unit	÷	direct labor hours required to produce one unit

22 If availability of one resource limits production, profits are maximized by producing the product with the highest contribution margin per unit of input of that resource, even though other products may have a higher contribution margin ratio.

23 In cost-volume-profit analysis the following simplifying assumptions are made: (a) sales price remains constant, (b) the sales mix of products remains constant, (c) fixed expenses remain constant, (d) variable expenses are a constant percentage of sales revenue, and (e) the number of units produced is equal to the number sold.

Thus, changes in these relationships should be closely monitored, for the cost-volume-profit relationships will need to be revised as these conditions change.

TEST YOURSELF ON COST-VOLUME-PROFIT ANALYSIS

True or False

For each of the following statements, circle the T or the F to indicate whether the statement is true or false.

T F   1 Cost-volume-profit analysis is a historical concept of analyzing what costs and revenue were during the last accounting period.

T F   2 When cost-volume-profit analysis is

used, the need for standard costs and budgets is eliminated.

T F 3 A volume index may be based upon either units of input or units of output.

T F 4 When a product is handmade, the manufacturer would probably view direct labor as a variable cost.

T F 5 A "mixed cost" is one that is partially tax deductible and partially nondeductible.

T F 6 The property taxes paid on a factory are fixed costs.

T F 7 Direct costs are generally fixed costs.

T F 8 Indirect costs (for example, factory overhead) are always fixed costs.

T F 9 Variable costs vary directly and proportionately with volume.

T F 10 Operating a tractor costs $3,000 plus 90 cents per mile per year. The semivariable cost of operating the tractor is $3,000.

T F 11 Cost-volume relationships may not hold true outside of the relevant range of volume.

T F 12 If item A has a higher contribution margin than item B, item A must have a higher contribution rate than item B.

T F 13 The break-even point on a cost-volume-profit graph occurs at the level of volume where total revenue equals total variable expenses.

T F 14 If a business has a $100,000 margin of safety, the business will still be profitable unless net income declines by more than $100,000.

T F 15 A cost-profit-volume graph assumes that the number of units produced is equal to the number of units sold.

T F 16 When the availability of direct labor limits the volume of production, profits will be maximized by producing the item with the highest contribution margin per hour of direct labor rather than the item with the highest contribution rate.

Completion Statements

Fill in the necessary words or amounts to complete the following statements:

1 Direct labor and fuel consumption are examples of _____ costs, while plant security and property taxes are _____ costs.

2 Miles driven is an example of a _____ _____ which could be used in analyzing the cost of operating an automobile.

3 Semivariable costs are also called _____ costs and have both a _____ portion (minimum level) and a _____ portion that responds to changes in volume.

4 The cost of producing bottled beer for Green Beer Company is $2,000,000 plus 6 cents per bottle of beer. If 10,000,000 bottles are produced, the _____ costs will be $600,000, the _____ costs will be $2,000,000, and the average unit cost will be $____ per bottle.

5 The number of dollars by which the sales price of one unit exceeds the variable expenses relating to the unit is called the ____ _____ _____ .

6 The contribution rate is the percentage that each dollar of _____ contributes to the _____ _____ and to the _____ _____ of the business.

7 Product X sells for $5 per unit and requires variable expenses of $2 per unit. Product Y sells for $10 per unit and requires variable expenses of $4.70 per unit. For product X, the contribution margin is $_____ and the contribution rate is _____ . For product Y, the contribution margin is $ _____ , and the contribution rate is _____ .

8 Referring to the last question, assume the total fixed costs to produce either product are the same. If total dollar sales are expected to be the same no matter which product is produced and sold, it would be more profitable to produce product _____ .

9 The margin of safety is the amount by which total dollar _____ could _____ and still allow the business to _____ _____ .

Multiple Choice

Choose the best answer for each of the following questions and enter the identifying letter in the space provided.

_____ 1 The volume index that would be used to determine the unit cost per item sold would be:
a Total direct labor hours.
b Total dollar sales.
c Total unit sales.
d None of the above.

_____ 2 Which of the following average costs per unit will usually decrease by the greatest percentage with an increase in the volume of units produced?
a Average fixed cost per unit.
b Average semivariable cost per unit.
c Average variable cost per unit.
d Average total cost per unit.

_____ 3 Within the relevant range of production, average variable cost *per unit* will tend to:
a Vary inversely with the level of production.
b Remain relatively constant.
c Vary directly and proportionately with the level of production.
d Fluctuate drastically.

_____ 4 When a cost-volume-profit graph is prepared, the break-even point will always be found:
a At 50% of normal capacity.
b At the volume resulting in the lowest average unit cost.
c At the volume where total revenue equals total fixed expenses.
d At the volume where total revenue equals total fixed expenses plus total variable expenses.

_____ 5 Which of the following assumptions is not made in the analysis of a cost-volume-profit graph?
a Unit sales price remains constant.
b Variable expenses per unit increase proportionately to increases in unit sales.
c Fixed expenses remain constant at all levels of production within the relevant range.
d If more than one product is sold, the product mix remains constant.

_____ 6 Super Glue sells for $2.00 per tube and has related variable expenses of $1.20 per tube. The fixed expenses of producing Super Glue are $48,000 per month. How many tubes of Super Glue must be sold each month for the Super Glue Company to have a monthly income (before income taxes) of $60,000?
a 45,000
b 60,000
c 90,000
d 135,000

_____ 7 The contribution margins of product A and product B are $7 and $6, respectively. Total fixed expenses are the same when either item is produced. Which of the following statements will always be true?
a The contribution rate is higher for product A than for product B.
b The company could break even by selling less units if it sold only product A than if it sold only product B.
c The contribution margin per hour of direct labor is higher for product A than for product B.
d If total sales will be $600,000 no matter which product is sold, it will be more profitable to sell product A than product B.

_____ 8 Product Z sells for $20 per unit and requires two hours of direct labor per unit to manufacture. The contribution rate for product Z is 40%. The contribution margin per hour of direct labor is:
a $12
b $ 8
c $ 6
d $ 4

Exercises

1 The information below relates to the Filtron Corporation:

Sales price per unit $26.00
Variable expenses per unit $20.00
Fixed expenses . . . . $54,000.00 per month
Maximum capacity . . . . 32,000 units per month

Complete the following statements:
a To break even, Filtron Corporation must produce and sell _____ units per month.
b If Filtron sold 20,000 units, operating income would amount to $ _____ per month.
c The maximum operating income that Filtron can expect to make with its present capacity is $ _____ per month.
d Assuming the cost of direct labor increased by $1 per unit, Filtron's maximum operating income would be $ _____ per month.

2 Digital Corporation manufactures three products sold exclusively to the government. The total production of Digital Corporation is limited by the fact that only 4,000 hours of direct labor per month are available.
a Compute the following schedule:

Product	Sales Price per Unit	− Variable Costs per Unit	= Contribution Margin per Unit	÷ Direct Labor Hours Required per Unit	= Contribution Margin per Hour of Direct Labor
X	$200	$120	$___	5	$___
Y	___	80	40	2	___
Z	80	___	30	___	15

b The Government will buy all of Digital Corporation's production up to the following quantities:

Product X   600 units per month
Product Y   400 units per month
Product Z   500 units per month

Determine how many units of each product Digital Corporation should produce each month to maximize operating income.

Product	Units Produced	Direct Labor Hours Used on Product	Contribution Margin per Hour of Direct Labor	Total Contribution Margin of Each Product
			$	$
Total direct labor hours: 4,000			Total contribution margin: $	

28

RELEVANT INFORMATION, INCREMENTAL ANALYSIS, AND CAPITAL BUDGETING

HIGHLIGHTS OF THE CHAPTER

1 Identifying the relevant considerations in a business decision requires both logic and judgment, as well as an understanding of accounting information. The only financial information relevant to a decision is that information which *varies* among the alternative courses of action being considered. Costs or revenue which *do not vary* among the alternative courses of action are *not relevant* to the decision.

2 The additional costs that will be incurred by pursuing one course of action rather than another are called *incremental costs*; the additional revenue that will be earned is called *incremental revenue*. By identifying the incremental costs and revenue, we may compare the relative profitability of two alternative courses of action. This approach is called *incremental analysis*.

3 Special orders may be profitably produced and sold if the sales price of an order exceeds the incremental costs of producing it. Factory overhead which would exist *whether or not* the special order was produced is not a relevant cost. The decision should be based upon a comparison of *additional costs incurred* with the *additional revenue generated* by each special order.

4 Manufacturing businesses are often confronted with the decision of whether to make or buy a component part of their product. The relevant costs in determining the cost of making the part are the incremental costs per unit of manufacturing the

component. Again, factory overhead, which will continue whether or not the part is made, should not be included in the unit cost of making the part for purposes of any make-or-buy decision.

5 *Opportunity costs* are the value of benefits *not received* but that *could have been received* if another course of action had been taken. For example, if you go to work for $6 an hour when you could be working for $10 an hour, you are incurring a $4 an hour opportunity cost. Opportunity costs are not recorded in accounting records, but ignoring them when making decisions can be a costly mistake.

6 In deciding whether to close a department or discontinue a product line, management should consider the contribution margin that would result from an alternative use of the plant facilities. The contribution margin resulting from an alternative use is an opportunity cost of not closing the existing department. This opportunity cost may be the most important factor in this type of a decision.

7 *Sunk costs* are those costs which have been irrevocably incurred sometime in the past. An *out-of-pocket cost* is an expenditure that will have to be made from current funds. *Sunk costs are irrelevant to future decisions because they cannot be changed no matter what decision is made.*

8 We have seen that a product's contribution margin is relevant to such decisions as whether or not to discontinue a product line and also to cost-volume-profit analysis. Through a technique called *variable costing*,

a cost accounting system may be modified to show contribution margins and other cost-volume-profit relationships.

9 In a conventional cost accounting system, *all* manufacturing costs are charged to the Goods in Process account and eventually flow into the Cost of Goods Sold account. This traditional costing approach is called *full costing*.

10 Variable costing is an alternative to full costing. Under variable costing, *fixed* manufacturing costs are treated as *period expenses* rather than as product costs. Thus, only *variable* manufacturing costs flow into the Cost of Goods Sold account.

11 In an income statement using variable costing, the cost of goods sold (variable manufacturing costs) is deducted from revenue to determine the *manufacturing margin*. Variable selling and administrative expenses are deducted from the manufacturing margin to determine the *contribution margin* of the units sold. Operating income then is determined by subtracting the fixed manufacturing costs and fixed operating expenses from the contribution margin.

12 Variable costing is a useful managerial tool for cost-volume-profit analysis, but it is *not acceptable* for use in financial statements or income tax returns. A company which uses variable costing must make adjusting entries at the end of the period to convert from variable costing to full costing.

13 The process of planning and evaluating proposals for investment in plant assets is called *capital budgeting*. Capital budgeting decisions are important because large amounts of money are committed for long periods of time and because these types of decisions are often difficult or impossible to reverse once the funds have been committed. Three common capital budgeting techniques are: payback period, return on average investment, and discounted cash flow analysis.

14 The *payback period* is the length of time necessary to recover the entire cost of an investment from the resulting annual net cash flows. When annual cash flows are uniform, the payback period is computed by dividing the amount of the investment by the annual cash flow. Short payback periods reduce risk of loss from changing economic conditions. A shortcoming of the payback

period is that it ignores the total life and therefore the total profitability of an investment.

15 The *rate of return on average investment* is the average annual net income from an investment expressed as a percentage of the *average* amount invested. The *average amount invested* is one-half of the *sum* of the original cost of the investment plus the estimated salvage value. Alternative investment opportunities may be ranked according to their respective rates of return on average investment. Return on average investment considers the profitability of an investment but ignores the *timing* of the cash flows.

16 *Discounting* future cash flows is the process of determining the *present* value of the future net cash flows to be received from an investment. This technique considers both the *amount and the timing* of the future cash flows.

17 The present value of a future cash flow is the amount that a knowledgeable investor would pay today for the right to receive that future amount. The present value of a future cash flow is always *less* than the future amount, because money on hand today can be invested to become equivalent to a larger amount in the future.

18 The present value of a future cash flow depends upon (a) the amount of the future cash flow, (b) the length of time until the future cash flow will occur, and (c) the rate of return *(discount rate)* required by the investor.

19 A *table of present values* shows the present value of $1 *to be received at various times in the future*, discounted at various required rates of return. To find the present value of a larger future cash flow, the present value of $1 is multiplied by the amount of the future cash flow. An *annuity table* shows the present value of $1 *to be received annually* for a given number of years, discounted at various discount rates. An annuity table can be used to find the present value of a series of *uniform* annual cash flows. A table of present values and an annuity table are illustrated in your text; you should become familiar with their use.

20 The *discount rate* used in finding present value may be viewed as the investor's required rate of return. The present value of the future cash flow is the maximum

amount that the investor may pay for the investment and still expect to earn the required rate of return. Thus, an investment is desirable when its cost is *less* than the present value of the expected future cash flows and undesirable when its cost is greater.

21 The net present value of a proposal is the difference between the total present value of the future net cash flows and the cost of the investment. When the net present value is zero, the investment provides a rate of return exactly equal to the discount rate. A *positive* net present value means that the rate of return is *higher than the discount rate*; a negative net present value means that the rate of return is *lower*. The investment with the highest net present value is considered the most desirable.

TEST YOURSELF ON RELEVANT INFORMATION, INCREMENTAL ANALYSIS, AND CAPITAL BUDGETING

True or False

For each of the following statements, circle the T or the F to indicate whether the statement is true or false.

T F 1 The only costs relevant to business decisions are those costs that can vary depending upon the course of action selected.

T F 2 The difference between the cost of two alternatives is called the *incremental cost*.

T F 3 Special orders are profitable only if the unit sales price exceeds the average unit cost of production.

T F 4 Sunk costs are costs that provide no benefit.

T F 5 Marvo Co. is considering discontinuing Product X so that those plant facilities may be used to produce Product Y. The contribution margin that would result from selling Product Y represents an opportunity cost of continuing to make and sell Product X.

T F 6 It is easier to determine whether a product is selling above or below the break-even point from a full costing income statement than from a variable costing income statement.

T F 7 A full costing income statement is a

useful management tool, but variable costing must be used for income tax purposes and in published financial statements.

T F 8 When variable costing is used, all fixed manufacturing costs are treated as period costs.

T F 9 If full costing is used to determine the unit cost of an item, it may still be profitable to manufacture the item rather than to buy it from a supplier at a price less than the unit manufacturing cost.

T F 10 The present value of a future cash flow is always less than the future amount.

T F 11 Able Company estimates a proposal involves $3 million in incremental revenue, $1 million in incremental costs, and $4 million in opportunity costs. The proposal is profitable, but Able Company should still select another course of action.

T F 12 The return on average investment method of evaluating investment proposals takes into consideration both the amount and the timing of future earnings.

T F 13 The present value of a sum of money to be received 7 years from now is more than the present value of the same amount to be received 10 years from now.

T F 14 Discounting future cash flows takes into consideration both the amount and the timing of cash flows.

T F 15 The most desirable investment is the one with the lowest net present value.

T F 16 A product that has a positive contribution margin might still be unprofitable to produce if discontinuing the product would eliminate some fixed costs.

T F 17 Making decisions on purely quantitative grounds will ensure that long-run profits are maximized.

T F 18 In deciding whether to replace old equipment, two important considerations are (a) the cost of the new equipment and (b) the cost of the old equipment.

T F 19 The investment proposal with the shortest payback period is not necessarily the most profitable.

Completion Statements

Fill in the necessary words to complete the following statements:

1 The increase in _____ costs that results from taking a certain course of action is called the _____ _____ of that action. This cost should be compared to the estimated _____ _____ to determine the profitability of the action.

2 John Hamilton owns a vacant lot in downtown New York. Ajax Corporation offered Hamilton $5,000 a year to use the vacant lot for parking, but Hamilton declined. Hamilton is therefore incurring an _____ _____ of $5,000 per year by not renting out the lot.

3 Beverly Corporation is considering replacing some old machinery which originally cost $300,000. The $300,000 is an example of a _____ _____ , and is _____ to the decision of whether to replace the machinery.

4 It might be profitable to discontinue a product with a small contribution margin if discontinuing the product would cause some _____ _____ to be _____ .

5 The variable (or direct) costing method treats all _____ _____ costs as _____ costs and all _____ _____ _____ _____ costs and selling and administrative expenses as _____ costs.

6 In an income statement using variable costing, the _____ _____ costs of the units _____ are deducted from sales to arrive at the _____ _____ . When _____ selling and administrative expenses are deducted from this figure, we have the _____ _____ . Next, _____ costs and expenses are deducted to arrive at _____ _____ .

7 The process of planning and evaluating investments in plant assets is called _____ _____ . Three techniques often used in this process are: (a) _____ _____ , (b) _____ _____ _____ _____

and (c) _____ _____ _____ _____ .

8 The present value of a future cash flow depends upon the _____ of the cash flow, the _____ _____ _____ until the cash flow will occur, and the _____ _____ used in determining the _____ _____ .

9 When the present value of future cash flows exceeds the cost of an investment, the _____ __ _____ from the investment is greater than the _____ _____ . The difference between the present value of the future cash flows and the cost of the investment is called the _____ _____ _____ .

Multiple Choice

Choose the best answer for each of the following questions and enter the identifying letter in the space provided.

_____ 1 The acceptance of a special order will improve net income whenever the revenue from the special order exceeds:
a The variable costs of producing the order.
b The marginal cost of producing one unit.
c The incremental cost of producing the order.
d The direct labor costs of producing the order.

_____ 2 The Multi-Product Company manufactures 10,000 units of product D per year. Each unit of product D sells for $5 and has a contribution margin of $2. If product D is discontinued, $14,000 of fixed overhead would be eliminated, and net income would:
a Decrease by $20,000.
b Decrease by $6,000.
c Increase by $20,000.
d Increase by $6,000.

_____ 3 Which of the following does *not* affect the net present value of an investment proposal?
a The timing of the future cash flows.
b The cost of the investment.
c The method of depreciation used for tax purposes.
d The method of depreciation used for accounting purposes.

_____ 4 A weakness in the return on average investment capital budgeting technique is that this method ignores:
a The cost of the investment.

b The average income earned from the investment.

c The life of the investment.

d The timing of the future cash flows.

_____ 5 Leader Company makes one product with variable manufacturing costs of $3 per unit and fixed manufacturing costs of $2 per unit. In the current year, 100,000 units were produced, and 80,000 units were sold. Using full costing, the manufacturing costs deducted from revenue in the year would amount to:

a $500,000

b $400,000

c $440,000

d Some other amount.

_____ 6 Referring to question *4*, if Leader Company used variable costing, the manufacturing costs which would be deducted from revenue in the current year would amount to:

a $500,000

b $400,000

c $440,000

d Some other amount.

_____ 7 Finch Corporation manufactures 4,000 units of product A each year at an average unit cost (full costing) of $20. The company sells all the product A it can produce for $30 per unit. Instead of manufacturing 4,000 units of product A, Finch Corporation could manufacture 10,000 units of product B at an average unit cost of $7. Finch Corporation could also sell all the product B it could produce for $13 per unit, with no change in selling and administrative expenses. Switching to the production of product B would increase Finch Corporation's annual operating income by:

a $ 0

b $ 20,000

c $ 60,000

d $130,000

Exercises

1 J Company uses 10,000 units of part X in their product each year. Part X currently costs J Company $12 per unit to produce, determined as follows:

Direct materials	$ 16,000
Direct labor	25,000
Variable factory overhead	20,000
Fixed factory overhead.	59,000
Total costs	$120,000
Cost per unit ($120,000 ÷ 10,000 units).	$ 12

J Company finds that an outside supplier will provide part X at a price of $10 per unit. If J Company stops producing part X, all the direct materials, direct labor, and variable factory overhead will be eliminated, as will $10,000 of the fixed factory overhead. Use incremental analysis to determine whether J Company should make or buy part X:

	Make the Part	Buy the Part	Incremental Analysis
Manufacturing costs:			
Direct materials	$ 16,000	0	$ 16,000
Purchase price ($10 per unit)	_____	_____	_____
Totals	$ _____	$ _____	$ _____

Conclusion:

2 Barker Corporation is planning to buy new equipment to produce a new product. The equipment will cost $375,000 and have an estimated 10-year life with a $25,000 salvage value. Estimated annual operating results from producing the new product are:

Incremental revenue		$250,000
Incremental expenses:		
Expenses other than depreciation	$190,000	
Depreciation (straight-line basis)	35,000	$225,000
Incremental net income		$ 25,000

All revenue and expenses other than depreciation will be received or paid in cash. Compute for this proposal:

a The annual net cash flow.

b The payback period.

c The return on average investment.

d The net present value, discounted at an annual rate of 10%. (Present value of $1 due in 10 years, discounted at 10% = .386; present value of $1 received annually for 10 years, discounted at 10% = 6.145).

CHAPTER 1

True or False

1 T	4 F	7 T	10 F	13 T
2 T	5 T	8 T	11 F	14 F
3 F	6 F	9 T	12 F	15 F

Completion Statements

1 Income statement, balance sheet. 2(a) Recording, (b) classifying, (c) summarizing. 3 Generally accepted accounting principles. 4 Audit. 5 Securities and Exchange Commission. 6 Financial Accounting Standards Board. 7(a) Profit, (b) solvent. 8 Internal control. 9 Single proprietorships, partnerships, corporations. 10 Name of the company, name of the statement, date. 11 Going-concern, objectivity, replacement, historical. 12 Creditors, owners, residual. 13 Assets, liabilities, owner's equity. 14 Assets, $80,000. 15 Understated, understated, correct. 16 Investment, profits. 17 Increase.

Multiple Choice

1 b	3 c	5 c
2 a	4 c	6 d

Solutions to Exercises

1

	Assets					=	Liabilities		+	Owner's Equity
	Cash	Accounts Receivable	Land	Building	Pool Tables		Notes Payable	Accounts Payable		Robert Neal, Capital
July 1	+$20,000									+$20,000
3	− 10,000		+$21,000	+$30,000			+$41,000			
Balances	$10,000		$21,000	$30,000			$41,000			$20,000
10	− 6,000				+$10,000			+$4,000		
Balances	$ 4,000		$21,000	$30,000	$10,000		$41,000	$4,000		$20,000
14	+ 500	+$ 500			− 1,000					
Balances	$ 4,500	$ 500	$21,000	$30,000	$ 9,000		$41,000	$4,000		$20,000
20	− 2,000							− 2,000		
Balances	$ 2,500	$ 500	$21,000	$30,000	$ 9,000		$41,000	$2,000		$20,000
24	+ 200	− 200								
Balances	$ 2,700	$ 300	$21,000	$30,000	$ 9,000		$41,000	$2,000		$20,000
30	− 600				+ 600					
Balances	$ 2,100	$ 300	$21,000	$30,000	$ 9,600		$41,000	$2,000		$20,000

2

McCALL COMPANY
Balance Sheet
December 31, 19___

Assets		Liabilities & Owner's Equity	
Cash	$ 7,000	Liabilities:	
Accounts receivable	24,000	Notes payable	$ 53,000
Land	29,000	Accounts payable	21,000
Building	45,000	Total liabilities	$ 74,000
Delivery equipment	12,000	Owner's equity:	
Office equipment	6,000	Daniel McCall, capital	49,000
Total assets	$123,000	Total liabilities and owner's equity	$123,000

CHAPTER 2

True or False

1 F	5 T	9 F	13 F	17 T
2 T	6 F	10 F	14 T	18 F
3 T	7 F	11 T	15 F	19 T
4 T	8 T	12 T	16 T	20 F

Completion Statements

1 Title, debit side, credit side. 2 Debit, credits, debits.

3 Left, ledger account, right. 4 Left, debit, right, credit. 5 Cash, Notes Payable, debit, credit. 6 Debit. 7 Book of original entry. 8(a) Date, (b) account, debited, (c) account, credited, (d) explanation. 9 Trial balance, debit balances, credit balances. 10 L/P (ledger page), posted, numbers, cross-reference. 11 e, b, a, d, c.

Multiple Choice

1 a	3 b	5 c	7 c
2 c	4 d	6 b	8 a

Solutions to Exercises

1

Journal Entry	Dr	Cr	Assets	= Liabilities +	Owner's Equity
a Cash	1,230		+1,230		
Accounts Receivable		1,230	−1,230		
Effect of transaction			0 =	0 +	0
b Cash	5,000		+5,000		
Ray Scott, Capital		5,000			+5,000
Effect of transaction			+5,000 =	+	+5,000
c Cash	3,800		+3,800		
Notes Payable		3,800		+3,800	
Effect of transaction			+3,800 =	+3,800 +	
d Accounts Payable	350			− 350	
Cash		350	− 350		
Effect of transaction			− 350 =	− 350 +	
e Land	9,000		+9,000		
Cash		1,000	−1,000		
Notes Payable		8,000		+8,000	
Effect of transaction			+8,000 =	+8,000 +	

2

Cash			
(a)	70,000	(c)	40,000
(b)	12,000	(g)	3,000

Notes Payable		
	(b)	12,000
	(c)	50,000

Land	
(c) 30,000	

Accounts Payable			
(f)	600	(d)	6,000
(g)	3,000	(e)	5,000

Building	
(c) 60,000	
(e) 5,000	

Vivian DuPar, Capital	
	(a) 70,000

Office Equipment		
(d) 6,000	(f)	600

RIVIERA COMPANY
Trial Balance
September 30, 19___

	Debit	Credit
Cash	$ 39,000	
Land	30,000	
Building	65,000	
Office equipment	5,400	
Notes payable		$ 62,000
Accounts payable		7,400
Vivian DuPar, capital		70,000
	$139,400	$139,400

CHAPTER 3

True or False

1	T	5	F	9	T	13	T
2	T	6	T	10	T	14	T
3	F	7	F	11	T	15	F
4	T	8	T	12	F	16	F

Completion Statements

1 Profits, losses, investment. 2 Revenue, expense.
3 Cost, depreciation. 4 $49,000; $68,000; $57,000.
5 Producing revenue, decrease, owner's equity. 6 Net income, increase. 7 Owner's capital, credits. 8 Closing entries. 9 Decrease, drawing, increase, capital.

Multiple Choice

1	c	3	d	5	c
2	c	4	a	6	b

Solutions to Exercises

1 a

SPEEDLINE AUTO REPAIR
Income Statement
For the Month Ended May 31, 19___

Repair revenue		$21,000
Expenses:		
Rent expense	$ 900	
Wages expense	14,000	
Supplies expense	2,000	
Utilities expense	100	
Depreciation expense: garage equipment	200	17,200
Net income		$ 3,800

b

SPEEDLINE AUTO REPAIR
Balance Sheet
May 31, 19___

Assets		
Cash		$ 2,900
Accounts receivable		12,400
Garage equipment	$24,000	
Less: Accumulated depreciation	7,600	16,400
		$31,700
Liabilities & Owner's Equity		
Liabilities:		
Accounts payable		$ 9,100
Wages payable		800
Total liabilities		$ 9,900
Owner's equity:		
Robert Leo, capital, Apr. 30, 19___	$19,200	
Net income for May	3,800	
Subtotal	23,000	
Less: Withdrawals	1,200	
Robert Leo, capital, May 31, 19___		21,800
		$31,700

2

Error	Total Revenues	Total Expenses	Net Income	Total Assets	Total Liabilities	Total Owner's Equity
1	NE	U	O	O	NE	O
2	O	NE	O	O	NE	O
3	NE	U	O	O	NE	O
4	NE	NE	NE	O	O	NE
5	NE	U	O	O	NE	O
6	NE	NE	NE	NE	NE	NE

CHAPTER 4

True or False

1 F	5 F	9 T	13 F	17 F
2 T	6 T	10 T	14 T	18 F
3 T	7 F	11 T	15 T	19 T
4 F	8 F	12 F	16 T	

Completion Statements

1 Recorded costs, unrecorded expenses, recorded revenue, unrecorded revenue. 2(a) Allocates, expense, (b) asset, Unexpired Insurance. 3 Revenue, expense.

4 Debit, expense credit, asset. 5 Debit, asset, credit, liability. 6 Debit, expense, credit, liability. 7 Debit, expense, credit, asset, liability. 8 Debit, asset, asset, liability. 9 Debit, credit, debits, credits, credit. 10 Management Fees Receivable, Management Fees Earned, Cash, Management Fees Receivable, $200, Management Fees Earned, $200. 11 Salaries Payable, Salaries Expense, January 1, Year 5.

Multiple Choice

1 b	3 c	5 c	7 d	9 b
2 a	4 c	6 a	8 d	10 c

Solutions to Exercises

1

	Trial Balance Debit	Trial Balance Credit	Adjustments Debit	Adjustments Credit	Adjusted Trial Balance Debit	Adjusted Trial Balance Credit	Income Statement Debit	Income Statement Credit	Balance Sheet Debit	Balance Sheet Credit
Cash	5,100				5,100				5,100	
Accounts receivable	17,300				17,300				17,300	
Unexpired insurance	360			(a) 60	300				300	
Office supplies	900			(b) 650	250				250	
Office equipment	4,800				4,800				4,800	
Accumulated depreciation:										
office equipment		560		(c) 40		600				600
Notes payable		8,000				8,000				8,000
Accounts payable		1,800				1,800				1,800
Unearned commissions		1,500	(e) 800			700				700
Steven Nuccio, capital,										
May 31, 19___		16,000				16,000				16,000
Steven Nuccio, drawing	1,000				1,000				1,000	
Commissions earned		15,000		(e) 800		15,800		15,800		
Rent expense	2,400				2,400		2,400			
Salaries expense	11,000		(f) 200		11,200		11,200			
	42,860	42,860								
Insurance expense			(a) 60		60		60			
Office supplies expense			(b) 650		650		650			
Depreciation expense:										
office equipment			(c) 40		40		40			
Interest expense			(d) 50		50		50			
Interest payable				(d) 50		50				50
Salaries payable				(f) 200		200				200
			1,800	1,800	43,150	43,150	14,400	15,800		
Net income							1,400			1,400
							15,800	15,800	28,750	28,750

2

19__		**General Journal** **Adjusting Entries**		
		a		
June	30	Insurance Expense	60	
		Unexpired Insurance		60
		To record insurance expired during June.		
		b		
	30	Office Supplies Expense	650	
		Office Supplies		650
		To record consumption of office supplies during June.		
		c		
	30	Depreciation Expense: Office Equipment	40	
		Accumulated Depreciation: Office Equipment		40
		Depreciation expense for June ($4,800 ÷ 120 months).		
		d		
	30	Interest Expense	50	
		Interest Payable		50
		To record interest expense for June.		
		e		
	30	Unearned Commissions	800	
		Commissions Earned		800
		To record commissions earned during June.		
		f		
	30	Salaries Expense	200	
		Salaries Payable		200
		To record salary expense and related liability as of June 30.		
		Closing Entries		
	30	Commissions Earned	15,800	
		Income Summary		15,800
		To close the revenue account.		
	30	Income Summary	14,400	
		Rent Expense		2,400
		Salaries Expense		11,200
		Insurance Expense		60
		Office Supplies Expense		650
		Depreciation Expense: Office Equipment		40
		Interest Expense		50
		To close the expense accounts.		
	30	Income Summary	1,400	
		Steven Nuccio, Capital		1,400
		To close the Income Summary account.		
	30	Steven Nuccio, Capital	1,000	
		Steven Nuccio, Drawing		1,000
		To close the drawing account.		

CHAPTER 5

True or False

1	F	5	T	9	F	13	F	17	T
2	F	6	F	10	T	14	T	18	T
3	T	7	T	11	T	15	F	19	F
4	T	8	T	12	T	16	T	20	F

Completion Statements

1 Perpetual, physical count, periodic. 2 Cost of goods available for sale, ending inventory, cost of goods sold. 3 Gross profit. 4 Sales Returns and Allowances, Cash, Accounts Receivable. 5 $1,960, $1,960, debit, Sales Discounts, $40, Accounts Receivable, $2,000. 6(a) Liability, (b) Sales, Sales Tax Payable. 7(a) Current assets, (b) plant and equipment, (c) other assets. 8 Working capital, current ratio, solvency. 9 Operating cycle. 10 Multiple-step.

Multiple Choice

1	d	3	c	5	d	7	b
2	b	4	b	6	d		

Solutions to Exercises

1

Sales ($155,000 net sales + $4,500 + $1,500)		$161,000
Sales returns & allowances	$ 4,500	
Sales discounts	1,500	6,000
Net sales		$155,000
Cost of goods sold:		
Inventory, Jan. 1	$ 22,000	
Purchases $98,500		
Less: Purchase returns and allowances $3,100		
Purchase discounts 2,000 5,100		
Net purchases $93,400		
Add: Transportation-in 3,600		
Cost of goods purchased	$ 97,000	
Cost of goods available for sale	$119,000	
Inventory, Dec. 31	$ 26,000	
Cost of goods sold ($155,000 net sales − $62,000 gross profit)		93,000
Gross profit on sales ($155,000 Net sales x .40)		$ 62,000
Operating expenses ($62,000 gross profit − $15,500 net income)		$ 46,500
Net income ($155,000 net sales x .10)		$ 15,500

2

	Net Sales		Ending Inventory	Cost of Goods Sold	Gross Profit	Operating Expenses	Net Income or (Loss)
a	400,000	325,000	*75,000*	250,000	*150,000*	*170,000*	(20,000)
b	700,000	*500,000*	90,000	*410,000*	290,000	235,000	*55,000*
c	250,000	210,000	*32,000*	*178,000*	72,000	105,000	*(33,000)*
d	*550,000*	*412,000*	82,000	330,000	*220,000*	185,000	35,000

CHAPTER 6

True or False

1 F	6 F	11 T	16 T
2 T	7 T	12 T	17 F
3 T	8 F	13 F	18 T
4 F	9 T	14 T	19 T
5 T	10 F	15 F	20 T

Completion Statements

1 Administrative, accounting. 2 Collusion. 3 Subdivision, organization, serially numbered, competent, internal audit. 4 Purchase order, receiving report. 5 Sales, purchase, purchase order. 6 Debit memorandum, credit memorandum. 7 $4,900, debit, Purchase Discounts Lost, $100, $5,000.

Multiple Choice

1 d	3 b	5 a	7 b
2 a	4 b	6 b	

Solutions to Exercises

1   **Problem Situations**

e   Paid a supplier for goods that were never ordered.

f   Sales department makes credit sales to customers who do not meet the company's minimum credit standards.

c   Paid a supplier for goods that were never received.

x   Sales clerk makes an error in giving change to a cash customer.

a   Accounts receivable department is unaware that receivables from several customers were never recorded because copies of the sales invoices were misplaced before being sent to the accounts receivable department.

d   An inventory clerk conceals a shortage of merchandise by understating the balance of the Purchases account.

e   Prices charged by a supplier exceed the amount that the company had agreed to pay.

b   Management is unaware that the company often fails to pay its bills in time to qualify for the cash discounts offered by suppliers.

2

Sequence	Department	Procedure
8	a	File paid invoice.
1	e	Prepare purchase requisition.
7	b	Send check to vendor.
3	d	Count and inspect goods upon arrival.
4	a	Perform steps to verify purchase invoice.
6	a	Record purchase and liability to vendor.
2	c	Issue purchase order.
5	a	Initial the invoice approval form.

CHAPTER 7

True or False

1 F	5 T	9 F	13 T	17 F
2 F	6 T	10 T	14 F	18 F
3 F	7 F	11 T	15 F	19 T
4 T	8 T	12 F	16 T	

Completion Statements

1 Posting. 2 Purchases, general, debit. 3 Debit, Accounts Receivable, credit, Sales. 4 Sales invoices, invoices, general, controlling. 5 Input, program. 6 Not be posted. 7 Occurs frequently. 8 Control total, limit test.

Multiple Choice

1 d	3 c	5 c	7 b
2 a	4 a	6 b	8 c

Solutions to Exercises

1   **2**

	S
a	S
b	CP
c	CP
d	CR
e	J
f	J
g	J
h	CP
i	J
j	CR
k	P
l	J
m	J
n	J

	Debit	Credit
a	P, CP	J
b	J	J, CR
c	J	CP
d	J	S, CR
e	J, CP	J
f	CR	J
g	J, CP	P, J
h	S	CR, J
i	CR	CP
j	J	J

CHAPTER 8

True or False

1	T	4	T	7	T	10	F	13	T
2	F	5	F	8	T	11	T	14	T
3	T	6	T	9	F	12	F	15	T

Completion Statements

1 Checks, bank accounts. 2 Maintenance of accounting records. 3 Deposited intact. 4 Collusion of two or more persons. 5 Outstanding checks, deposits in transit. 6 Not Sufficient Funds, Accounts Receivable. 7 Deducted from, bank statement, added to, bank statement, deducted from, depositor's records, added to, depositor's records. 8(a) Voucher register, Telephone Expense, Vouchers Payable (b) check register, Vouchers Payable, Cash. 9 Accounting, finance, payee, perforated, accounting.

Multiple Choice

1	c	3	c	5	c	7	b	9	a
2	c	4	a	6	c	8	b	10	b

Solutions to Exercises

1

__7__ Voucher reviewed by treasurer and check signed and mailed.

__3__ Preparation of voucher, including verification of prices, quantities, terms, and other data on vendor's invoice.

__2__ Receipt of goods and preparation of receiving report.

__1__ Issuance of purchase order.

__4__ Purchase and related liability recorded in voucher register.

__9__ Voucher filed in paid voucher file.

__5__ Voucher filed in unpaid voucher file by payment date.

__8__ Voucher and supporting documents perforated to prevent reuse.

__6__ Preparation of check for signature and payment recorded in check register.

2
HUNTER CORPORATION
Bank Reconciliation
July 31, 19____

Balance per depositor's records, July 31, 19____			$11,364
Add: Note receivable collected for us by bank			1,800
			$13,164
Deduct: Service charge	$ 6		
NSF check of Jay Kline	264		
Error on check no. 295.	108		378
Adjusted balance			$12,786
Balance per bank statement, July 31, 19____			$17,018
Add: Deposit on July 31.			1,950
			$18,968
Deduct: Outstanding checks:			
No. 301	$2,500		
No. 303	600		
No. 304	1,800		
No. 306	1,282		6,182
Adjusted balance (as above)			$12,786

3

Sept. 11	Petty Cash	300	
	Cash		300
Sept. 30	Postage Expense	48	
	Travel Expense	26	
	Miscellaneous Expense	55	
	Cash		129

CHAPTER 9

True or False

1	T	6	T	11	T	16	T	21	T
2	T	7	T	12	F	17	T	22	T
3	F	8	F	13	F	18	T	23	F
4	T	9	T	14	F	19	F	24	T
5	F	10	T	15	F	20	T	

Completion Statements

1 Matching costs and revenue, net income. 2 Over-stated, overstated, overstated. 3 Uncollectible accounts expense, allowance for doubtful accounts. 4 $15,940, debit, Interest Expense, $60, $16,000. 5 15%. 6 Accrued Interest Receivable, Interest Revenue, Interest Revenue. 7 $4,032, debit, Credit Card Discount Expense, $168, credit, Accounts Receivable — Global Express, $4,200. 8 Contra-liability, deducted, interest expense. 9 Contra-asset, deducted, notes receivable, interest revenue. 10 $10,075, $10,075, $10,150, $10,150.

Multiple Choice

1 d   3 d   5 b   7 d
2 a   4 d   6 c   8 d

Solution to Exercises

1

	Accounts	
	Debited	Credited
	A,C	X
1	D	C
2	A	E
3	A,J	C
4	A,I	B
5	C	D
6	I	G
7	A,F	E
8	A	C
9	E,G,I	A
10	I	F

2

a $280 ($12,000 × .14 × $\frac{60}{360}$)
b $315 ($8,400 × .18 × $\frac{75}{360}$)
c $120 ($4,000 × .12 × $\frac{90}{360}$)
d $375 ($9,000 × .125 × $\frac{120}{360}$)
e $975 ($13,000 × .15 × $\frac{180}{360}$)

CHAPTER 10

True or False

1 T	6 T	11 T	16 T	21 T
2 T	7 F	12 F	17 T	
3 T	8 F	13 F	18 T	
4 F	9 F	14 F	19 F	
5 T	10 T	15 F	20 F	

Completion Statements

1 Title, seller, buyer. 2 $5,000; $37,000; $18,000.
3 Specific identification, average cost, first-in, first-out, last-in, first-out. 4 Replacement, replacement, historical, overstating. 5 Replacement cost, reinvested, inventory, fifo. 6 Decrease, replacement, increase, replacement. 7 Lifo. 8 Retail, cost, ratio (or percentage).
9 Inventory, (a) Sales, sales, (b) Cost of Goods Sold, Inventory, cost.

Multiple Choice

1 c   3 b   5 b   7 b
2 b   4 a   6 c

Solutions to Exercises

1

	Revenues	Costs and/or Expenses	Net Income	Assets	Liabilities	Owner's Equity
a	NE	NE	NE	U	U	NE
b	NE	U	O	O	NE	O
c	NE	O	U	U	NE	U
d	NE	O	U	U	NE	U

2

	Inventory	Cost of Goods Sold
a	$6,300	$16,600
b	$6,250	$16,650
c	$5,000	$17,900
d	$5,725	$17,175

3

Cost of goods available for sale:

Beginning inventory, January 1 . . . . $60,000
Purchases, January 1 through March 8 39,600
  Cost of goods available for sale $99,600
Deduct: Estimated cost of goods sold:
 Net sales $81,000
 Cost percentage (100% − 40%) 60%
  Estimated cost of goods sold 48,600
Estimated inventory, March 8 . . . . $51,000

4

a 64%   ($480,000 ÷ $750,000)
b $400,000   ($750,000 − $350,000)
c $256,000   ($400,000 × 64%)

CHAPTER 11

True or False

1 T	6 T	11 F	16 F
2 T	7 T	12 F	17 T
3 F	8 F	13 T	18 T
4 T	9 F	14 F	
5 T	10 T	15 F	

Completion Statements

1 Depreciation, cost. 2 Units-of-output, straight-line, fixed percentage on declining balance, sum-of-the-years'-digits. 3(a) Physical deterioration, (b) obsolescence. 4 Capital revenue, understated. 5 $40,000; $35,000; $37,000. 6 1981, income tax, not acceptable. 7 Current value, historical, overstate.

Multiple Choice

1 b	3 b	5 d
2 a	4 c	6 c

Solutions to Exercises

1		Year 1	Year 2
a	$11,000 - $1,000 \times \frac{1}{4} \times \frac{9}{12}$ . . .	$1,875	
	$10,000 \times \frac{1}{4}$		$2,500
b	20,000 × 10 cents	$2,000	
	40,000 × 10 cents		$4,000
c	$10,000 \times \frac{4}{10} \times \frac{9}{12}$	$3,000	
	$10,000 \times \frac{4}{10} \times \frac{3}{12} + ($10,000		
	$\times \frac{3}{10} \times \frac{9}{12})$		$3,250
d	$11,000 \times 50\% \times \frac{9}{12}$	$4,125	
	$11,000 - $4,125 \times 50\%$		$3,437.50

2

19__	General Journal		
Jan. 4	Machinery	4,000	
	Cash		1,000
	Notes payable		3,000
	Purchased machine for cash and 8% note due in 90 days.		
6	Machinery	250	
	Cash		250
	Moving and installation costs.		
Apr. 4	Notes Payable	3,000	
	Interest Expense	60	
	Cash		3,060
	Paid note due, including interest at 8% for 90 days.		
June 30	Depreciation Expense	180	
	Accumulated Depreciation: Machinery		180
	Depreciation for 6 months: ($4,250 - $650) \times \frac{6}{120}		

CHAPTER 12

True or False

1 T	5 F	9 T	13 T	17 T
2 T	6 F	10 F	14 T	18 F
3 F	7 T	11 F	15 F	
4 T	8 F	12 T	16 T	

Completion Statements

1 Original cost, Accumulated Depreciation. 2 Basis. 3 Book value, additional amount. 4 Subsidiary ledger, identification number, inventory. 5 Amortized, straight-line, 40. 6 Present value, excess, purchased.

Multiple Choice

1 a	3 d	5 c
2 c	4 c	6 c

Solutions to Exercises

1

	General Journal		
a	Cash	4,000	
	Accumulated Depreciation	1,800	
	Loss on Disposal of Equipment	200	
	Equipment		6,000
b	Cash	3,500	
	Accumulated Depreciation	2,700	
	Gain on Disposal of Equipment		200
	Equipment		6,000
c	Equipment	7,300	
	Accumulated Depreciation	3,600	
	Equipment		6,000
	Cash		4,900

2 "Normal" earnings ($12,000,000 × .20) = $ 2,400,000
Excess earnings ($3,120,000 − $2,400,000) = $ 720,000
Goodwill ($720,000 ÷ .25)   = $ 2,880,000
Price offered ($12,000,000 + $2,880,000) = $14,880,000

CHAPTER 13

True or False

1 F	5 F	9 F	13 T	17 T
2 F	6 T	10 T	14 T	18 F
3 T	7 F	11 T	15 F	
4 F	8 F	12 F	16 T	

Completion Statements

1 Contractor, employee. 2 Liability. 3 Gross earnings (or gross pay), deductions, take-home pay.

4 $4,420; $4,000. 5 W-2, Internal Revenue Service. 6 FICA (or social security taxes), federal income taxes withheld, other deductions (such as union dues, retirement plan, insurance premiums, etc.). 7 FICA taxes, federal unemployment insurance tax, state unemployment insurance tax. 8 Employee's earnings record. 9 Padding the payroll.

Multiple Choice

1 c	3 a	5 b
2 d	4 b	

Solutions to Exercises

1

Employee	Cumulative Earnings for Year up to Current Period	Payroll for Current Period	FICA Taxes	FUTA Taxes		Total Taxes on Employer
				State	Federal	
Adams	$ 45,000	$ 5,000	—0—	—0—	—0—	—0—
Barnes	37,800	4,200	$154.00	—0—	—0—	$154.00
Corey	4,800	1,200	84.00	$ 32.40	$ 9.60	126.00
Daniel	18,900	2,100	147.00	—0—	—0—	147.00
Eliot	5,400	1,800	126.00	43.20	12.80	182.00
Ford	11,250	1,250	87.50	—0—	—0—	87.50
Gray	—0—	1,900	133.00	51.30	15.20	199.50
Totals	$123,150	$17,450	$731.50	$126.90	$37.60	$896.00

2

19__	General Journal		
Jan. 15(a)	Office Salaries Expense	30,000	
	FICA Taxes Payable		2,100
	Liability for Income Taxes Withheld		5,700
	Accrued Payroll		22,200
	To record payroll and related deductions for pay		
	period ended Jan. 15.		
15(b)	Payroll Taxes Expense	3,150	
	FICA Taxes Payable		2,100
	State Unemployment Taxes Payable		810
	Federal Unemployment Taxes Payable		240
	To record payroll taxes on employer for pay		
	period ended Jan. 15.		

CHAPTER 14

True or False

1	T	8	F	15	F	22	F
2	F	9	T	16	T		
3	T	10	F	17	T		
4	T	11	T	18	T		
5	T	12	F	19	T		
6	F	13	T	20	T		
7	T	14	F	21	F		

Completion Statements

1 American Institute of Certified Public Accountants, Financial Accounting Standards Board, American Accounting Association, Securities and Exchange Commission. 2 Going-concern. 3 Objectivity, consistency, disclosure. 4 Cost, market. 5 Audit, opinion, fairness. 6 During production, when production is complete, when the sale is made, when cash is collected from customers. 7 Purchasing power, decreases. 8 Understate, overstate. 9 Loss, gain. 10 General price index, current dollars, purchasing power, replace.

Multiple Choice

1	d	4	c	7	d
2	b	5	a	8	c
3	b	6	b	9	c

Solutions to Exercises

1

	Assets	Liabilities	Owner's Equity
a	NE	NE	NE
b	D	NE	D
c	NE	NE	NE
d	I	NE	I
e	NE	NE	NE
f	NE	NE	NE
g	I	NE	I
h	D	NE	D

2a $(\$70,000 \times \frac{155}{140}) + \$153,000 = \underline{\$230,500}$

b   140,000 units sold $\times$ \$1.70 per unit = $\underline{\$238,000}$

CHAPTER 15

True or False

1	T	5	F	9	T	13	F	17	T
2	F	6	F	10	F	14	T	18	F
3	T	7	T	11	F	15	T		
4	F	8	F	12	T	16	T		

Completion Statements

1 Mutual agency. 2 Debit, \$10,000, credit, \$10,000.
3 \$27,000, \$2,000. 4 \$(6,000) loss, \$24,000.
5 \$9,000. 6 \$5,000, \$0, \$7,000.

Multiple Choice

1 a   3 c   5 c
2 c   4 b   6 a

Solutions to Exercises

1		A's Share	B's Share
First situation:	a	$24,000	$ 36,000
	b	39,720	20,280
	c	32,400	27,600
Second situation:	a	$ (8,000)	$ (8,000)
	b	2,400	(18,400)

2 a

Income Summary	. . . .	25,000	
C, Capital	. . . .		15,000
D, Capital	. . . .		10,000
C, Capital	. . . .	11,000	
C, Drawing	. . . .		11,000
D, Capital	. . . .	16,000	
D, Capital	. . . .		16,000

b

C & D
Statement of Partners' Capitals
For Year 1

	C	D	Total
Balance, beginning of year . . .	$18,400	$17,750	$36,150
Add: Net income for year . . .	15,000	10,000	25,000
Subtotal	$33,400	$27,750	$61,150
Less: Withdrawals	11,000	16,000	27,000
Balance, end of year	$22,400	$11,750	$34,150

3 a

K, Capital	. . . .	16,000	
L, Capital	. . . .	16,000	
M, Capital	. . . .		32,000
b Cash	. . . .	54,000	
K, Capital	. . . .		2,000
L, Capital	. . . .		2,000
M, Capital	. . . .		50,000
c Cash	. . . .	39,000	
K, Capital	. . . .	3,000	
L, Capital	. . . .	3,000	
M, Capital	. . . .		45,000

CHAPTER 16

True or False

1	F	5	T	9	F	13	F	17	T
2	T	6	F	10	T	14	T	18	T
3	T	7	T	11	T	15	T	19	T
4	F	8	F	12	T	16	F	20	F

Completion Statements

1 Stockholders, certificate. 2 Stockholders' equity.
3 Heavy taxation, greater regulation. 4 The amount of their investment. 5 Capital stock, retained. 6 Increased, decreased, dividends. 7 Par value, credited, Common Stock, credited, Paid-in Capital in Excess of Par. 8 Legal capital. 9 Callable. 10 Preferred Stock, Common Stock, Paid-in Capital in Excess of Par.

Multiple Choice

1 b   3 b   5 b   7 c
2 b   4 b   6 a   8 b

Solutions to Exercises

1

Net income for Year 2	$180,000
Less: Deficit at beginning of Year 2	20,000
Retained earning available for dividends	$160,000
Less: Dividends on preferred stock for 2 years (10,000 shares × $10)	100,000
Available for common stock	$ 60,000
Less: Balance in retained earnings at end of Year 2	25,000
Dividends paid on common stock.	$ 35,000
Dividends per share: $35,000 ÷ 10,000 shares .	$3.50

2 Stockholders' equity:

$9 preferred stock, $100 par, 1,000 shares issued and outstanding	$100,000
Common stock, no par value, 50,000 shares issued and outstanding	200,000
Paid-in capital in excess of par: preferred stock	10,000
Donated capital	65,000
Total paid-in capital	$375,000
Retained earnings	128,000
Total stockholders' equity	$503,000

CHAPTER 17

True or False

1	F	5	F	9	T	13	T	17	T
2	F	6	F	10	F	14	T	18	T
3	F	7	F	11	T	15	F	19	T
4	T	8	F	12	F	16	T		

Completion Statements

1 Income, extraordinary items. **2** Primary, weighted average, fully diluted. **3** Prior period adjustment, statement of retained earnings, retained earnings, beginning. **4** Footnote. **5**(a) $1,020,000; **(b)** $440,000; **(c)** $740,000. **6**(a) $900,000; **(b)** $0.20; **(c)** before; **(d)** $2,358,800; **(e)** $21 [($103,400 + $94,000) ÷ 9,400 shares].

7

Transaction or Event	Increase	Decrease	No Effect
a Declaration of cash dividend		✓	
b Distribution of a 20% stock dividend		✓	
c A 4 for 1 stock split		✓	
d Net income is reported for latest year	✓		
e Additional stock is sold at $8 per share		✓	
f Treasury stock is acquired at $12 per share		✓	
g Additional stock is sold at $14 per share	✓		

Multiple Choice

1 d	3 b	5 d	7 d	9 c
2 c	4 c	6 a	8 c	10 b

Solutions to Exercises

1

AXEL COMPANY
Income Statement
For the Current Year

Sales	$4,200,000
Cost of goods sold (70%)	2,940,000
Gross profit on sales (30%)	$1,260,000
Operating expenses [$1,260,000 − ($210,000 ÷ .6)]	910,000
Operating income before taxes ($210,000 ÷ .6)	$ 350,000
Income taxes ($350,000 × .4)	140,000
Income from continuing operations ($4,200,000 × .05)	$ 210,000
Loss from discontinued operations, net of income tax benefit	(300,000)
Net loss	$ (90,000)
Per share of capital stock:	
Income from continuing operations	$ 2.10
Loss from discontinued operations	(3.00)
Net loss	$ (.90)

2 Earnings from continuing operations:

    ($490,000 − $60,000) ÷ 100,000 shares $4.30

  Net earnings:

    ($672,000 − $60,000) ÷ 100,000 shares $6.12

3

General Journal			
Year 1			
Mar. 1	Retained Earnings	200,000	
	Dividends Payable		200,000
	Declared cash dividend of $0.80 per share on 250,000 shares.		
21	Dividends Payable	200,000	
	Cash		200,000
	Paid dividend declared Mar. 1.		
Aug. 10	Retained Earnings	500,000	
	Stock Dividend to Be Distributed		62,500
	Paid-in Capital from Stock Dividends		437,500
	Declared 5% stock dividend on 250,000 shares of $5 par value stock.		
Sept. 2	Stock Dividend to Be Distributed	62,500	
	Common Stock		62,500
	Distributed 12,500 share stock dividend.		
Dec. 21	Retained Earnings	1,312,500	
	Common Stock		1,312,500
	Declared and issued 100% stock dividend on 262,500 shares of $5 par stock.		
30	Treasury Stock	30,000	
	Cash		30,000
	Purchased 1,000 common shares for treasury.		

CHAPTER 18

True or False

1 F	6 F	11 T	16 T	21 F
2 F	7 T	12 F	17 F	
3 T	8 T	13 T	18 T	
4 T	9 F	14 T	19 T	
5 T	10 T	15 T	20 F	

Completion Statements

1 Less, greater. 2 Premium, discount. 3 $1,000;
twice. 4 $92\frac{1}{2}$. 5 Present value, less, larger. 6 Multiplying, carrying value, effective interest rate, contractual.
7 Increases, decreases. 8 Rental Expense, off-balance-
sheet, liability. 9 Lease Payments Receivable, Sales,
present value, interest revenue, Lease Payments Receivable.

Multiple Choice

1 a	3 c	5 d	7 a
2 a	4 b	6 b	

Solutions to Exercises

1 a $32,000 ($600,000 × 16% × $^4/_{12}$)

b The premium amounted to $5,800 ($637,800 −
$600,000 − $32,000)

c $48,000 ($600,000 × 16% × $^6/_{12}$)

d $32,000 ($600,000 × 16% × $^4/_{12}$)

e $5,500 [$5,800 less amortization of $50 ($5,800 ÷
116) per month for six months]

f $47,700 (interest on $600,000 at 16% for six
months, $48,000, less the amortization of pre-
mium for six months, $300)

2	Year 1	General Journal		
a	July 1	Cash	637,800	
		Premium on Bonds Payable		5,800
		Bonds Payable		600,000
		Bond Interest Payable		32,000
		To record issuance of bonds.		
b	Sept. 1	Bond Interest Payable	32,000	
		Bond Interest Expense	16,000	
		Cash		48,000
		To record payment of interest for six months, including		
		$32,000 which was accrued on date bonds were issued.		
	1	Premium on Bonds Payable	100	
		Bond Interest Expense		100
		To amortize premium for July and August at $50 per month		
		($5,800 ÷ 116).		
c	Dec. 31	Bond Interest Expense	32,000	
		Bond Interest Payable		32,000
		To accrue interest for four months.		
	31	Premium on Bonds Payable	200	
		Bond Interest Expense		200
		To amortize premium for four months at $50 per month.		

3
  a $42,376 discount ($800,000 − $757,624)
  b $104,000 ($52,000 × 2)
  c 13% ($104,000 ÷ $800,000)
  d 7% ($53,034 ÷ $757,624)
  e $106,449 ($53,183 + $53,266)
  f Bonds payable $800,000
     Less: Discount on bonds 37,787 $762,213

Completion Statements

1 Bond Interest Receivable. 2 $80, dividing, $8,400, 105 shares. 3 Return, risk, diversification, risk.
4 Cost, unrealized, sold. 5 Net income, dividends, cash. 6 Controlling, entity. 7(a) Consolidated, (b) is not. 8 $300,000 ($80,000 ÷ .10 = $800,000; $800,000 − $500,000 = $300,000). 9 $2,050,000, $2,300,000.

CHAPTER 19

True or False

1 F	6 T	11 T	16 F	21 F
2 F	7 T	12 F	17 T	22 T
3 F	8 F	13 T	18 T	23 F
4 T	9 T	14 F	19 F	24 F
5 F	10 T	15 F	20 T	

Multiple Choice

1 b	3 d	5 b	7 d	9 d
2 d	4 b	6 d	8 c	10 b

Solutions to Exercises

1	General Journal		
Year 5			
Sept. 1	Accrued Bond Interest Receivable	1,000	
	Investment in Bonds	88,250	
	Cash		89,250
	Purchased $100,000 par value of World Airlines 12% bonds at		
	87¾ and accrued interest, plus commission of $1,000.		
Dec. 31	Accrued Bond Interest Receivable	4,000	
	Bond Interest Earned		4,000
	To accrue bond interest earned to Dec. 31 ($100,000 $\times$ 12% $\times$ $^{4}/_{12}$).		
Year 6			
Feb. 1	Cash	6,000	
	Accrued Bond Interest Receivable		5,000
	Bond Interest Earned		1,000
	Received semiannual bond interest on World Airlines bonds		
	($100,000 $\times$ 12% $\times$ ½).		
Apr. 1	Accrued Bond Interest Receivable	2,000	
	Bond Interest Earned		2,000
	To accrue interest to date of sale of investment in World Airlines		
	bonds ($100,000 $\times$ 12% $\times$ $^{2}/_{12}$).		
Apr. 1	Cash	92,500	
	Investment in Bonds		88,250
	Accrued Bond Interest Receivable		2,000
	Gain on Sale of Investments		2,250
	To record sale of $100,000 par value of World Airlines 12% bonds at 91		
	plus accrued interest of $2,000 and minus commission of $500.		

2	General Journal		
Year 1			
Dec. 31	Unrealized Loss on Marketable Securities	24,000	
	Valuation Allowance for Marketable Securities		24,000
	To establish valuation allowance for decline in market value of marketable		
	securities as current assets. ($325,000 − $301,000 = $24,000)		
Year 2			
Dec. 31	Valuation Allowance for Marketable Securities	9,000	
	Unrealized Gain on Marketable Securities		9,000
	To reduce valuation allowance as a result of partial recovery of market		
	value of securities in current portfolio. ($270,000 − $255,000 = $15,000		
	required amount of allowance.)		
Year 3			
Dec. 31	Valuation Allowance for Marketable Securities	15,000	
	Unrealized Gain on Marketable Securities		15,000
	To eliminate valuation allowance as a result of recovery of market value		
	of marketable securities.		
Year 4			
Jan. 2	Cash	52,000	
	Gain on Sale of Marketable Securities		7,000
	Marketable Securities		45,000
	To record sale of marketable securities at a realized gain.		

3

PAR CO. AND SUBSIDIARY
Consolidated Balance Sheet
April 30, Year 4

Assets

Cash	$ 190,000
Other assets	1,050,000
Goodwill	90,000
Total assets	$1,330,000

Liabilities & Stockholders' Equity

Liabilities	$ 640,000
Capital stock	300,000
Retained earnings	390,000
Total liabilities & stockholders' equity . .	$1,330,000

CHAPTER 20

True or False

1 F	4 T	7 F	10 F	13 T	16 T
2 F	5 F	8 T	11 F	14 F	17 T
3 F	6 T	9 T	12 T	15 T	18 T

Completion Statements

1 Higher percentage. 2 Individuals, corporations, estates, trusts. 3 Income, sales, property, excise.
4 Information. 5 Constructively received. 6 Interest, taxes, contributions, medical expenses, casualty losses, production, income. 7 Interperiod income tax allocation, taxable, timing.

Multiple Choice

1 a	3 c	5 b	7 c	9 c
2 b	4 a	6 d	8 d	10 a

Solutions to Exercises

1

Income before taxes		$100,000
Add: Long-term capital loss		
(not deductible)	$ 8,000	
Amortization of goodwill		
(not deductible)	5,000	13,000
Subtotal		$113,000
Less: 85% of $20,000 (dividends		
from other corporations)	$17,000	
Interest received on municipal		
bonds (not taxable)	4,500	21,500
Taxable income		$ 91,500

2   ROBERT AND BETTY HILL
Computation of Taxable Income for 19___

Gross income:

Salaries	$44,000	
Dividends ($580 − $200)	380	
Interest on savings account	1,320	
Net long-term capital gain		
($8,200 − $4,200)	4,000	$49,700

Deduction to arrive at adjusted gross income:

Long-term capital gain deduction (60%		
of $4,000 reported in gross income)	$ 2,400	
Two-earner married couple deduction		
($22,000 × 10%)	2,200	4,600
Adjusted gross income		$45,100

Deduction from adjusted gross income:

Itemized deductions:

Sales taxes	$ 400	
State income taxes paid. . .	2,300	
Contributions	800	
Property taxes on residence	1,650	
Interest on mortgage and		
personal loan	6,520	
Medical expenses, $1,800		
less $1,353 (3% of		
$45,100)	447	
Subscription to investment		
advisory service	200	$12,317
Less: Zero bracket amount		3,400
Excess itemized deductions		$ 8,917
Personal exemptions (8 × $1,000) . . .	8,000	16,917
Taxable income		$28,183

CHAPTER 21

True or False

1 F	5 T	9 F	13 T	17 T
2 T	6 T	10 T	14 T	18 F
3 T	7 F	11 T	15 F	19 T
4 F	8 F	12 F	16 T	

Completion Statements

1 Financial position, sources, uses, working capital.
2 Cash flow. 3 Declaration, use, source, use.
4 Added, net income, provided by operations. 5 Non-current. 6 Current. 7 Accrual, cash. 8 Decrease, increase, increase.

Multiple Choice

1 d	3 c	5 a	7 c
2 b	4 b	6 d	

Solutions to Exercises

1 __U__ Paid semiannual interest on bonds payable.

__N__ Recognized depreciation expense.

__U__ Made monthly payment on operating lease.

__N__ Paid six months' rent in advance.

__U__ Declared cash dividend for payment in the next accounting period.

__N__ Declared a stock dividend for distribution in the next accounting period.

__SU__ Outstanding convertible preferred stock is converted into common stock.

__S__ Sold treasury stock at a price below cost.

__U__ Sold marketable securities (a current asset) at a price below carrying value.

__SU__ Issued common stock in exchange for the net assets of another corporation.

2   PATRIOTIC FIREWORKS CORPORATION
Statement of Changes in Financial Position
For Year Ended December 31, Year 2

Sources of working capital:

Operations:

Income before nonoperating gain and loss		
($112,000 − $20,000 gain + $30,000 loss)	$122,000	
Add: Expenses not requiring use of funds —		
depreciation	25,000	
Total working capital provided by operations	$147,000	
Sale of land	60,000	
Total sources of working capital		$207,000

Uses of working capital:

Purchase of equipment	$84,000	
Declaration of cash dividend	50,000	
Total uses of working capital		134,000
Increase in working capital		$ 73,000

3

Net income		$100,000
Add: Depreciation expense		40,000
Amortization of patents		5,000
Subtotal		$145,000
Less: Gain on sale of plant assets		
(net of taxes)	$20,000	
Amortization of premium on		
bonds payable	2,500	22,500
Working capital provided by operations		$122,500

Note: The entire proceeds (including the gain) from the sale of plant assets should be reported as a nonoperating source of funds. Interest revenue, accrued salaries and wages, and income tax expense are properly included in the net income figure since each of these items either increased or decreased working capital.

4 a $316,000 ($320,000 − $4,000)
  b $204,000 ($200,000 + $7,000 − $3,000)
  c $79,750 ($90,000 − $8,000 − $1,000 − $1,250)
  d $32,250 ($316,000 − $204,000 − $79,750)

CHAPTER 22

True or False

1 T	5 T	9 F	13 F
2 F	6 F	10 F	14 T
3 T	7 F	11 F	15 T
4 T	8 T	12 T	16 T

Completion Statements

1 Dollar, percentage, component percentages, ratios.
2 Short-term creditors, long-term creditors, preferred stockholders, common stockholders. 3 Price-earnings ratio. 4 Equity ratio. 5(a) $150,000, (b) $50,000, (c) $75,000. 6 Long-term creditors, income from operations, interest expense. 7 Return on assets, low. 8 Inventory, inventory turnover. 9 Inventory, accounts receivable, operating cycle.

Multiple Choice

1 c	3 d	5 c	7 c
2 d	4 a	6 c	8 d

Solutions to Exercises

1 a D
  b D
  c D
  d NE
  e NE
  f D
  g I
  h I
  i D
  j I

2

GULFSTREAM COMPANY
Comparative Balance Sheet
Year 1 and Year 2

Assets	Year 2	Year 1	Increase (or Decrease) Amount	Percentage
Current assets	$150,000	$120,000	$ 30,000	25%
Investments	160,000	80,000	80,000	100%
Plant and equipment (net)	360,000	300,000	60,000	20%
Intangibles	80,000	100,000	(20,000)	(20)%
Total assets	$750,000	$600,000	$150,000	25%

Liabilities & Stockholders' Equity				
Current liabilities	$ 76,000	$ 80,000	$ (4,000)	(5)%
Long-term debt	116,000	100,000	16,000	16%
Capital stock, $5 par	250,000	200,000	50,000	25%
Retained earnings	308,000	220,000	88,000	40%
Total liabilities & stockholders' equity .	$750,000	$600,000	$150,000	25%

3 a $280,000 by $105,000
  b $140,000 by $105,000
  c $800,000 by $60,000 [($50,000 + $70,000) ÷ 2]
  d $490,000 by $135,000 [($140,000 + $130,000) ÷ 2]
  e $150,000 by $7,000
  f $150,000 by $657,500 [($700,000 + $615,000) ÷ 2]
  g $515,000 by $700,000
  h $84,000 by $492,500 [($515,000 + $470,000) ÷ 2]
  i $84,000 by 60,000 shares
  j $42 by $1.40
  k $0.65 by $42
  l $515,000 by 60,000 shares
  m $310,000 by $800,000

CHAPTER 23

True or False

1	F	5	T	9	F	13	F	17	T
2	F	6	F	10	T	14	F	18	T
3	T	7	T	11	F	15	T	19	F
4	F	8	F	12	T	16	T	20	T

Completion Statements

1 Under their control.   2 Cost center, profit center.
3 Expenses, revenue.   4 Separate departmental, general ledger, balance.   5 Direct, indirect.   6 Contribution to the indirect expense.   7 Equity (or proprietorship), Home Office, asset, North Branch.

Multiple Choice

1	c	3	a	5	d
2	b	4	c	6	c

Solutions to Exercises

1

STYLESETTER CORPORATION
Departmental Expense Allocation Sheet
Current Year

	Total Expenses	Women's Dept. Direct	Women's Dept. Indirect	Men's Dept. Direct	Men's Dept. Indirect
Sales force salaries	$240,000	$150,000		$ 90,000	
Advertising expense	90,000	45,000	$22,500	15,000	$ 7,500
Building expense	75,000		45,000		30,000
Buying expense	115,000	65,000		50,000	
Administrative expense	130,000	40,000	30,000	40,000	20,000
Totals — direct and indirect	$650,000	$300,000	$97,500	$195,000	$57,500

Totals for each department:

Women's Department	$397,500
Men's Department	252,500
Total — direct and indirect	$650,000

2

Events	Branch Books		Home Office Books	
Example: Home office opens East Branch and transfers $10,000 cash and $1,500 store supplies to branch	Cash	10,000	East Branch	11,500
	Store Supplies	1,500	Cash	10,000
	Home Office	11,500	Store Supplies	1,500
1 Merchandise purchased by branch from outside supplier for $16,000	Purchases	16,000	No entry	
	Accounts Payable	16,000		
2 $10,000 in sales on account made by branch	Accounts Receivable	10,000	No entry	
	Sales	10,000		
3 Rent expense of $1,200 paid by branch	Rent Expense	1,200	No entry	
	Cash	1,200		
4 Wages expense of $4,000 at branch is paid by home office in cash to avoid cash shortage at branch	Wage Expense	4,000	East Branch	4,000
	Home Office	4,000	Cash	4,000
5 Cash sales of $8,000 made by branch	Cash	8,000	No entry	
	Sales	8,000		
6 Branch collects $7,000 of branch accounts receivable	Cash	7,000	No entry	
	Accounts Receivable	7,000		
7 Branch remits $5,000 cash to home office	Home Office	5,000	Cash	5,000
	Cash	5,000	East Branch	5,000
8 Branch closes Income Summary with $3,200 debit balance at end of period: home office also records net income (loss) of branch	Home Office	3,200	Losses — East Branch	3,200
	Income Summary	3,200	East Branch	3,200

CHAPTER 24

True or False

1	T	5	T	9	F	13	T	17	T
2	F	6	F	10	T	14	T	18	F
3	T	7	F	11	F	15	F	19	T
4	F	8	T	12	T	16	F	20	F

Completion Statements

1 Cost of finished goods manufactured, purchases.
2 Raw materials used, direct labor, factory overhead.
3 Product, expenses. 4 Debit, cost of finished goods manufactured, Income Summary. 5 Factory overhead, direct labor. 6(a) $50,000 ($450,000 − $400,000), (b) $120,000 ($400,000 − $80,000 − $200,000), (c) $430,000 ($450,000 − $20,000), (d) $437,500 ($430,000 + $7,500). 7 Manufacturing Summary, debited, beginning. 8 Debits, credits, Manufacturing Summary.

Multiple Choice

1	c	3	d	5	b
2	b	4	d	6	a

Solutions to Exercises

1 **a** Factory overhead rate $= \dfrac{\$200,000}{\$160,000} = \dfrac{5}{4}$, or 125%

b
Raw materials used ($1,000 × .70 × 20)	$14,000
Direct labor ($2,000 × .20 × 20)	8,000
Factory overhead ($8,000 × $\frac{5}{4}$)	10,000
Ending inventory, goods in process	$32,000

2

Statement of Cost of Goods Manufactured		
Goods in process (beginning of year)		$ 27,500
Raw materials used	$ 84,500	
Direct labor	160,000	
Factory overhead	200,000	
Total manufacturing costs		444,500
Total cost of goods in process during the year		$472,000
Less: Goods in process (end of year—from Exercise 1)		32,000
Cost of goods manufactured		$440,000
Income Statement		
Sales		$700,000
Cost of goods sold:		
Finished goods (beginning of year)	$ 60,500	
Cost of goods manufactured	440,000	
Total cost of finished goods available for sale	$500,500	
Less: Finished goods (end of year)	55,000	
Cost of goods sold		445,500
Gross profit on sales		$254,500
Operating expenses:		
Selling expenses	$ 90,000	
General and administrative expenses	130,000	
Total operating expenses		220,000
Net income		$ 34,500

CHAPTER 25

True or False

1 F	5 F	9 T	13 T	17 F
2 T	6 T	10 T	14 T	18 T
3 F	7 T	11 F	15 T	19 F
4 T	8 F	12 T	16 F	

Completion Statements

1 Department, process, job, lot. 2 Unit, control, cost. 3 Subsidiary ledger, invoices, requisitions.
4 Factory overhead, factory overhead, $4,500. 5 Job cost sheets. 6 Overhead application rate, budgeted, budgeted direct labor. 7 Underapplied, cost of goods sold, understated. 8 Equivalent full units. 9(a) Equivalent full units, (b) units, costs, (c) unit. (d) completed, goods in process.

Multiple Choice

1 b	3 d	5 d	7 c
2 a	4 a	6 a	

Solutions to Exercises

1 a
Raw material	$40,000
Direct labor	15,000
Overhead ($15,000 × .6).	9,000
Total cost	$64,000

b Underapplied by $16,000. Actual overhead was $208,000. Overhead applied was 60% of direct labor of $320,000, or $192,000, leaving $16,000 of actual overhead not charged to jobs.

c The underapplied overhead of $16,000 should be deducted from the year's revenue.

2 a
Raw Materials Inventory	$119,000	
Accounts Payable.		$119,000

To record materials purchased in March.

b
Goods in Process: Cutting		
Department	102,900	
Goods in Process: Assembly		
Department	19,100	
Raw Materials Inventory		122,000

To record materials used in March.

c The Raw Materials Inventory account at March 31 has a debit balance of $11,000, which would appear on the balance sheet as a current asset and also in the schedule of cost of goods manufactured.

CHAPTER 26

True or False

1 F	5 T	9 T	13 T	17 F
2 T	6 F	10 T	14 F	18 T
3 F	7 T	11 F	15 T	19 F
4 T	8 F	12 T	16 T	20 F

Completion Statements

1 Financial plan. 2(a) Responsibility budget, (b) capital budget, (c) master budget, (d) flexible budget. 3(a) Corrective action, (b) evaluating performance. 4 Should be, unfavorable, variance. 5 Unfavorable, quantity variance, $1,100. 6 Favorable, usage variance, unfavorable, rate variance. 7 Unfavorable controllable, favorable volume variance. 8 Debit, $1,400, credit, Labor Usage Variance, $200, credit, $1,200.

Multiple Choice

1 c	3 a	5 c	7 a
2 b	4 c	6 b	

CHAPTER 27

True or False

1 F	5 F	9 T	13 F
2 F	6 T	10 F	14 F
3 T	7 F	11 T	15 T
4 T	8 F	12 F	16 T

Completion Statements

1 Variable, fixed. 2 Volume index. 3 Mixed, fixed, variable. 4 Variable, fixed, $0.26 5 Contribution mar-

Solutions to Exercises

1   EAGLE CORPORATION
          Cash Budget
    For the month of December 19___

Cash balance at beginning of month		$ 18,000
Receipts:		
Collections from customers		
($120,000 × .90)	$108,000	
December cash sales ($200,000 × .25)	50,000	158,000
Total cash available		$176,000
Disbursements:		
Fixed expenses ($30,000 − $6,000) .	$ 24,000	
Variable expenses ($200,000 × .62). .	124,000	
Note payable	12,000	
Total cash disbursements		160,000
Cash balance at end of month		$ 16,000

2 a $32,500 ($30,000 + $3,000 − $500)
   b $44,500 ($40,000 + $2,000 + $2,500)
   c $87,300 ($90,000 − $1,500 − $1,200)
   d 15,800 units [($160,000 − $2,000) ÷ $10]

gin. 6 Sales, fixed costs, operating income. 7 $3.00, 60%, $5.30, 53%. 8 X. 9 Sales, decrease, break even.

Multiple Choice

1 c	3 b	5 b	7 b
2 a	4 d	6 d	8 d

Solutions to Exercises

1 a 9,000 units ($54,000 − $6 per unit)
   b $66,000 ($520,000 − $400,000 − $54,000)
   c $138,000 ($832,000 − $640,000 − $54,000)
   d $106,000 ($832,000 − $672,000 − $54,000)

2 a

Product	Sales Price per Unit	− Variable Costs per Unit	= Contribution Margin per Unit	÷ Direct Labor Hours Required per Unit	= Contribution Margin per Hour of Direct Labor
X	$200	$120	$80	5	$16
Y	120	80	40	2	20
Z	80	50	30	2	15

b

Product	Units Produced	Direct Labor Hours Used on Product	Contribution Margin per Hour of Direct Labor	Total Contribution Margin of Each Product
Y	400	800	$20	$16,000
X	600	3,000	16	48,000
Z	100	200	15	3,000
		Total direct labor hours: 4,000	Total contribution margin: $67,000	

CHAPTER 28

True or False

1	T	6	F	11	T	16	T
2	T	7	F	12	F	17	F
3	F	8	T	13	T	18	F
4	F	9	T	14	T	19	T
5	T	10	T	15	F		

Completion Statements

1 Total, incremental cost, incremental revenue.

2 Opportunity cost. 3 Sunk cost, irrelevant. 4 Fixed costs, eliminated. 5 Variable manufacturing, product, fixed manufacturing, period. 6 Variable manufacturing, sold, manufacturing margin, variable, contribution margin, fixed, operating income. 7 Capital budgeting, (a) payback period, (b) return on average investment, (c) discounted cash flow analysis. 8 Amount, length of time, discount rate, present value. 9 Rate of return, discount rate, net present value.

Multiple Choice

1	c	3	d	5	b	7	b
2	b	4	d	6	c		

Solutions to Exercises

1

	Make the Part	Buy the Part	Incremental Analysis
Manufacturing costs:			
Direct materials	$ 16,000	0	$ 16,000
Direct labor	25,000	0	25,000
Variable factory overhead	20,000	0	20,000
Fixed factory overhead	59,000	$ 49,000	10,000
Purchase price ($10 per unit)	0	100,000	(100,000)
Totals	$120,000	$149,000	$ (29,000)

Conclusion: Continue to make part X.

2 a $60,000 ($250,000 − $190,000)

b 6¼ years ($375,000 ÷ $60,000)

c 12½% $\left[\dfrac{\$25,000}{(\$375,000 + \$25,000) \div 2} \right]$

d
Present value of annual cash flows ($60,000 × 6.145)	$368,700
Present value of salvage value ($25,000 × .386)	9,650
Total present value	$378,350
Less: Cost of investment	375,000
Net present value of proposal	$ 3,350